The DANISH SECRET to HAPPY KIDS

How the Viking Way of Raising Children Makes Them Happier, Healthier, and More Independent

HELEN RUSSELL

Published by Sourcebooks
P.O. Box 4410, Naperville, Illinois 60567–4410
(630) 961-3900
sourcebooks.com

Cataloging-in-Publication Data is on file with the Library of Congress.

Printed and bound in the United States of America.
VP 10 9 8 7 6 5 4 3 2 1

FOR THE MINI-VIKINGS

(Sorry about the bubble machine.)

FOR PARENTS-TO-BE

(It'll all be okay. And don't worry if you can't keep basil alive. I can't keep basil alive. Or any houseplant, despite following instructions. Green-fingered friends persist, buying plants they assure me are foolproof. These inevitably brown and wilt, and we both look like fools. Houseplants? No. But children? Yes! Three of them! So don't worry if you can't do basil. You can still do parenting. Here's how Vikings do it.)

Contents

∿

INTRODUCTION: The Accidental Dane — vii

1: Congratulations! It's a Viking! — 1

2: A Viking Is Born — 17

3: Baby Dane — 31

4: Bringing Up *Børn* — 47

5: No Such Thing as Bad Weather — 67

6: Foraging and Family Meals — 83

7: Singing, *Samfundssind*, and the Social Brain — 101

8: Show, Don't Tell: Discipline Danish Style — 121

9: Play (Well) — 145

10: Risk (a.k.a. Viking Health and Safety) — 163

11: Digital Blind Spot — 181

12: The New Norse Sagas — 197

13: Schooltime (Barely) — 213

14: *God Ferie!* Holidaying Like a Viking 233

15: Let's Get Physical 253

16: Teen Viking 267

EPILOGUE 287

BONUS CHAPTER: How to Party Like a Viking 303

NOTES 318

INDEX 347

ACKNOWLEDGMENTS 363

ABOUT THE AUTHOR 365

Introduction

〰

THE ACCIDENTAL DANE

I KNEW I'D PASSED THE point of no return when googling "best axe for children" in a coffee shop while my babies slept outside in their carriage. Munching on rye bread, jam, and cheese (together... welcome to Denmark), I was feeling the creeping sensation of caffeine working its magic when an email pinged up from my son's scout group. I was expecting pre-camp paperwork or an invitation to bake something. Instead, it read:

On Wednesday, we build bonfires! Bring daggers!

No, he hasn't joined a gang. In the land of Vikings, children are regularly tooled-up fire starters. Something that could earn him jail time in the UK is normal for mini Vikings, who are packing blades every Wednesday. By the age of six, the eldest already had his own dagger and tool kit, complete with hammer, saw, screwdrivers—flat head and cross head. He couldn't read or write; Scandinavians aren't fussed about "book learning" before the age of eight. But he was *killing it* at boat building and kindling campfires.

It wasn't supposed to be like this. The girl about town, convinced she couldn't have children, never expected to become a mother of three living in rural Scandinavia. I lived and worked for twelve years as a journalist in London, and I had no intention of leaving until out of the blue one wet Wednesday, my husband was offered his ideal job working for Lego in Denmark. I was skeptical to start with. I had a career I'd worked hard for. We had a decent apartment, good friends, close family—I had a life. Okay, so my husband and I both worked long hours, ran on adrenaline, and barely had time to see each other. We regularly had to bribe ourselves to get through the day, and we'd both been ill on and off for the past six months.

But that was normal, right? We thought we were living the dream. In reality, we were burnt out. We'd also been trying to start a family of our own with years of fertility treatment, only it never seemed to work. So when this other-life possibility was dangled in front of us—the chance to swap everything we knew for the unknown—we stopped in our tracks.

Denmark had just been voted the happiest country in the world, and I became fascinated by this. How had a tiny Nordic nation managed to pull off the happiest nation on earth title? Was there something in the water? Could beer, bacon, and pastries really make life so much better? I discovered that Denmark had regularly been voted one of the happiest countries in the world in studies going back to the 1970s.

We visited one weekend, just to check the place out, and as soon as I stepped off the plane, I noticed that there was something different about the Danes we met. They didn't look like us for starters, quite apart from the fact that they were all strapping Vikings, towering over me. They looked more relaxed and healthier.

They walked more slowly.

They took their time to stop and eat together.

Or talk.

Or just...breathe.

And we were impressed. My husband—a walking Patagonia catalog—was sold on the idea. He begged me to move, promising we'd relocate for my career next time. And I found myself agreeing. I quit my job as editor of marieclaire.co.uk to go freelance and decided I would give it a year, investigating the Danish happiness phenomenon firsthand, looking at a different area of living each month to see what Danes did differently—from food and family life to day care, education, and design. Each month, I would throw myself into "living Danishly" to see if it made me happier and if I could change the way I lived as a result. I would seek out sociologists, historians, scientists, economists, politicians, psychologists, everyone to try to uncover the secrets to living Danishly. And we emigrated, swapping the bright lights and bustle of the UK's capital for rural Jutland in the middle of winter. I didn't know anyone, didn't speak the language, and had no job. My "Lego Man" husband left to go to work at 7:30 a.m., and I was all on my own. Almost. Our dog—a woolly mutt of unknown origin (his mother being something of a local belle)—had come along for the ride. But canine conversational skills are substandard, and I started to worry that I'd just made the biggest mistake of my life. But that was ten years ago. And I'm still here.

The cultural gap between the UK and Denmark has only

widened since I wrote about my initial experiences in *The Year of Living Danishly* (2013). Since then, we've had Brexit, Boris, and the Trump years. My first book ended with a newborn in tow; now I'm a mother of three.

Born here, my children—a redhead and IVF twins—have only ever experienced the Viking way. Despite their dad and I both hailing from the UK and planning on just a year of living Danishly, here we are a decade later. Mostly because we're incredibly disorganized, time has flown by, and it's all our children know. So I have an alarming amount of skin in the Viking parenting game—whether we end up staying or not.

Parenting Danishly is strangely anachronistic at times, like an Enid Blyton book without the bigotry. And mini Vikings are different from children back home. They eat differently. They learn differently. They play, dress, even sleep differently. They sing (all the time), run, jump, climb, fall, and get up again, out in nature, for hours a day. It's cold and wet and uncomfortable—often. But they cope.

In Denmark, children play outdoors, schools have no gates, and babies are left to nap outside in their carriages. That's because 79 percent of Danes trust *most* people—a statistic I found extraordinary (I don't trust 79 percent of my immediate family).[1] Okay, so Denmark is a small country of just 5.8 million. But that's about the size of South London—and I didn't trust most people there either.

In the UK and the US, levels of trust have fallen dramatically in the past sixty years, from around 60 percent to 30 percent.[2] I grew up in the 1980s and '90s with the full force of the "stranger danger" campaign. Along with generations of schoolchildren, we were taught to trust *less*, with annual police talks on the perils of people we didn't know. My American friends had McGruff, a hard-boiled crime dog with a gravelly voice who warned of danger at every turn. To be a child in the 1980s was to be acutely aware that you could be done for on any given day. But in the Nordic countries? Less so.

Trust in Denmark has always been high and has actually been on the rise by a few percent in recent years. Children are taught that the world is an essentially good place and most people are not out to get them. Which is ~~madness, delusional~~ *liberating*. "If you trust the people around you, you can be more relaxed," as my oldest Viking friend put it. She's a formidable flaxen-haired Nordic goddess with three children who gets things done, apparently effortlessly, and is surprised when others (i.e., me) don't. But she has a heart of pure Viking gold and has been helping me decode the Danish way ever since our arrival. And this much I learned early on: Vikings typically trust that children will figure things out, learn how to use their bodies, and manage their surroundings.

Internationals always joke that there's no such thing as health and safety for Nordics (contrary to what Brexiteers would have us believe about Europe). Instead, there are lit candles everywhere, four-year-old children saw wood, and six-year-olds walk the family dog or bike to school by themselves. As my Veteran Viking friend says, "Our children grow up free because they trust."

This trust seems to be a self-fulfilling prophecy: Denmark is the least corrupt country in the European Union, and even politicians, notoriously untrusted in most countries, enjoy a relatively good reputation. Nordic countries regularly top the UNICEF rankings in terms of happiness, education, and equality.[3] And children in Nordic countries generally have the highest rates of well-being globally.

By contrast, youngsters in the US and the UK are more likely to suffer from mental ill health than in almost any other rich country, according to UNICEF.[4] A report from the Children's Society charity shows that the number of UK children who are unhappy with their lives continues to rise.[5] While in the US, a third of all teenagers now have symptoms that meet the criteria for an anxiety disorder, according to Harvard data.[6]

The US and UK models aren't working. So what are Vikings doing differently? What are the secrets to Viking parenting? And what can the rest of us learn from them? From pregnancy and birth to toddlerhood and school, I want to find out what it's like for children and their caregivers in Denmark, Norway, Sweden, Iceland, and Finland.

"Wait," I hear you cry. "Are Finns Vikings too? And is Scandinavian the same as Nordic?"

To which I say, "It's complicated" and "Not quite."

There's often confusion about the Scandinavian countries, and conversations about my relocation regularly go something like this:

Friend: How's the Dutch coming along?

Me: I'm in Denmark. They speak Danish.

Friend: Oh. Okay then. How's the *Danish* coming along?

Me: [*points to the middle distance*] Look! A bird!

(Danish is tricky, and I still suck at it.)

But generally? The bewilderment runs deep. Google "Is Denmark..." and the most searched terms that come up are

...*an island?*

...*English speaking?*

...*part of Sweden?*

(Answers: nope.)

There are three Scandinavian countries—Norway, Denmark, and Sweden—whose languages share common characteristics. But there are five Nordic countries: Norway, Denmark, Sweden, Finland, and Iceland. *Nordic* is the term used to describe anything related to them, like Nordic design or Nordic cuisine. *Norse* is used to refer to the ancient people who were native to these five countries and their common culture.

Friend: What about those guys with the horned helmets and hipster beards?

Me: Do you mean Vikings?

Friend: [*nods vigorously*]

Despite every cartoon depiction ever, Vikings never wore horned helmets. We only think they did because of the German composer Wagner. For the 1876 production of his Ring Cycle, based on the Norse sagas, the costume designer included horned helmets. The show was such a hit that Vikings with horned helmets became standard.

So it's all Wagner's fault.

Friend: Huh! Who were Vikings, then?

Well, Vikings were seafaring folk who roamed northern Europe from 800 to 1066 CE. The word *Viking* comes from the Old Norse *vikingr*, or "to pirate."

Friend: So was it all marauding, sex, and dragons?

Me: Are you thinking of *Game of Thrones*?

Friend: Could be. [*adopts faraway look*] Mmm, Jon Snow.

At this point, I bust out a portable projector for Viking 101. Over the years of living Danishly, I've done my fair share of Viking geekery, visiting burial sites and racking up more rune stones than I remember. I've ventured east, following the Norsemen and Norsewomen's route to the Arab world, to see firsthand picture stones that show images of Viking life as it was recorded at the time, cutting out the guesswork. I've hung out with archaeologists and historians who have attempted to school me. I've learned how Vikings traveled extensively on iconic longships (the ones with the oars and the big bendy sails) and how their impact on the history of Europe is widespread. Millions of Viking descendants exist today, many unaware of their genetic background (it could be you!). Even the names of our days come from the Nordic tradition. Sunday is named after Sunna, the Norse goddess of the sun. Monday comes from "moon day," named after the god of the moon. Tuesday is Tyr's day, named for the god of war and law. Wednesday is Woden's day, named after the Norse god Woden, a.k.a. Odin. Thursday is named after probably the best-known Norse god, Thor (the one with the hammer). Friday gets a little hazy (doesn't it always?), but it's either named after the Norse god Freyr or the Norse goddesses Freya or Frigg.

Friend: What about Saturday?

Me: I think they were probably tired from all the marauding by then—Saturday is just named after the Roman god Saturn.

Vikings originated in what is now Denmark, Norway, and southern Sweden. They traveled west to trade, spending time in Finland at ports along the southern coast en route to Russia. So, the history of early Finland is surprisingly Viking heavy. The archaeologist Marika Mägi who teaches at Tallinn University argues that the Baltic Finns were Vikings too, but the world ignores this fact because Finns missed their moment.

Vikings really became popular in Europe at the end of the nineteenth century when Scandinavians started writing about them. But Finns were busy being an autonomous grand duchy of the Russian Empire around then. It was only after Finnish independence in 1917 that they could start talking about their Viking ancestors, but by then it was too late.

Friend: Gutted!

Me: I know!

The story was already being told, the souvenirs sold, and the T-shirts printed throughout Scandinavia.

Friend: What about Iceland? Didn't you mention Iceland?

I did! I flick back through my PowerPoint and pick up the laser pen no one needs and only uses for teasing cats to point at the volcanically active island in the North Atlantic. I explain how the country we now call Iceland was unpopulated before Norse settlers arrived in 874 CE. Today, it has a population similar to that of Cleveland, Ohio, one hundred words for wind, and a restaurant that serves exclusively tomatoes. So Iceland is in the Viking club.*

Friend: Got it. Scandinavia is Norway, Sweden, and Denmark. The Nordic countries are Iceland, Finland, Norway, Sweden, and Denmark.

At this stage, I put away my laser, lest local cats congregate, and send the newly minted Viking enthusiast on their way. I've got scouts to shuttle, axes to sharpen, and wood to whittle (the whittling never ends). All before another round of coffee and *kanelsnegle*

---

* Greenland, however, isn't. Greenland's current population is descended from the Thule culture, which arrived in the 1200s. The Faroe Islands are also not in the Viking gang, having been settled three hundred years before Vikings arrived.

(cinnamon swirls). But it's not all baked goods, hot drinks, and hygge. The Nordic countries may be among the happiest on earth according to the latest UN report, but Vikings face the same challenges as the rest of us.

The region has changed since I first arrived, in step with the rise of nationalism across Europe and the US. And my experiences won't be the same as everyone else's. But there are common trials and troubles that we face the world over. Because trying to "do life" right is hard. Parenting while sleep deprived and poorer than in your previous life is hard. Relationships, once children come along, are *insanely* hard.

The latest figures from Statistics Denmark show that around 40 percent of marriages ended in divorce.[7] Getting unhitched can be done online in Denmark for just 775 Danish kroner (DKK), which is about $111 USD, so divorce tends to be less acrimonious. But there are also cultural factors at play. The Nordic countries are famed for gender equality, and female employment has long been a given. Since both sexes work and tend to be paid a livable wage, women don't depend on their husbands for money. And Danes rank highest in Europe for overall life satisfaction. So although no one sets out to get divorced, it isn't the end of the world if you do. And Danes are happy to give marriage another go. Denmark is the fifth country in Europe with regard to remarriages, and as my neighbor put it, "Danes really like getting married, so we don't mind doing it more than once."[8]

"The great thing about Denmark is that there are lots of different ways to be a family," a fellow school mom tells me. In fact, there are thirty-seven different types of family units in Denmark, according to government records, from same sex couples to single parents and more.[9] The wicked stepmother trope holds no truck in Denmark, where a growing majority of families include a "bonus" mom, dad, sister, or brother. As Rasmus Kjeldahl of Børns Vilkår, Denmark's children's rights association, puts it, "You can have happy children *despite* the high divorce rate in Denmark."[10]

Sweden, Norway, and Iceland have more births outside marriage than within it, and 69 percent of Icelandic babies are born to parents who aren't married.[11] In the US and the UK, these family formations are associated with being worse off and can attract stigma, but in the Nordic countries, more flexible arrangements are embraced. Former Finnish prime minister Sanna Marin was raised by two female parents. She had a baby in 2018, came to power in 2019, and *then* married in 2020. Mette Frederiksen became Denmark's youngest prime minister in 2019 as a single mother of two. She has since married and now lives with her husband plus his three children in a household of seven ~~which must be total chaos~~ as a happy blended family.

Even those who aren't Danish see the appeal of raising Viking children. The country famed for Lego, Nordic noir, and perfect pastries has another major export: sperm. Danes currently send their sperm to a hundred countries worldwide. Shipments to the UK have been increasing year after year and now account for 40 percent of all new imported donors in what's being termed "the gentle Viking invasion."[12] A friend in the UK going through the process now with Danish sperm tells me, "They make it easier to go it alone in the Danish system, and the idea of a Viking baby doesn't hurt either." It's not that everyone looks like Mads

Mikkelsen or Nikolaj Coster-Waldau in Denmark. It's just that, well, a fair few do.

But there's more to it than that, I think, watching my children scale trees and generally maraud, fearless, free...and *happy*? Here's hoping. I want to find out the secrets of Danish parenting and what I can learn from the Nordic approach.

Some aspects of Viking parenting can be applied wherever we are. Some can act as inspiration. Some may be an insight into a different way of living—exotic, even, in some cases (see "jam and cheese"). So this is a tale of fish-out-of-water parenting. With me, clueless in both parenting *and* the Viking way.

Because let me be clear: I have no idea what I'm doing.

Forget conscious parenting. I'm more of a lurching parent, ricocheting from one calamity to the next. My most commonly used emoji is the facepalm. My most commonly used phrase is "Oh shit! I forgot about [insert relevant item or event here]." I drop balls *daily*. Despite a decade of living Danishly, I still have an outsider's perspective, albeit with insider information from friends who take pity on me regularly and explain what on earth is going on.

When raising small people, every phase is new. Each life stage brings distinctive difficulties and rewards. I am learning all the time. There's plenty of talk about "self-parenting" these days, but if we weren't raised with an inner core of Viking grit, is it something we can learn as adults? I want to find out. With you. And snacks preferably. Sitting comfortably? Then let's begin.

CONGRATULATIONS! IT'S A VIKING!

I'M PEERING DOWN A MICROSCOPE at what looks like a party. Single and ready to mingle, densely packed shapes move about. Women in lab coats and squeaky Crocs navigate tanks of liquid nitrogen and fridges graffitied with tadpoles. Nearby, straws of genetic material are poked into pastel-colored tubes before being sent to fertility clinics across the world.

"We send them by DHL usually," one Croc wearer tells me as she places vials of semen in a smoking vat of liquid nitrogen. "Or, if it's only a short distance, via UPS in a ziplock with ice packs."

"Ice packs? Like in a cool bag for Popsicles?"

"Sort of, but chilled to negative 196 degrees. And for sperm."

This is Cryos, the epicenter of the international sperm trade. And it's just up the road from me. I'm not exactly a regular visitor, but I first took tea with the man responsible for seventy thousand babies in 2015. No, not the reincarnation of Genghis Khan but Ole Schou, the business student turned sperm magnate who in 1987 set up Cryos in the Danish city of Aarhus.

"I had a dream," he told me when we met.

That one day every valley shall be exalted?

"No, about frozen sperm. I could just see it, as clear as I see you now, so I started reading all I could about the process of freezing sperm. I got a business loan, and here we are!"[1]

The market developed and demand increased, helped by the supposed virility of Danish men and their unusual willingness to donate sperm. Cryos isn't the only sperm bank in Denmark, but it's the biggest. And demand is so great that all Denmark's sperm banks are kept busy. Cryos currently sends its seed to "every continent except Antarctica," according to Ole, but some countries import more Viking genes than others. In the UK, one in three donor-conceived children have biologically Danish fathers.[2] There's a limited supply of the home-grown stuff since 2005 legislation outlawed anonymous donation, putting off many would-be donors. But Vikings are less easily deterred.

Denmark holds the world record in fertility treatment thanks to generous state funding that made reproduction a national project rather than just an individual endeavor. Since 2007 in Denmark, women without children have been granted access to state-funded IVF regardless of marital status or sexuality.

Today in Denmark, one in ten children is conceived in a fertility clinic—a statistic I've contributed to.[3] After failed fertility treatments in the UK, I was finally helped to start a family by the Danish system. Thrice. The first picture I have of my twins is two cells in a petri dish. But whereas I made my babies with boring old British sperm, the Viking variety is rampaging far and wide.

To find out why, I'm back at Cryos on the fifth floor of an

unassuming building on a busy street. In reception, there are fridges of bottled water, glass bowls of free muesli bars, and Post-its reminding me to *Be Awesome!* It's the hottest day of the year, so I'm delighted to see they're also serving ice cream (vanilla, mango, or salted caramel).

It feels inappropriately intimate to be sitting on a plush gray sofa just a couple of yards from the donor cabins with lights above the doors that glow red when occupied. Each has a rack of porn mags, excellent internet, and virtual reality goggles. Cryos was the first sperm bank in Denmark to invest in virtual reality porn at a cost of about 20,000 DKK per headset (around $2,800) after studies showed that users experienced "a strong positive effect on the number of motile sperm in an ejaculate."[4] Also, the longer they take to create their sample, the better the quality, I learn from the literature.

A steady stream of Vikings pass through reception, picking up a sample cup, then hovering until the light turns green on one of the rooms. I try very hard to be a grown-up but catch the eye of a twentysomething Alexander Skarsgård look-alike. We exchange an awkward smile, then I glance at my watch to appear busy, ignoring the fact that he's off to beat one out before a mango sorbet.

Only 5 to 10 percent of applicants are accepted into the donation program. "But getting turned down doesn't mean you can't be a father. It just means you can't be a donor," Ole always reminds men. Sperm is divided into IUI (intrauterine insemination) or ICI (intracervical insemination) straws according to the motility and quality. For IVF, you need fewer good sperm in each sample since you're injecting it directly into an egg. For IUI and ICI, it's more of a scattergun "send 'em up and set 'em free" approach. (And I should know: I've tried both.)

Donors apply online, then give a sample. This is analyzed, and if approved, donors discuss family history and rule out any serious hereditary disorders. Doctors take blood and urine samples, which are analyzed by geneticists. All before a psychosocial interview to assess the maturity and mental state of the donor.

From getting to know donors at Cryos and other Danish sperm banks (for research, I hasten to add), I've gleaned that Vikings spreading their seed can loosely be divided into three groups: family guys, donor disciples, and young bucks.

A third of donors already have their own family. "My girlfriend and I tried for eighteen months before we got pregnant the first time," says one family guy, "so I know how hard it can be. After I experienced becoming a parent, well…it just does something to you. I think that everyone who wants kids and can take care of them should be able to have them."

Then there are donor disciples, those with firsthand experience of donor families. "My sister has a little girl by a donor," one tells me, "so when I was talking to my mom about getting a job when I started university, she said, 'Have you thought about donating sperm?' My sister was inseminated because she wasn't interested in finding a husband or a boyfriend but she wanted a baby. So I wanted to help other women like her who wanted a family."

The third group are the young bucks: carefree men in their early twenties who may not be mad about babies but are happy to help out and assure themselves that they're virile.

"'Is your sperm good enough?' was the headline that first got me interested," one young buck tells me. "It was a leaflet for the clinic saying, basically, 'Are you man enough to have good quality sperm?' I came here really just to see how my sperm were. I didn't expect much after I heard how only the top 5 percent actually have the quality of sperm to be a donor, but I went through all the tests and got to thinking it would be a good thing to do. And get paid for it."

How much a donor is paid depends on the quality of the sperm and whether they have an anonymous "non-ID release" profile or become an open "ID release" donor. Remuneration starts at 250 DKK (around $36) for a basic profile with low motility—fewer forward-moving sperm in a millimeter of semen. It goes up to 500 DKK (around $71) for an ID-release profile with high motility. But studies show that it's not about the money for most Danes.

"Donors tend to have more altruistic motivations," says Ole. "Perhaps it's something about being raised here. We do things differently." Denmark has a world-famous welfare state, tax-funded healthcare and education, high levels of trust and volunteering (42 percent of Danes do volunteer work in their spare time[5]). There's a strong tradition of being community minded—46 percent of the Danish sperm donors also donate blood.[6]

And there's no stigma to being a donor in Denmark. "I'm pretty open about it and know other guys who do it too," says one young buck. "I ran into a friend when I was donating once. It was a bit funny, but we found it pretty easy to talk about it. I'm currently seeing someone, and I talk to her about it. I think it's something you want your partner to know because if it turns serious, she might be surprised when you turn forty and all of these biological donor-kids get in touch. It's difficult to say how you're going to feel when that happens. I can't even imagine being forty!"

"Same" (Side-eye.) It occurs to me that although I could technically be his mother, it would have caused a great deal of family strife and societal judgment in my hometown in the 1990s. *So there's that.*

Those who elect to release their ID are encouraged to carefully consider how they'll feel when children conceived with their sperm come knocking.

"I could have twenty kids on my doorstep within the space of four years," another young buck who has chosen to be an open donor tells me. As he talks, I get the sneaking suspicion that he quite likes the idea. "It's a lot," he admits, "so it's something I think about."

When children conceived with non-anonymous donor sperm turn eighteen, they are given the name, address, and birth date of their donor. Then it's up to them. Cryos doesn't facilitate meetings.

There's been a debate in Denmark about whether anonymous donors should still be allowed. Many children conceived with anonymous donor sperm have spoken in public about the disadvantages of knowing just half of their genetic makeup.

"That affected me," says a young buck who decided to be non-anonymous as a result. He tells me how he was raised by a solo mother and says, "It's strange, not knowing half of what made you."

I understand this. Not having a relationship with my own dad means that when I look in the mirror, I wonder how much of him is in there. It's the same with my children. One of them has olive skin that definitely didn't come from my Irish blue-hued maternal side nor my husband's Yeti complexion, honed by a misspent youth in the not-so-sunny town of Middlesborough in Northern England.

So is the olive skin from my father? A man my son's never met?

"It makes you wonder," says the young buck/potential father of twenty. "And I have no doubt at all that these children are much wanted and will be looked after to the best of these parents' abilities. If there is any confusion when they meet me, I'll say, 'Hey! You have a great family already! The ones that love you most are over there!'"

All the donors I have met over the years are, as my grandmother would have said, "thoroughly nice boys." So nice, in fact, that knowing where to begin when choosing between eight hundred hopefuls vying to spread their seed on the Cryos website seems impossible. A friend in the UK who has been through the process of buying Cryos sperm for her own Project Baby tells me, "It's a lot like online dating. You start with the basics, so looks, height, eye color, etc., then nose around at their hobbies." These are extensive, but a brief browse informs me that

Nikolas likes diving and jiu-jitsu.

Emil enjoys Frisbee.

and

In his free time, Kasper enjoys most things.

Most things, Kasper? Pick a lane! Commit!

Badminton is wildly overrepresented in the sperm donor community. (Know a Great Dane who's fond of a shuttlecock? Chances are he's shuttling sperm in his spare time.) And profiles also cover favorite holidays and films as well as staff impressions. Here, the Cryos team share their thoughts on donors—a bit like a bookstore's staff picks. You can learn that

Ulrik is chatty.

Svend has kind eyes.

Lars resembles a mix between the American actor James Franco and the singer Joe Jonas.

Or this gem:

Aksel has good muscle tone in his arms. He has an attractive triangular body shape and a roughness to his appearance that adds a lot of charm. Aksel has sparkling green eyes and a flirty smile. The sun is giving him crow's-feet around his eyes, which adds a pinch of wisdom to Aksel's appearance.

Dear staff member: I think you should date Aksel.

If you're looking for a donor with a specific facial feature, like a curve of the nose, you can ask for a manual photo match. "Generally, people want a better-looking, smarter version of themselves," says Helle Sejersen Myrthue, CEO at Cryos.[7]

And are some donors more popular than others?

Helle laughs. "You'd be surprised! Sometimes we get people in, we'll see the photos or their profiles, and someone might say, 'I can't sell him.' But then someone else in the office will love them. There really is someone for all of us!"

Prospective parents can also see personality test results, handwriting samples, donor baby pictures, and adult photographs. The latter are behind a paywall—"to stop their friends browsing just for fun"—and there's a lot of interest in the adult donor photos from the UK. "It is by far the European country with the greatest number of people who have paid to access the images on our website," says Helle.

Once you've picked a donor, you click to buy a straw of sperm to be FedExed to your nearest fertility clinic. Each country sets its own rules on the number of children a donor can father. American guidelines recommend twenty-five children per population of 850,000, although there's no enforced national limit.[8] In Denmark, donors are subject to a twelve-family limit, so families can have multiple children by the same donor, but a donor can't donate to more than twelve different families.[9] And in the UK, there's a ten-family limit.[10] As long as a donor hasn't exceeded his country quota, he's all yours.

So, who are the women opting for Danish donors?

"We're seeing an avalanche of educated older women," according to Ole. "Eighty-five percent are aged between thirty-one and forty-five, and half have a master's degree or higher. More and more of them are going it alone." Cryos exports 96 percent of its sperm internationally, and the sperm shopping demographic is made up of 15 percent heterosexual couples, 35 percent same-sex couples, and 50 percent single women.[11]

I wonder about the resources needed to raise children alone as a single mother by choice in the land of Nord where the cost of living is dizzying. "It's actually easier to be a *solomor*—or single mother—in Denmark than elsewhere because society accepts and supports you," says Karin Erb, lab director at the fertility unit of Denmark's Odense University Hospital. "If you have a good network, babysitters, and family nearby willing to lend a hand, then there are ways to make it work."[12] There are currently 137,000 households headed up by single women with children in Denmark (and 32,000 headed up by single men, according to Statistics Denmark).[13]

Becoming a solo parent via donor conception isn't most people's plan A, and 90 percent of women surveyed wanted to have a child with a partner, according to a study by Copenhagen's University Hospital. Lone Schmidt, professor at the University of Copenhagen Department of Public Health tells me, "Two-thirds had a partner with whom they wanted to become pregnant, but their partners weren't ready." The average age of couples seeking help for fertility problems in Denmark is thirty-three, while the average age of single women is thirty-six. "In other words, women are waiting it out, and when it becomes clear that there isn't going to be a man in the picture, they're taking action themselves," says Lone.[14]

Back in 2015, I interviewed a series of elective single mothers in Denmark for the *Guardian* newspaper and have kept up with a few over the years. One of the growing tribe says, "I was so focused on finding the man and then having the child. The possibility of turning the order on its head hadn't crossed my mind." When it did, the choice became simple: "Having a child without a man and then hoping for a man to enter my life later became a rational solution." Another shares, "I'd always dreamt of having three or four kids, but the man I was in a relationship with in my thirties wasn't ready. I wasn't anti-men: I adore men! I just couldn't find one who wanted kids. I saw lots of friends choose to become pregnant with boyfriends they knew wouldn't last—purely because the desire to have a child took over. I also saw 'traditional' families breaking up all around me, so I thought, 'maybe I should just make this happen on my own.'"

These women asked themselves all the hard questions, like "Does the world need more people? Couldn't I adopt?" And most looked into it, but adoption is an expensive, lengthy process with no guarantee of a positive outcome. In Denmark, those over the age of forty-two aren't allowed to adopt babies.[15] Many considered a one-night stand—not a big deal in Denmark—but felt this would be somehow dishonest, "stealing" sperm from someone. This left donor conception.

The cost for the women looking to conceive with donor sperm varies based on circumstances and donor choice. A straw of sperm from an anonymous donor might cost the equivalent of $765, including donor costs, extensive screening, and shipping.[16] You might pay a local fertility clinic $710 for an IUI and get pregnant for $1,475 all in. Costs rise to $1,930 for a straw of sperm from an ID-release donor with an extended profile and upward of $1,245 for sperm micro injection in an IVF cycle. In this scenario, the total costs would be upward of $3,131 *per try*. It's a lot, but it's less than you'd pay elsewhere. In the UK, even IUI procedures cost between $874 and $2,000 per try—excluding donor sperm.[17] And same-sex couples must go through six attempted inseminations before they can receive government support. "So it's just much harder," says one British woman who has elected to be inseminated in Denmark instead.

Henriette Cranil got lucky the first time. A striking woman with piercing blue eyes who also happens to be a solomor by donor conceived sperm, says, "I was in my thirties, my relation-ship ended, but I wanted kids, and to be a single mom has been an available option in Denmark for a long time. I was at a party with a lesbian couple, and one was pregnant, and I thought, 'I could do that too.'" Henriette had a successful insemination with an anonymous donor, but during her first scan, the nurse looked confused. "She could see two tiny flashing hearts. Twins." There was a moment of concern about how Henriette would cope with two babies as a single mom. "I could see the worry in the nurse's eyes—and the doctors' notes! We all knew this was going to be hard. But I felt really looked after." She had weekly scans, and the babies were born at thirty-six weeks. "We were in the hospital for two weeks, then we went home, and my parents came to babysit for an hour every day so I could sleep."

An hour of uninterrupted sleep a day is hardly ideal, but it's better than no hours. Any newborn is hard. Two newborns? Psychedelically so.

"I was *extremely* exhausted for the first seven"—she corrects herself—"eight...no, *nine* months. Then I went back to work as a psychologist, and they went to a very good day care. I was totally knocked out, but I got used to it." Henriette recommends baby-proofing your life as a single mother: "Finding other adults who you can share the small moments in life with is key." The hospital where she gave birth had a Facebook group for single mothers, "so from day one, I've had a community." There are around twenty thousand donor-conceived children in Denmark today. "And we hang out with other donor families, so it's normal for us." The only real difficulty? Dating. "Being a single parent locks you in, romantically speaking. There's a window of time you can go everywhere you want with a huge carriage, but it's not ideal for dating."

No. Talk about intimidating: my twin transporter was the size of a tank and just as menacing rolling toward you. Shoppers would scatter in anticipation.

Henriette is now married to a former colleague. "Early on, he was aware we needed to make some big decisions. Everything is more complicated with children involved. Of the women I know who are single moms, life is primarily work and children," she says before adding, "I'm sure if they could have had their children with a great love, they'd have preferred that. But not to have had their children? That would have been far worse."

This, I understand. When baby fever began to consume me, at age twenty-six, the idea of a "great love" became far less important than my preoccupation with procreation. (Sorry to my boyfriend at the time. I get it: I was A Lot.)

The solo moms of donor children spend years researching the pros and cons of single parenting before starting treatment—including the psychological impact on a child. There's a traditional idea that children of single parents suffer, but this tends to be based on lone mothers bringing up children post divorce or after unplanned pregnancies, explains Professor Susan Golombok of the Centre for Family Research at Cambridge University in *Modern Families: Parents and Children in New Family Forms.*[18] "Unelective" single mothers may be statistically more at risk of mental health struggles due to the stress of a split, conflict with a former partner, or financial anxiety. But single mothers by choice are spared all this. Children conceived through medically assisted reproduction (MAR), such as IVF, are at no more risk of developing emotional or behavioral problems than those conceived naturally, according to London School of Economics research.[19] A collaboration between University College London and the University of Helsinki looked at 280,682 children born between 1995 and 2000 and found that children conceived by MAR actually did better at school.[20] This could be because parents who elect to pay for fertility treatment tend to be highly educated themselves and so prioritize education. But still, researchers agree that donor children are likely to be okay—as long as they're told the truth about where they come from.

Henriette has been honest with her twins from the start. "We've always talked about it, and I haven't tried to take away the sadness at not having a dad. That's just how it is. Life isn't perfect."

Twenty-six-year-old Emma has known she was donor-conceived for as long as she can remember. "Mom and Dad made me a children's book when I was two and explained how they loved each other very much and wanted a child but couldn't have one. They went to a doctor and found out that Daddy didn't make enough sperm, so a nice man gave us some of his to put on Mommy's egg. They read this to me as a bedtime story, and I could ask all the questions I wanted." And she did. "Mom still has the drawings of the egg and sperm cells I did when I was five, explaining it all to my classmates."

Goodness. How did that go down?

"They were fine about it!"

I wonder whether she's ever felt different as a donor-conceived child.

"Never. Donor-conceived children are the most wanted and hard won. I've always felt super loved."

This is wonderful to hear. Any assisted reproduction is tough, I know—with daily injections, painfully invasive treatment, a tsunami of hormones, and 75 percent of all fertility treatments failing. It's never the easy option.

Many of the sperm donors—even the young ones—realize this. A young buck with sandy hair says, "I know parents will have given it a lot of thought and will give all their love to this donor child." A family guy agrees: "There's been prejudice against lesbian couples and single mothers in the past, but if it's two women or one woman, then I don't think that should decide whether or not you have children. We're liberal in Denmark, and we're not going to stand and giggle about it. If I told someone in the street that I was a sperm donor, they'd say, 'Great! Good for you.'"

At the end of my time at the clinic, I'm back in reception when the Alexander Skarsgård look-alike finally emerges from the donation room. *Blimey.* I look at the clock: *he's been in there a while.* I remember what I was told earlier: "The longer it takes, the better the quality."

Wow. Good job.

Skarsgård and I exchange a smile and both pretend that he hasn't been furiously masturbating for the duration of my interview. He's walking toward me, and for a moment, I contemplate a "Hej!" or even a high five, then see him reaching for the hand sanitizer and think better of it.

Instead, I pick up a packet of Post-its reminding me to *Be Awesome!* and make my way down ten flights of stairs, back out to the busy street.

WHAT I'VE LEARNED ABOUT HOW TO RAISE A VIKING FROM CELL CLUSTER ONWARD

◆ **Embrace science when necessary**. Nature is great. We all love nature. But isn't it amazing that humans can give it a helping hand once in a while? Without science, I wouldn't have two-thirds of my family. I am exceedingly grateful that fertility treatments were accessible to me and worked. Thank you, science.

◆ **Be honest about where your small person has come from.** For much of human history, brushing things under the carpet was the modus operandi for many parents. Adoptees weren't told they were adopted. Children conceived with fertility treatments or surrogates were kept in the dark. But now we are (allegedly) enlightened, and children are pretty liberal and accepting. Tell a child their origin story early and they're unlikely to blink an eyelid.

◆ **Keep an open mind.** A loving family comes in many forms. Baby Mette may have two moms; Svend may be raising his son single-handedly; Lars and Ingrid may have used donor sperm. Each of their families will have strengths and flaws, just like ours. Learning more about the Nordic approach to family has shifted some deep-seated private shame that I had no idea I'd been carrying around with me for the past forty years. Growing up the only child of a single mom, I was often made to feel that my family was "lesser" somehow and I internalized this. Believed it, even. But it's not true. It can't be. What matters is how much we're loved. We know enough by now to appreciate that the traditional setup is no guarantee of future happiness. And conventional couplings don't have the monopoly on well-adjusted children.

A VIKING IS BORN

IN A SCANDI MODERN GLASS house with the Danish flag flying outside and a view of the Baltic Sea, it finally happened. After years of trying came two blue lines. And life changed forever.

Thanks to a centralized healthcare system and a handy yellow ID card, after the first doctor's appointment, I was officially in the system and on autopilot. I was assigned a midwife, my appointments were scheduled, and I was enrolled at the local hospital. My progress was tracked in a yellow journal, used by every expectant mother in Denmark. And I learned early on that Danes use fewer needles, tests, exams, or any other medical procedures than elsewhere. Because Vikings go old school—as typified by visits to my midwife.

Following a cursory chat about how I was doing and a good deal of linguistic creativity (my gynecological Danish being below par), she came at me with an ear trumpet. "Now, we listen for the heartbeat!"

I had been expecting a scanner, but apparently Pinard's horn worked just fine. And aside from encouragement to eat a vegetable once in a while, dietary and lifestyle advice was minimal. Consequently, other internationals expressed horror at some (all) of my life choices during pregnancy.

"Coffee! You're drinking coffee? What about the baby?"

The blood rose in my cheeks. *Had I mistaken coffee for crack?* I checked the guidelines in my yellow journal: *Coffee: No more than two to three cups a day.*

"I think a single shot latte is probably okay."

"In *Denmark*, maybe."

The following week, lumbering to a Japanese restaurant with friends, I was ambushed by the judgy international again.

"Sushi? You're eating sushi?"

I got out my yellow journal to show him how pregnant women are advised not to eat sushi made from fish that has not been frozen. But in Denmark, all fish has been previously frozen, "so it's safe to eat sushi when pregnant in Denmark." *Actually...*

The only restrictions—other than alcohol and smoking—are around two major Danish food groups: *leverpostej* (liver pâté) and *lakris* (licorice). The former contains too much vitamin A, while the latter can increase blood pressure and cause fluid retention. I don't know about you, but I retain plenty of fluid all by myself, so I steered clear. But Danes confine themselves to the smallest smear of pâté and limit licorice to fifty grams a day in pregnancy. Then, for the most part, it's business as usual.

Vikings don't change their lifestyle just because they're pregnant. They don't blast babies with Bach or Gregorian chants in utero. There's no pressure to do daily affirmations or burn a candle that smells like your vagina (for instance). Danes are happy to cycle, run, and swim up until birth. In Norway, they also ski. "Until around six months pregnant at least," a mother of two in Oslo told me. Despite looking like I'd been inflated with a bicycle pump by the second trimester, I did my best to keep up with my Nordic neighbors.

Whereas friends in the US and the UK increasingly shower mothers-to-be leading up to birth, Vikings simply assemble a few essentials themselves. It's normal to welcome hand-me-downs or buy preloved baby gear, and Danes are a thrifty bunch. There's no eBay or Amazon in Denmark, but sites such as dba.dk and reshopper.dk are popular for all manner of secondhand items from toys to car seats.

Since 1938, Finland's expectant mothers have been offered baby showers by the state in the form of a "baby box." This contains a mattress, sheet, blanket, sleeping bag, insulated mittens, and booties. "There's also a hooded suit, socks, a knitted hat, and a balaclava," says mother of one, author, and journalist Katja Pantzar in Helsinki. "There are bodysuits, romper suits, a hooded bath towel, nail scissors, a hairbrush, a bath thermometer, nappy cream, a washcloth, nappies, muslin squares, a picture book, bra pads, condoms—"[1]

"Condoms?" *I think that horse has bolted.*

"Basically, everything you need—for free!"

The contents of Finland's baby box have changed over the years, offering an insight into Viking parenting norms. In the 1970s, with more mothers working, disposable diapers and easy-to-wash baby clothes in colorful patterns replaced white nonstretch garments that took an age to launder. Then in 2006, cloth diapers were reintroduced to assuage environmental concerns, and the bottle was left out to encourage breastfeeding.

Once Finns have unpacked their boxes, the new arrival can sleep in it. Since the 1990s, it's been recommended that parents don't sleep with babies due to the increased risk of sudden infant death syndrome (SIDS). My sister died this way in the 1980s, so this has always been an issue close to my heart—and one I worried about from the moment I discovered I was pregnant. The risk of SIDS is highest in the first six months of life, when parents are the most exhausted and the least equipped to make safe sleep choices. So Finns figured out that giving families a portable place to put sleepy babies made parents more likely to follow guidelines. Finland now has one of the lowest infant mortality rates in the world—two deaths per one thousand live births, compared with a global rate of thirty-eight in one thousand, according to the UN.[2]

But this isn't just about a box. Finland's baby kits were introduced at the same time as prenatal care, so pregnant women had to attend clinics to qualify for the package. At the start, the baby box was only for Finland's poorest families, and only 31 percent of pregnant women received prenatal care. By 1949, the package was offered to all expectant mothers, "and coverage has been 99 to 100 percent in recent decades," says Professor Mika Gissler of the Finnish Institute for Health and Welfare.[3] The baby boxes are symbolic of Finland's wider healthcare system and a dedication to combating inequality—something the UN secretary general called one of the four biggest challenges facing the world today. (Along with the cost of living, "crumbling" trust levels, and the fact that our "planet is burning." Good times.)[4]

Finland's baby boxes spawned imitators in England, Canada, Australia, India, Scotland, and South Africa. But these initiatives can't make up for the structural inequalities outside the Nordic countries. "You're always taken care of here" is how one Swedish friend puts it. "You feel safe. However much you earn, however rich or poor your parents are, you get looked after. So in pregnancy, you can just, well, relax." This was my experience.

"Hello, darling!" my mother FaceTimed in a frenzy a month from my due date. "You look tired."

"Thanks."

"Have you *nested*? You must *nest*! Defrost the freezer! Deep clean the bathroom! Get it all done now, and you'll thank yourself later!"

I won't.

"What about your hospital bag? Have you packed your hospital bag? It could be any day now!"

It wasn't. My firstborn was eleven days overdue.

"Pack your hospital bag today!"

I walked to the bathroom, picked up my electric toothbrush, and dropped it into my handbag. "Done."

"That's it?"

"That's it."

The hospital-bag packing list in Denmark is as follows:

Toothbrush

End of list. You *can* pack more if you like, but there's nothing you *need* since the hospital has it sorted.

"What about a birth plan?" my mother asked. "Sarah from work had a paddling pool with U2 playing! Would you like a paddling pool with U2 playing?"

I would not.

"I don't think they do birth plans here." They didn't, at the time.

"About as close as we get is a white scarf in the car," says my oldest Danish friend and mother of three, Veteran Viking. She tells me this while rustling up dinner for five and watching a YouTube tutorial on how to fix a U-bend (like I say, she gets stuff done).

A white scarf? Surely labor is no time for Hollywood glamour? Or a Marilyn Monroe tribute?

"Traditionally, you'd hold a white scarf out of the car window if you were having a baby, then it was accepted that you could skip the traffic."

"Was that legal?"

"Sure. Still is, as long as it's an emergency and you get police permission."

This is so entrenched in Danish life that it's officially illegal to dangle anything white out of your car, except in a crisis.[5] Which all meant no Marilyn Monroe chic for me.

"I'm not sure I can face the fashion police and labor all in one day." I wasn't sure I could face labor at all. I already knew from friends that Viking childbirth tended to be au naturel. Everyone seemed to agree that it was a good idea to take birth preparation classes, but these weren't an option where I lived (Sticksville) back in the Middle Ages (2014). So instead, I talked to my midwife.

"What are my pain relief options?"

"What would you like?"

"Everything?"

"We will write 'oxygen as a last resort.'"

I had rather assumed oxygen as a given—something I enjoyed on a daily basis.

"You could also try a heat pad."

"*A hot water bottle?*"

"Or a bee sting? This is where water is injected under the skin with a very small needle so that you're distracted from the big pain by a smaller, different pain."

"Does it work?"

"For around half of all women giving birth, yes!"

I didn't love those odds. "What about an epidural?"

"The princess stick?"

This, it transpired, was Viking for *epidural*.

"A princess stick is serious."

"Isn't having a baby serious?"

"Ha ha ha ha ha!" she laughed. I did not.

Veteran Viking told me matter-of-factly that having a baby was "like being kicked by a horse" before adding, "but I've done it three times now so it can't be that bad."

"What if I don't want to be kicked by a horse?"

She shrugged. "It's not always optional."

She was right. It wasn't.

———

Baby number one emerged after eighteen hours of labor with a shock of red hair and the biggest lungs in the hospital, so the nurses told me. Second time around with twins, I had a C-section at thirty-eight weeks.

"I'll be with you every step of the way," Lego Man told me before fainting at the glint of the surgeon's knife.

I was grateful to swap eighteen hours of labor for a seven-minute C-section, but recovery was agony.

Nanna Schultz, founder of the Danish pregnancy and birth community Momkind, describes her experience of new motherhood as "shell shock."

"I loved my new baby, but I was surprised by how difficult I found it all. I felt like, 'I'm brave! I'm adventurous!' and then I had this kid and suddenly, I didn't feel like I was any of those things. I didn't feel like I was doing anything right."

Feeling out of control conflicted with the idea Nanna had of herself. "Here in Denmark and the Nordic countries, women are supposed to be 'strong.' We have careers; we can do everything; we are Vikings! So suddenly, when I felt like I couldn't do everything, when I didn't feel strong...well, it was a real shock."[6] Nanna felt inspired to share the lows of parenting as well as the highs, setting up Momkind to help other Danish parents through the process.

I wonder what makes a "good Viking birth," so I get in touch with Louise Simsick, midwife and mother of three, including my son's *second* best friend from kindergarten (when you're small, these things matter). I make her tea and she tells me, "I think many women here find it difficult to be out of control, and having a baby can feel very out of control." So what should we do? "I want women to have thought through what they expect, what they're scared of, and what they look forward to," says Louise. And when she speaks, women listen. Midwifery is notoriously competitive to get into in Denmark, requiring the highest grades in the country for just a few prized places, so midwives enjoy a phenomenal level of respect in Danish society. I had my babies in the same hospital where Louise works and experienced firsthand the expertise of her colleagues.

Once a baby has been delivered and the professionals have made sure everyone's okay, there is the ceremonial new-baby breakfast tray, with bread, jam, cheese, juice, and a Danish flag on a wooden stand. This isn't purely a sign of patriotism but of celebration—used to mark every birthday in Denmark.

After I'd been fed and watered, I was given my own room, and Lego Man was invited to stay over on a spare bed. "But if you're going to be here, you have to help," an excellently brusque Danish nurse told Lego Man after the birth of our first. She handed him a leaflet titled *A Partner's Role During Hospitalization*. He read aloud: "Responsibilities include changing bed linen as needed, picking up clean clothes and towels, collecting food and drink, and fetching things?"

"Like what?" I asked.

"Anything you need," said the nurse.

The corridors of power in Viking maternity wards are lined with cupboards containing clothes, diapers, washcloths, industrial postbirth sanitary pads, sick bags, breast pumps, vases for flowers, and mysterious-looking packets marked "fishnet panties."

"You haven't worn these before?" The nurse took in our surprised expressions.

I looked at Lego Man. Then the nurse. Then at Lego Man again.

"I mean I may have, one time…"

"They can be very useful if you soil yourself," the nurse went on.

What? I'd have thought fishnet would be the very last fabric advantageous in any sort of accident. It's basically a sieve...

"Because then you just toss them away."

"Oh!" Lego Man was quicker off the mark. "You mean disposable underwear?"

"What did you think I meant?"

"Just that," I mumbled.

Next time the brusque nurse was passing, she brought me several enormous pairs of ruched-leg panties, definitely more surgical mesh than Victoria's Secret. I thanked her profusely.

During my time in the hospital, nurses and midwives were unfailingly patient and generous in teaching me how to care for my new baby.

"How do I clean"—I stared at a tiny bottom covered in what looked like curried yogurt—"*this*? Are there wet wipes? I'm sure I've seen people using wipes."

"No. We use *skumvaskeklude*!"

"Scum—? What did you say?"

"*Skumvaskeklude*!" These turned out to be small sponge slices to be run under water, then used to wipe away whatever it is you need to wipe away, without chemicals.

Okay, I told myself. *I can do this! Bring on the skum!*

I got the hang of changing but struggled with breastfeeding, resulting in a chest that became so full, it turned square. Two stony-faced nurses in their fifties took turns pummeling me like bread to encourage letdown. Because Vikings, I learned, are big on nursing. Icelandic hospitals even import supplies of breast milk from Denmark for preterm babies whose mothers are unable to breastfeed.[7] This is great for babies but can be tough for the Nordic mothers I speak to who feel that their worth and identity are tied to their ability to breastfeed.

New mothers who are ready to leave the hospital but are experiencing lactation issues have an opportunity to stay on at the "stork hotel" or "patient hotel" for around 300 DKK a night ($42) with a nurse on call. A friend who gave birth in the US was incredulous at this when she called to ~~compare war stories~~ share the miracle of birth.

"Wait, so you can just...*stay*? Being *looked after*? With someone else doing the cooking and cleaning and newborn poopsplosion laundry? With professionals on hand for any emergencies or existential crises at one a.m. because your baby won't latch and you've never felt more alone in your life? For *forty dollars*? Tell me you're staying?!"

I had to disappoint her here too. Once my son was out of special care and I could urinate without a catheter, I elected to go home. But whereas new parent friends in the US left the hospital with a hefty bill, in Viking land, childbirth is free.

"Presumably you pay for it with your crazy taxes though?" asked incredulous US friend.

"Yes and no," I told her.

The average Dane pays 35.4 percent of their income in taxes, compared with the Organization for Economic Cooperation and Development (OECD) average of 24.6 percent.[8] But the average monthly salary is 45,500 DKK ($6,500).[9] This means Danes are taking home an average of around 31,000 DKK a month after tax ($4,433).[10] In the US, the average monthly wage is $5,048 *before* tax (35,313 DKK).[11]

Of course, tax rates vary, and there are regional differences in income. But even in US states like Florida, with no income tax, the average worker has less disposable income than someone living in high-tax Denmark. According to the Forbes tax calculator (every American's best friend come April), a worker in Florida with an average monthly salary of $5,048 is only taking home $4,242 after tax (or 29,675 DKK).[12] In summary: less than the average Dane.

Yes, the cost of living in Denmark is 7 percent higher than in the US, but rent in Denmark is, on average, 33 percent lower than in the US.[13] Danes also get free healthcare, free education, and free dental treatment up to the age of twenty-two. Oh, and although the official working week is thirty-seven hours, OECD figures show that the average Dane is only putting in thirty-three hours a week.[14]

"So, you know," I told my incredulous US friend, "it's not bad."

The high tax and the redistribution of wealth make for less inequality too, which in turn makes Danes happier. Americans are also happier when there's more economic equality. Shigehiro Oishi from the University of Virginia studied General Social Survey data from 1972 to 2008 and found that Americans were—on average— happier in the years with less national income inequality.[15] He found that happiness remained stable until the 1990s, then began to drop as income inequality grew.

Social epidemiologists Richard Wilkinson and Kate Pickett believe that trying to maintain self-esteem and status in a more unequal society can be highly stressful and that growing inequality worldwide is even leading to a rise in addiction.[16] Whereas in Denmark and the Nordic countries where tax is high and there's less inequality, there's less animosity between the (relatively) rich and the (relatively) poor. And I can leave the hospital without paying a thing.

"I shall have to try very hard not to punch you in the face next time I see you," incredulous US friend told me.

"I love you too," I told her.

Bag packed, disposable underwear in place, I stood and prepared to leave, held together by stitches and codeine. We were going home. To somehow take care of a brand-new baby all by ourselves.

"And I can't even keep basil alive," I murmured.

"Nobody panic," muttered Lego Man as he tried to navigate the car seat and the small pink thing started hollering. "No need to panic." But his eyes, very clearly, said, "Panic!"

WHAT I'VE LEARNED ABOUT HOW TO RAISE A VIKING FROM THE INSIDE OUT

- There is no easy way to get a baby out. Worse luck. Pregnancy and birth are unpredictable, regardless of best-laid plans. There may not be whale music or scented candles or U2 playing a private concert in a paddling pool, but that's okay. We'll have some impressive new scars, mesh underwear, and war stories to share instead.

- There's no need to buy all the stuff advertised to new parents. We are a captive, scared, susceptible market, making babies in a madly capitalist age. There are plenty who seek to exploit us. But just because a schoolfriend on Facebook bought a Bugaboo doesn't mean I need to.

- It's worth reframing "high taxes" as "reducing inequality and investing in the next generation," Nordic style. Sharing really is caring and a baby is not a commodity. It shouldn't arrive with a price tag.

BABY DANE

WE BEGAN LIVING LIKE MOLES, blackout blinds drawn, a wooden stork outside the front door—as is the custom in Denmark—warning the postman to tread lightly for a while. I experienced moments of pure joy, visceral love, and a lot of laundry. The basil plant on the windowsill shriveled and died. Time bent and particles suspended as I heaved my broken body through a new world of erratic sleep and mind-blowing responsibility. I noticed parts of the day—and night—that I had somehow skipped for the preceding decades.

"My God, *owls* are loud, aren't they?"

"Mmm." Lego Man made a noise into his pillow.

Two hours later.

"Jeez, dawn's bright, isn't it?"

"Uh-huh." A thick, muffled sound came from under the duvet.

When the redhead cried in the night, one of us would slide heavily out of bed, wondering whether the other had heard or noticed. Resenting. Forgiving. Then resenting again. Delirious with exhaustion. When the health visitor came to visit, I dissolved: "I didn't know days could be like this! I didn't know love could be like this!" I told her about the smell that came off my newborn's head and how it was the most phenomenal sensory explosion that had ever existed and, "Did people *know* about this? *Everyone* should know about this! This stuff could stop *wars!*"

She smiled and said gently, "I know." Then, "Do you need a hug?"

I did.

Extra help was offered, from baby physical therapy to psychotherapy and lactation consultants. One friend was assigned a male lactation consultant who brought his own puppet to demonstrate (a frog, just FYI). Another friend had a lactation nurse called Lone Wolf—to this day, my favorite Danish name ever ("You never forget Lone's latch!" is still a catchphrase round my way). But there was less attention paid to the mothers' physical recovery postbirth. In the early days of parenting, I asked my Veteran Viking friend about postpartum pelvic health options, only to be met with a look of disdain.

"We're not *French!*"

Intrigued, I took to Google and read with envy how France's state-subsidized "perineal re-education" program helped strengthen a new mother's pelvic floor. But Vikings, I discovered, were more about the hearts and minds of new parents.

"Do you have enough support?" my health visitor always asked.

I didn't. But then, do any of us? The upheaval of a newborn is like nothing else, and today we're expected to manage it within the four walls of our home. This is why the next part of the Danish setup usually works well. When new parents are at their most vulnerable, sleep deprived and eating peanut M&Ms like it's their last supper, a health visitor sets them up in a mother's group.

Four or five other mothers who've given birth at roughly the same time meet weekly to support one another, with some municipalities offering fathers' groups and family groups too. The health visitor joins the first gathering to encourage parents to tell their birth story and how it's all going so far. Basically: therapy. Talking about the birth ~~trauma~~ *experience* helps to develop a narrative around it and so begin to process it. As the psychotherapist Julia Samuel explains to me, "in enunciating the words, the feelings emerge."[1] So a chatty mothers' group is a pretty good plan. Some work better than others. Embarking on friendships purely because you had an amniotic explosion around the same time isn't always successful. In my first mothers' group with the redhead, everyone else's babies slept like logs, waking only occasionally to guzzle clotted cream–grade breast milk. Mine did not sleep. Instead, he cried and thrashed continuously, refusing both milk and sleep. One of the other mothers asked, "Have you thought about swaddling?" just as I was in fact swaddling, to the best of my ability. I went home soon after for a cry.

"It's potluck," says my Danish friend Camilla, a tall, willowy artist and mom of two. "My first group was a lot of talk about *bleer* [diapers in Danish]. But the women I was with for my second baby were a lot more fun. The day we all peed our pants with laughter, I remember thinking: 'I found my people!' We talked about everything from life to men, work, and 'by the way, I had a baby!'"

It was second time lucky for me too. We'd moved house, away from Sticksville-on-Sea to the "porny pony" town,* where there was more going on and a bigger pool of new mothers to be matched with.

Capes flying in the wind, legs askance, with dry ice pumping out of every possible nook, my second mothers' group after twins were grade A superheroes. We talked about everything, and even on days when we collectively had breath like stale milk and armpits that smelled of potato chips, we were there for one another. The day the twins got a stomach bug and the dog ended up chin to tail in vomit (the bathroom looked like a Jackson Pollock painting), the super-heroes dropped off lasagna. When another told us, "I'm so tired, I might be sick," then was, we rallied with *skumvaskeklude*, the sponge slices I'd been surprised to find Danes use instead of wet wipes.

We tended to meet in coffee shops, late morning since it took hours to pack all the baby gear. Fortunately, there was no need to pack light, with plenty of space for diapers, pacifiers, food, blankets, if not a week's worth of groceries, under Danish baby transit. Viking babies don't do strollers. They are wheeled around in huge Mary Poppins–style carriages or *barnevogne* (child wagons). This is because it's considered crucial for Vikings to be able to lie down flat rather than be bent banana shape in a buggy or car seat.

"Isn't it rather cumbersome?" asked a skeptical bachelor friend who never knowingly wears a shirt without unbuttoning it to his navel. He pointed with horror at my huge Mary Poppins carriage on an early visit from London. "How are you getting *that* in a restaurant?"

---

* The prominent local landmark being a stallion on two legs bearing its full-frontal glory, surrounded by cats with breasts. When I see you, I'll show you pics.

I explained that parenting in rural Denmark involved remarkably few restaurants.

He held my hand and looked sad for me. Deep V thinks all babies look like potatoes and would tolerate no such sacrifice. "Okay then, a café? How are you getting *that* in a café?"

"I'm not."

Danes trust one another so much, they're happy to leave their babies outside in a carriage to nap while they pop in for a flat white or to grab a sandwich. Families living in apartments—especially in Copenhagen or the big cities—even leave babies sleeping in communal courtyards. And yes, when I first heard about this, pre-parenthood, I was shocked too.

"Won't it take you a long time to get down there if the baby needs anything?" I asked a new-mom friend as we sat drinking coffee on the balcony of her fifth-floor walk-up.

"Yep." She nodded, taking a long, slow sip of her latte.

It sounded insane. But Finnish researchers found that babies sleep longer when they nap outdoors,[2] and all the Nordic countries are big believers in the importance of fresh air. Giving mini Vikings great gulps of it from around two weeks old at every opportunity is thought to help lungs develop. There's no "cry it out" approach in Denmark. Viking babies always have their needs attended to, with new parents schooled in the principle that "you can't spoil a baby." But when it comes to napping? They're out in the cold. Often literally, since babies are allowed to sleep outside until it's around minus twenty degrees Celsius. Wim Hof has nothing on Viking babies.

"Isn't it dangerous?" I hazarded early on "What if someone… takes them?"

"No one steals babies in Denmark," Veteran Viking assured me.

In fact, the last reported case was in 1966 and came as such a shock that it made the *New York Times*.[3] The baby was returned alive and well four weeks later, and since then? Nothing. Today, putting babies outside to nap is still common practice in Denmark. But not so elsewhere.

A Dane in New York was famously arrested for placing her baby outside in her carriage to nap. On a May evening in 1997, Anette Sørensen parked her baby daughter outside a restaurant in Manhattan's East Village while she and the baby's father, a New York–based playwright, were inside. Both parents were arrested for child endangerment. The episode sparked outrage in the US, with Americans astounded at the idea of parents leaving a child alone. But Danes were equally stunned by the concept of criminalizing alfresco naps. All charges against Anette were eventually dropped, but the case is symbolic of the cultural differences between the Nordics and North America.

I get in touch with Anette, now fifty-five, who has the same wide smile, large eyes, and brown curls as the young mother in the press clippings I've read from the 1990s.[*]

"The whole thing was a shock," she tells me with characteristic Danish understatement. "I just didn't think about it. Leaving babies outside to sleep in their carriages was very normal to me. But the US press were all against me. And although the Danish media was on my side, it was overwhelming." Anette grew up in the Danish countryside, the daughter of farmers, and so was used to a lot of

---

[*] And her book, *Ormen i æblet: En barnevogn i New York* (*A Worm in the Apple: The Pram-case of New York*).

freedom. "We played outside all day long and were trusted to do so." Because that was the Danish way. "I always go back to this idea of *tillid*." This is a Danish word that translates to both "trust" *and* "faith." "The whole society in Scandinavia is based on *tillid*," says Anette. "Our parents had faith in us, and we had faith in ourselves. But the opposite of trust and faith is anxiety, and I don't want to live like that," says Anette. "Of course, we shouldn't be naïve. It's important that we are awake and can be critical. But at the same time, I still believe trust and faith have to be the headline in our lives."

After my first year of living Danishly, I already felt more trusting and happier—with faith, even, in a more equal society. But I still couldn't imagine leaving my tiny, squalling redhead outside in his carriage to sleep. I wasn't quite there yet. Then one day, I did. And it was okay.

And then I had twins.

And as Henriette, the psychologist and solomor found out, getting a twin carriage in anywhere is nigh on impossible. So if my twin babies were sleeping, they stayed outside, and I'd take a window seat, keeping an eye out for twitching blankets. Some of the superheroes had baby monitors ("a newfangled idea" according to my neighbor), but many relied on their ears or the kindness of strangers to alert them to any stirrings.

And then, at a time when many parents are thinking about childcare provision and returning to work, Vikings elect *not* to.

Parents get fifty-two weeks of parental leave in Denmark. Mothers take four weeks before the birth, then each parent has eleven weeks of nontransferable, use-it-or-lose-it leave, with the remaining twenty-six weeks to share.

In Norway, parents are also entitled to a year, with mothers getting three weeks before birth and six weeks after. Then there's a shared period (*fællesperiode*) divided between parents and a paternal quota (*fædrekvote*). Parents in Iceland are entitled to six months each with one transferable month, so one parent could take seven months and the other five. But a major chunk of the leave is nontransferable with both parents encouraged to be actively involved. Finns get fourteen months with the "parent who has been pregnant," as the inclusive legislation terms it, getting forty days more to recover than the "parent who has not been pregnant."

Want to know who's winning on parental leave? Sweden. Swedes have 480 days paid parental leave, and Swedish fathers use the most parental leave in the world—120 days per child on average. "Today, 90 percent of all Swedish fathers use some parental benefit, and the term 'housewife' doesn't exist anymore," says Niklas Löfgren from the Swedish Social Insurance Agency (Försäkringskassan). "In the late 1950s, there were one million housewives in Sweden. Now the term is obsolete—and there is no desire from women to go back there."[4]

Sweden was the first country in the world to give both parents the same opportunities to be at home with their child back in 1974, with ninety days of parental leave for the mother and ninety for the father. "But you were allowed to transfer them from the father to the mother, so everyone did. Men were *very* reluctant indeed," says Niklas. It would take another twenty years to reach a point where men would use even 10 percent of it. In 1995, the first *pappamånad* (daddy month) was introduced, with thirty days of leave reserved for the father on a use-it-or-lose-it basis. "Almost every father spends time at home now. If you don't, it's thought of as a bit strange." There's even a nickname, latte papas, used to describe the well-turned-out dads hanging out in coffee shops with a baby in tow.

I ask how Niklas persuaded the men of Sweden to get on board with this plan, and he laughs. "Well, there weren't protests on the street with men holding signs! It's important to stress that this was *not* a change driven by fathers. Men had to be encouraged to take this time. They haven't chosen to do so from the start. It was because politicians dared to push for this change even though they may have lost votes."

Brave politicians? Making unpopular decisions for the greater good? Now there's a thought.

Politicians weren't prompted purely by a sense of fair play, however. There was an economic imperative too. Educated women have always been a major resource, and losing them from the labor market makes poor financial sense. So shared parental leave and childcare in Sweden is a no-brainer. As Niklas says, "If you help women to be in the workforce, you get more taxes." The OECD, the European Union, and the World Economic Forum all encourage member nations to guarantee their workers paid parental leave and subsidize day care because shared parental leave has been unequivocally proven to be good for economic growth. (Let's get T-shirts printed! Or tattoos! Who's in?) The Norwegian government recently valued the contribution of working mothers to the country's GDP at $800 billion—equivalent to the value added by its oil reserves.[5]

"Plus, if you make it doable to have a career and a family," says Niklas, "you increase future tax income."

But are these rights subject to the whims of politicians? Could a new government turn back the clock?

"Not now," says Niklas. "We're seeing that the policies just make sense, so no one is going to argue with the bottom line. Even though there are political parties today that want to take away the 'use or lose days,' it isn't high on the political agenda."

That's not to say that the Nordics have it nailed. Even with all the emphasis on helping mothers go back to work, they're still less likely to work as CEOs than their male counterparts. An unintended consequence of generous leave is that while it allows women to stay at home without giving up work, it also keeps women out of the workforce for an extended period, something that can set anyone back in their careers but may be a particular problem for those in high-powered corporate careers.

Women make up almost half the workforce, but fewer management positions are held by women—36 percent in Finland, 34 percent in Norway, and 29 percent in Denmark at the time of writing.[6] In the UK, it's 32 percent.[7] But in the US? Where there's no parental leave? Women make up 40 percent of managers, according to Catalyst research. American women may be stressed and in need of a vacation, but they *are* making it up the slippery corporate pole (apologies for the phallic analogy).

So can career success only come at the expense of family life?

Well, no. Turns out it is possible to "have it all" with Swedish women making up 43 percent of managers.[8]

"This is largely down to Sweden's use-it-or-lose-it policy having been in place for the longest," says Lise Johansen, advisor on gender equality and family policies at the Danish Confederation of Trade

Unions, since for parental policy to work, governments need to effectively force men to take time off.[9] One study showed that a woman's earnings rose 7 percent for every month of leave her partner took.[10] And researchers have found that paternity leave also improves maternal health, because women have support and can take time to heal.[11] This is better for women, babies, and the economy—since depression and anxiety in new mothers costs an additional £17.5 billion in England alone, Birthrights analysis found.[12]

Denmark may lag behind the US on the CEO count, but with the introduction of use-it-or-lose-it paternity leave in 2022, it's hoped that the percentage of women in management roles will rise. And for decades now in Denmark, parents have been able to *have a life* as well as get on in life. Only 1 percent of employees work very long hours in Denmark compared to the OECD average of 10 percent.[13] Yet Danes are the second most productive workers in Europe—more productive than those in the US, Canada, and Japan.[14]

"There are still challenges," says Niklas, "like the sickness gap." A long-term study of men and women in Sweden showed that before becoming parents, there's no significant difference in terms of illnesses, poor health, and lower immune systems between the sexes. "But after the first child, women take much more sick leave— and this comes at a cost to society," says Niklas. This "sickness gap" carries on until a woman's youngest child reaches the age of ten, according to a study from Uppsala University.[15]

Is this just a Swedish thing?

"There hasn't been research from other countries to my knowledge," Niklas tells me.

But I begin asking every mother I meet, and it rings true: we are worn out. And the parent who's had a baby has also, you know, *had a baby*. Something now proven to take the same toll on the body as an ultramarathon or doing the Tour de France.[16] At the very time bodies are recovering from growing and pushing out a human, we're at our most sleep deprived. On returning to work, we pick up every bug going at playgroups and day care. I had the constitution of an ox before parenthood. Now I'm down with something most months. And my youngest are only five. Am I condemned to another five years of this? I'm not sure I can cope.

"I hear this a lot," Niklas sympathizes.

"Why aren't things...well, *better*? Even in Sweden?" What with all the shared parental leave and hot latte papas?

"Women still tend to be the project leaders of the family," says Niklas. "They stay home unpaid a lot more before kids go to day care."

So what's the solution?

"More paternity leave!" says Niklas.

The Danish Fathers Association found that many men who would like to go on parental leave don't feel able to, if they earn more, for example. But this is shortsighted, says Lise from the Danish Confederation of Trade Unions, "because about twenty years from now, they'll realize that fathers have missed out on time with their kids, women have missed out on promotions, and companies have missed out on all the skilled women who could have created more wealth for society."

"There also used to be the argument that kids can only attach to one parent and that parent was mother-shaped," adds Niklas, who raised his two children single-handedly. "We know now that this isn't true, but the cultural hangover remains." It's something he's working on. Now, Niklas speaks about the Swedish model around the world. "I've been to Korea, South Africa, Argentina, Ukraine, Moldova, Croatia—all over. People from different countries all have different starting points, but in common is the idea that we should be able to work and have children at the same time."

"What about the US?" I'm curious.

"I haven't been there. They haven't invited me."

"And the UK?"

"Same."

I tell him this is depressing. He tells me to hurry up and spread the word.

"I think what's most important to point out," says Niklas as I prepare to say goodbye, "is that for fathers, it's a *fantastic* opportunity to be at home with your own children. I would urge anyone to use it. It's a short time in your life, so if it's possible, you should go for it!"

———

Lego Man took ten weeks off back in 2014, fully paid, to care for the miniature redhead while I went back to work. Something he couldn't have done in the UK at the time, when paternity leave was a mere ten days. (UK parents are now entitled to share thirty-seven weeks paid.) Suddenly, I could drink coffee and pee whenever I wanted, once at the same time. I could regain a sense of self and navigate this new identity of "working mother," then go home to a fat-cheeked cherub who I could really enjoy spending time with. It was nice to see my baby too.*

Dads throughout the Nordic countries change diapers, cook, and do the day care run, "so much so that it's like you're not a real man if you haven't done your share of diaper duty," says photographer and Finnish father of three Johannes Romppanen.[17]

There's nothing inherent about women that makes us better at parenting. Neuroscientists from Tel Aviv University analyzed fourteen hundred MRIs and found no discernible difference between the male and female brains.[18] A study from Bar-Ilan University in Israel studied eighty-nine first-time parents and found that primary caregivers develop neural pathways in their brains that make them more responsive to the emotional cues of children in their care—regardless of their gender.[19] Brain scans show an increase in gray and white matter in the regions linked to nurturing, affection, and threat detection. Thanks to neuroplasticity, the same pathways develop in fathers who are primary caregivers. It's loving care and putting in the hours that counts. Men who take parental leave tend to have better relationships with their children and are more likely to pitch in with extra childcare once they return to work, according to a Swedish study.[20] Sharing the burden keeps everyone sane. Advisable, since you need your wits about you in the first six months of a Viking's life to avoid committing a crime. Let me explain.

In the Nordic countries, you must choose a name for your child from a preapproved government list. "If you really want something

---

* Joke.

that's not on the list, you need special permission—and creative spellings are rejected," the Veteran Viking instructed me. The official list is available at borger.dk, but many parents take to Google as a first port of call to see if a name they're considering is legal. Some of the results that appear when you search *Can I name my baby...* in Denmark include "Batman," "Disney," and "Shrek." To which the answer—I'll save you the trouble of searching—is no.

Thankfully, there are seven thousand other names that you *are* allowed to call your child. (This is generous. In Iceland, it's only thirty-five hundred.) If you want a name that isn't authorized, you have to justify it in an application to the local priest or choir director.

Who gave choir directors such power? I marveled.

If the name is approved, it's written on the list of approved names and can be used freely by anyone in future.

"I could become some sort of Shrek trailblazer!"

The baby looked livid.

"That'll never happen," Veteran Viking assured him. "The idea is that the name must not disadvantage the child. A kid's life shouldn't begin badly because their parents have bad taste."

This seemed fair, though the rules can appear arbitrary, disallowing some perfectly inoffensive monikers (incidentally, Monica *is* allowed). One Icelandic couple faced fines for calling their child Alex.

Being too tired to operate the TV remote, let alone face legal action, we stuck to the list. And then came twins. And we lost the remote control for two months and just watched an iPad through glazed eyes while feeding squalling babies day and night. The list came through for us again, none of my children were accidentally named Batman, and then there were five of us. A family. Come what may. Only the "may" part turned out to be rather a lot. As we're about to find out.

WHAT I'VE LEARNED ABOUT HOW TO RAISE A VIKING FROM BIRTH

◆ Dads can do this parenting lark too and shouldn't be treated like buffoons—or "babysitters." Having grown up without one of these fabled father creatures, I struggled slightly to know what to do with one when my own children came along. I've had to learn to share—everything from the parenting load to big decisions. It's a work in progress, but I'm trying. ("*Trying*? You're exasperating!" Lego Man tells me. I throw a satsuma at him. And so it goes on.)

◆ *Tillid* is everything. Parenting is a largely thankless task, so trust and faith in the future—in humanity even—are advised.

◆ A gang of other new parents helps. Friends at a similar life stage keep us sane when all around us are losing their shit (mostly babies. But once, me). Fellow parent friends can remind us to have a shower/sandwich/*snegl* once in a while. They can offer a counterbalance to the simmering resentments of parenthood. Fact: everyone hates their partner at some point in the trenches of new parenting. Friends to vent to are essential.

◆ Taking time to choose a name is smart. Shrek might have been called something sensible like 'Simon' had his parents not been quite so sleep deprived with a newborn at home.

BRINGING UP *BØRN**

* "Children" in Danish

I'M STANDING IN A FIELD, staring up at a tree. The tree contains several moldy apples, a broken bucket, and my youngest son. It is a blustery Tuesday, and I would really like to go home. But the universe has other plans.

"How long's he been up there?"

"He was with us for lunch?" offers a student helper at my son's *børnehave* (kindergarten). It's 3:00 p.m., so this isn't much help. I thought something might be amiss when he wasn't in the sand pit with his favorite mini Vikings. Neither was he etching on walls with chalk. Nor cooking up a feast in the "mud kitchen." This is because, it now emerges, he managed to find his way up a tree. But like cats in every *Fireman Sam* episode ever (or *Brandmand Sam* in Danish) he cannot, it seems, get down.

"*Kom nu!*" calls out the student helper, meaning "Come now!"

He does not move.

"*Kom nu!*" She tries again.

He still does not move.

"*Kom—*" she goes for a third round.

"I think," I stop her, "if he could *kom nu*, he would have *kom nu* by now." I look around for assistance, but all the other adults have children hanging off them like human monkey bars. These are pedagogues or early years educators—highly trained day care staff with a three-and-a-half-year bachelor's degree in social education who are used to children hanging off them like human monkey bars. They are less used to children stuck up trees. So this one's on me.

I try coaching my son down ("put one foot there, the other here...") but to no avail. I'm going to have to go up, I see now. I'm going to have to hitch my skirt and scale a tree. For the first time in thirty years.

The lower branches are easy enough, if an inelegant spectacle. The next are trickier. *Fair play*, I think, impressed that my five-year-old managed it. From my elevated vantage point, I see sunshine bouncing off glossy roof tiles and several dads ambling up the road to pick up offspring.

"Oh hej!" I wave and almost lose my grip.

"Are you okay?" one of them calls out. It's the one Lego Man always swears is "the spitting image of Peter Schmeichel." After googling "Who is Peter Schmeichel" and learning that he was a soccer player and famous goalkeeper for Manchester United, back in the day when Manchester United won things, I refuted this ("He's just tall and blond—like everyone here!"). Also, my husband wears thick glasses and has shockingly bad facial recognition. But he insisted, so the name stuck.

"Would you like help?" asks the Peter Schmeichel look-alike.

I would like help, actually. But a small girl dressed as Elsa from *Frozen* is looking up at me with saucer eyes.

I can't let Elsa down. We've only just started getting good Disney female leads. What would Mirabel do? Or Moana? They would not, no way, wait for a strapping Viking to come along and save them.

"*Nej tak*, I'm fine," I tell him in my now trademark Danglish (Danish-English), then manage, "*Jeg kan gøre det selv*," or "I can do it myself"—the phrase all good Danish Vikings learn from approximately age two.

"Sure?" Peter Schmeichel asks.

"Uh-huh," I waver in response. *Damn Nordic egalitarianism, making all damsel in distress action impossible!* "*Jeg er ok!*" ("I am okay") I lie.

There follows a few standard swears and minor splintering, but one grazed knee later, I make it down with my son. Hosiery laddered, pride intact. Ish.

"*Flot!*" a pedagogue with three children hanging off her calls out, which means "Nice!" And then, "*Tak for en rigtig god dag!*" or, "Thanks for a really good day!"

This is day care, Danish style. All children in Denmark attend high-quality, government-run day care five days a week from around ten months until they turn six, when they (finally) start school. And I mean "all." Even Prince Christian, the future king, attended public day care. Parents may opt for a babysitter or *dagplejemor* (day care mother) who can look after up to four children, although *vuggestue* (nursery) and *børnehave* (kindergarten) are the most common options.

Whatever has happened in the preceding hours, no matter how battered, bruised, or mud-caked your child appears at pickup, the response to the question "Did he/she have a good day?" will inevitably be "*Ja, rigtig god!*" ("Yes, really good!")

Your child may have a black eye and a fractured collarbone, but the response is still likely to be, "*Rigtig god!*"

"Are you sure?" a concerned parent may then ask. There will usually be a pause as they wait for more information about how the day was "really good" when their child now has Viking battle scars. But no explanation is usually forthcoming unless a visit to the hospital or the emergency dentist is needed. And I write from experience here.

Very occasionally, things go (more) awry. "My daughter found a hole in the fence and escaped," one dad tells me. "Mine got locked in day care after it shut" says another. And a pedagogue who will remain anonymous tells me firsthand how a child went AWOL during "forest time."

"A mother called the børnehave and said, 'Have you got Thunder Bear with you?'" [Sidebar: Thorbjørn is a hugely popular name in Denmark, from Thor, god of thunder, and *bjørn*, meaning bear. I know. It's too much. *Immediately changes name*] "So Thorbjørn's mom was on the phone, and the day care staff looked around, did a quick head count, and had to admit, 'Actually, no, we haven't got him with us.' 'No, you haven't,' the mother replied, 'because he's found his way home and he's outside my window.'" Remarkably, everyone was able to "see the funny side" by Friday and commend the boy on his resourcefulness.

Vuggestue or the "nursery room" for under-threes is fractionally less perilous, although with ten-plus children ranging in age from ten months to three years, it can be quite the kid soup. When little Frida or Karl are first dropped off aged ten months, they have to be very lucky indeed not to be trodden on by a hulk of a three-year-old as ages zero to three are all lumped together. The month of their third birthday, toddlers graduate to børnehave where they will be expected to ~~avoid being crushed alive~~ hold their own with children up to the age of six.

"It's fine though," a lovely pedagogue named Pia assured me after my son's first black eye, "because we have the step-by-step program that teaches them to read each other's emotions." Presumably so that they can ~~avoid being crushed alive~~ hold their own and survive the elemental clashes of toddler versus toddler.

Despite my skepticism, this approach has precedent. Anthropologist Abigail Page studies hunter-gatherer communities and found that mini "alloparents"—individuals other than parents who care for young—provide about a quarter of all young children's care in some places.[1] Psychologist Sheina Lew-Levy found that in central Africa, child-to-child teaching is much more common after infancy than adult-to-child teaching.[2] It's thought that multiage playgroups are important for helping children expand their horizons, gain social and emotional skills, and learn how to function in society. Other children tend to be better teachers and playmates than adults, since children naturally integrate play into learning and have skill levels closer to one another. So that's all lovely—as long as they can ~~avoid being crushed alive~~ hold their own.

"Teachers also practice being actively passive," says Lise Hansen, a smiley blond pedagogue who works at Valhalla Børnehave in Vejle (her Australian husband calls her "the Viking from Valhalla"). "We sit on our hands," she tells me. I assume she means this metaphorically. She doesn't. "So if a child joins a group where everyone's sitting on a chair and there's no chair for them, and they're about to get upset or have a tantrum, you sit on your hands. *Literally.* To send a signal. You might say something like, 'oh, sorry you can't find a chair. What can we do about that?' The nudge is to make other kids go and pull up a chair." Instead of fixing it, pedagogues expect that children will handle it themselves. "It works with the really little kids too," says Lise. "In nursery, if a baby is crying, you might say to the others, 'Oh, Anton is sad! Do you remember what we used to do when you were sad?' And a two-year-old might say, 'We would get a *sut* [a pacifier]?' I'd then say, 'Great! Can you find Anton a *sut*?' And this way, we're teaching them empathy too." Whereas in the UK and Australia, where Lise has also worked, "it's less about developing them as a person and more about reading and math—even from the age of four."

Nadine, a Danish mom of two in my town, spent ten years in Silicon Valley and recalls nurseries that specialized in Mandarin and extracurricular activities to get kids "Stanford-ready" *aged two.*

But for Vikings? "We prioritize play and time in nature," says Kitta, a statuesque Viking pedagogue who has looked after all three of my children. Kitta, fifty-one, started work in a kindergarten when she was eighteen years old and has worked her way up ever since, "apart from the three years I spent in prison."

I wonder whether I misheard. *Prison?*

"Yes! I spent so many years in kindergarten, I felt I should try something else. So I became a prison guard."

Jail, she tells me, is actually a lot like kindergarten.

"You're looking after people. You have to earn their respect, and you have to find a way to communicate." This makes sense. I once interviewed an FBI hostage negotiator who told me how everything he learned on the job could also be applied to toddlers.

So why didn't Kitta stay in prison, so to speak?

"Too boring!" she says. "I'd work from eight until four, and nothing really happened. Whereas kindergarten"—she holds her hands wide and blows air out of her cheeks—"it is never boring with children." In case a dozen mini Vikings weren't enough to contend with, Danish pedagogues actively encourage their charges to go berserk every now and again. "It's important for them to run wild and have *ramasjang* [hullabaloo]," says Kitta, "so we let them run up and down hills and make noise. How they move is how they learn to talk. If they don't use their body the right way, it's harder for them to learn speech." Studies show that while motor development does not *cause* language to emerge, they are related, and new motor skills can contribute to language development.[3]

The goal of day care in Denmark is to promote children's well-being, give the family flexibility, and prevent negative social inheritance, according to Denmark's Social Services Act. Swedish childcare is similarly based on the principle that early-years education is a form of poverty prevention. The OECD now advises that a better quality of childcare service contributes to a better start in life for children, and three decades of research shows that what happens between the ages of zero and five lays the foundations for our future health and happiness. This window of opportunity is when our brains are at their most receptive and adaptable. If we miss it, we pay down the line. London School of Economics researchers estimate the remedial steps to tackle mental and physical health issues in children "that might have been avoided through action in early childhood" cost £16 billion (or around $20 billion).[5] A year. In England alone. Which, we can all agree, is daft.

In the Nordic countries, they take a different approach. "You notice from the very beginning that the pedagogues are not 'babysitting.' They're bringing up people," says Finnish mother of one Katja Pantzar, "so they'll show kids how to bake, help out, put their dishes back on a tray after meals. Kids learn to participate."[6]

"Participation is key," agrees pedagogue Lise. "We have to make sure that all children can participate in all the activities at the same level."

I don't mean to come over all Maggie Thatcher, but doesn't this mean *no one* gets to thrive? Aren't some children held back when everyone is treated the same?

"No," Lise tells me firmly. "It's the opposite of everyone being squashed down and treated the same. They are all treated *differently* to get to the same level. Each child is treated as an individual with individual needs."

This sounds brilliant, but what does it look like in practice?

"Kids participate in the planning of the day, and we follow their interests, so if they love farms, we might read books about a farm or arrange a visit." Children are also offered any extra resources or help they might need. "You just have to snap your fingers and you can get a psychologist, a speech therapist, a physical therapist four different experts, even translators, to be with you for an hour-long meeting in a couple of days," says Lise.

"In Finland, if you are highly sensitive, have a speech impediment, are scared of loud noises, or find it tough to play with others, you get practical help to address the issue," says Katja.

How does this work with the idea of Viking spirit or Finnish *sisu*, often translated as "grit" or "resilience"? Isn't there a conflict here?

Katja wrote the book on *sisu*, twice (*Finding Sisu*, 2018 and *Everyday Sisu*, 2022), so she should know. "But actually," she says, "no—there is no conflict. You don't want to wait until you have a situation on your hands. You look at the early signs, and you find a solution. It's worth doing to ensure that there aren't bigger problems later on. This is part of the Nordic approach of helping each child fulfill their potential, regardless of income or birth circumstances."

As the former director general of the Finnish Ministry of Education Pasi Sahlberg writes in *Finnish Lessons*, "Kindergarten in Finland doesn't focus on preparing children for school academically. Instead, the main goal is to make sure that all children are happy and responsible individuals."[7]

So how much does all this cost? Well, in Denmark, the state pays 75 percent of the cost of childcare. For under-threes, parents pay around 3,588 DKK ($513) per month and for ages three to six, it's 2,036 DKK ($291). If your collective household income is lower than 576,799 DKK ($82,000), your childcare will be cheaper, and if it's below 185,701 DKK ($26,500), day care is free.[8] There's also a sibling discount, so if you have more than one child using childcare, you pay full price for the most expensive day care and half price for the other(s)—a lot like a Barnes & Noble book deal.

In Iceland, day care can start when a baby is six months old if you're a single parent or nine months for cohabiting or married couples. Monthly costs start at around $487 for a full-time place.

Norwegians attend day care from the age of one, and parents pay around $300 a month. Day care in Finland is free for low-income families, with costs capped at $289 per month. The gold medal goes again to Sweden where parents pay just 10 percent of the actual cost of day care, around $142 per month, with the rest financed through taxes.

At the time of writing, full-time nursery for children under the age of two in the UK costs almost two-thirds of a parent's weekly take-home pay in many areas. Britain has the second highest childcare costs in the developed world.[9] "I basically hand over my salary each week so that my son can bring home a new bug," says one friend with a particularly petri dish child. It's changing, slowly, thanks to work from the likes of Stella Creasy, a member of Parliament and the charity Pregnant Then Screwed. The UK government has pledged funding for all primary schools to provide wrap-around care from 8:00 a.m. to 6:00 p.m. by September 2026, but as many friends say, "I'll believe it when I see it."

In the US, there is no national childcare program. Which is bananas, since studies show that for every dollar invested in early childhood education, the broader economy gets back between $1.50 and $2.80.[10] In the Nordic countries, the high proportion of working mothers (82 percent in Denmark[11]) mean more tax revenue to fund the welfare state—including subsidized, high-quality childcare. Childcare pays for itself. Even better, in Viking land, it's automatic, and you don't have to be a Mensa member to navigate it. Childcare is organized by local government and only closes for a couple weeks over the summer, so parents can manage around their annual leave—usually five weeks paid holiday a year.

High-quality, state-run institutions heavily subsidized by taxes are now the norm, and the Danish ethos is that it's verging on child cruelty *not* to let your small person socialize from ten months. The same is true in many hunter-gatherer societies. For the Maya people of the Yucatán Peninsula in southeast Mexico, not letting others love your children is considered mean-spirited. The indigenous people of Kugaaruk, Canada, believe that just as parents need breaks from their offspring, toddlers get sick of their parents and should socialize regularly.[12] Kitta agrees: "You have to learn to be social. When children are at home for too long, it's so difficult for them to play with others. So it's important to start early." This isn't a sentiment you hear in the UK or the US. At least not these days.

During World War II, it was seen as a patriotic duty for both men and women to work in the UK and the US, so nursery education was presented as being beneficial for children. By 1943, 80 percent of married women were working, so both Britain and America provided nursery places to every child. But after 1945, men returning from war needed jobs—and women lost theirs. Nurseries were seen as an expensive wartime legacy and closed. In 1950, the World Health Organization commissioned a report by British psychologist John Bowlby on children separated from their parents as a result of war.[13] In the report, Bowlby condemned institutional care in France, the Netherlands, Sweden, and Switzerland, describing large orphanages incapable of meeting the needs of individual children. He extrapolated this argument, claiming that *any* maternal separation would adversely affect a child to some degree. (Bowlby didn't bother about fathers. He left the care of his four children entirely to his wife, Ursula.) In response to Bowlby's "findings," the World Health Organization claimed that nurseries and day care caused permanent damage to the emotional health of children. Only his findings showed no such thing. Quite apart from the fact that his research methods have been largely discredited, he was looking at the results of huge orphanages, filled with deeply unhappy children who had suffered conflict, loss, or abuse. Not *day care*.

US anthropologist Margaret Mead and British psychiatrist Michael Rutter were among many to dismiss Bowlby's ideas in subsequent years, only by then, "attachment theory" had taken hold in the UK and US.[14]

But not in the Nordics. There, governments wanted women in the labor force to contribute taxes, so they needed good childcare. Psychologist Henriette Cranil doesn't think this has done Danes any harm either. "There's a lot of attention to attachment in Danish day cares," she says, "and the focus should really be on the quality of care that children get. You could be with your child all day, every day, but it may not be quality time, if they're in front of a TV for large chunks of this, for example. Day care is good for helping children to learn self-regulation with the warmth of highly trained pedagogues."[15]

Alarmist headlines regularly claim that working mothers risk damaging their children, but Harvard studies since 2015 categorically debunk this. Researchers analyzing data from twenty-four different countries found that daughters of working moms have better careers, better pay, and more equal relationships than daughters of stay-at-home mothers.[16] And they're just as happy in adulthood as the children of mothers who stayed at home. A study from the University of North Carolina found that children develop better with a mother who is happy in her work than with a mother who is frustrated by staying at home.[17] By all means, stay home with children if you choose. But if you don't choose it, you shouldn't feel obliged to. Because a parent permanently seething with resentment isn't much fun for anyone. As economist Emily Oster put it in *Cribsheet: A Data-Driven Guide to Better, More Relaxed Parenting, from Birth to Preschool,* "the weight of the evidence suggests the net effects of working on child development are small or zero."[18]

My mother worked while I was growing up out of necessity, but most mothers didn't. We are all products of our upbringing, so at the beginning of my parenting path, I had all sorts of "rules" for myself to make it okay to put the mini redhead in day care. First, I decided he had to have more daylight hours with me each day than at *vuggestue*. When I realized that daylight was minimal in Denmark October to March (we're talking *Mordor*), I modified this to more *waking hours* with me each day than at day care. It's an ongoing tussle, but I know by now that I am a nicer, more fulfilled member of the human race when I have a work life and a home life.

"In Denmark, we believe that others can care for your children. You don't need to be on guard *all* the time," says lovely pedagogue Pia from my children's day care. "It's good to let grandparents, friends, or pedagogues take over sometimes." Also: men.

"My son goes to a day care with all male pedagogues," says Lise, the Viking from Valhalla. "This would be considered weird in the UK, but my son loves it. It's very outdoorsy, very physical." Mini Vikings spend their mornings running around the nearest forest, playing tag, building forts, making "art" with leaves and sticks, catching bugs, and generally rolling in mud. They'll break for lunch, then the older ones might do it all again in the afternoon. "I'm really grateful my son is getting that experience," says Lise. "The stigma around men working in childcare helps no one." *Hear hear.* My twins are currently dazzled by a man at their day care named Simon who can do a fishtail braid and draw a killer unicorn (when requested). He isn't a trained pedagogue—he's a student helper, seeing if he might want to work in the field.

"Every kindergarten will have one or two student helpers," Kitta explains. "They may not have the experience or the same training, but they bring energy and new ideas." All Danes have a criminal background check before working with children, but there is far more trust that people are essentially good.

Whereas British and US friends tell tales of biometric finger codes to enter nurseries and even CCTV, when my son started day care, we used a magnet system. And the word *system* is doing a lot of heavy lifting here. Each child had a magnet that parents could move along a whiteboard to show when they planned on swinging by later. If a grandparent or babysitter was picking up, parents could notify carers via a pen dangling from a string. Over the last couple of years, they've gone high tech, with an electronic system to check in and check out each child daily. But we *all* miss the magnets.

"I think it's amazing the trust this puts on the children too," says Lise. "We don't always even have gates on day cares, so we're relying on a three-year-old not to cross an imaginary line." Although for a good deal of the day, littler ones *can't*. Under-threes nap outside in their Mary Poppins–style perambulators under a shelter or in a "sleeping shed."

The sight of row upon row of carriages was startling when I first visited a Danish day care. Before I had children of my own, I met an American mother of three with perma glossy hair and distinctly North American dentistry who'd also found herself living Danishly. One afternoon, I joined her on the day care pickup. First stop? Swinging by the carriages to check if her smalls were still sleeping.

"They're strapped in so they can't escape," American Mom friend explained, pointing out the rein-like harnesses wrapped around still snoozing infants. "And some carriages even have hinged wooden bars over the opening so they stay put until a pedagogue comes to get them!" She demonstrated, lifting and lowering a small square. "Like baby cages!"

My eyes widened. "And...err...what's with the ladders?"

"Ah! Well, some Viking babies are...you know...*Vikings*," she explained. The three-foot ladders leaning against some carriages help sturdier toddlers make their own way up to sleep, thus saving pedagogues a trip to the chiropractor down the line. The whole thing looked archaic, but as American Mom put it with a flash of a Whitestrips-bright smile, "They nap like a dream!"

Babies are frequently checked on by pedagogues, and there's a monitor in the sleeping shed so the grown-ups can hear what's going on. Under-threes cozy up under a duvet and possibly extra blankets before being covered with a fly net.

"In winter?" I asked, surprised. "Do they have some kind of badass Viking flies here?"

"Well, no," American Mom told me, "but they do have cats." True story: one child woke up with a cat on his face before the year-round bug-net policy was implemented.

Most children are dropped off before 8:00 a.m. and collected between 3:00 p.m. and 4:00 p.m. The working day in most Danish offices is 8:00 a.m. to 4:00 p.m., but two-parent families often tag team so that one will work an hour later while the other picks up children. On a Friday, everyone winds down even earlier. I once had to collect the redhead at 4:00 p.m. on a Friday, and he was the only child left. Pia was ready for the weekend, and I was consumed by guilt. I never did it again. But there's generally a lot of love both ways between parents and pedagogues. Kindergarten staff in central Denmark even offered parents two hours' free childcare on a Thursday evening so that the parents could have "special adult time."[19]

It's pretty great. But there are challenges. "It used to be one pedagogue for every four kids in børnehave," says Kitta. "Now it's one for every seven or eight." This issue was brought to nationwide attention in a 2019 TV documentary by the Danish public service broadcaster, DR. *Hvem passer vores børn?* (Who is looking after our children?) showed one institution where three staff members were left to care for thirty-one children.[20] After the program aired, protests took place and a nationwide parents' movement was set up called *Hvor er der en voksen?* (Where is there an adult?). Campaigners began fighting for one adult to every three children in vuggestue and one to every six in børnehave. In 2020, the government agreed to meet the demands...in theory. But when a pedagogue is ill and a substitute comes in, Statistics Denmark registers this as two separate employees. The day care manager and kitchen staff are also counted. "We need more help," agrees Pia. "We need to attract more people to the profession and keep existing pedagogues working." But the real threat to the Danish day care system is admin.

"The toughest thing that has happened in my industry since I started is that we have to document everything now," says Pia, "from language accumulation to motor skills and the ability to share and communicate new ideas." The Danish government likes to have a handle on how its mini Vikings are faring, says Pia, "but that time comes away from the kids."

Kitta agrees that it's a problem. "Almost half want to leave the profession as there is now too much paperwork."

There's also a nudge toward the more central European and US approach of goals, says Pia, "around everything from social skills to language and more admin—which means less time with the children."

"And who is this coming from?"

"The government in part," says Pia, "and actually—" She hesitates.

"Go on?"

"Parents."

Oh.

"Expectations among parents are higher than they used to be," agrees the Viking from Valhalla, Lise. "We are slowly becoming consumers in Denmark—just like everywhere else. I think the influence of American TV and culture can really be seen here."

So how do we get back to a more balanced place?

"Well, what sets us apart is that we have equal opportunities," says Lise. "We need to hold on to that."

"And boundaries," adds Pia ominously. "I'd say parents under the age of forty are pretty bad at setting boundaries." *Ouch.* "But as adults, sometimes you just have to be firm, like when it comes to wearing the snowsuit in winter." This is the Maggie from *The Simpsons*–style zip-up padded onesie that all Danish children wear in varying sizes from birth until they're about ten. "You *have* to wear the snowsuit, because it's cold." There's no debate here: it's Baltic.

Boundaries are crucial for Kitta too. She's famed for her no-nonsense, firm-but-fair approach, inspiring awe and envy in all. ("Why, when *Kitta* asks them to put their shoes on, do they actually put their shoes on? How come when *Kitta* says 'wash your hands,' they actually wash their hands? When *Kitta* says 'no throwing rocks,' they actually stop throwing rocks!") I beg Kitta to tell me her secrets. ("Is it magic? It's magic! Isn't it?")

"Maybe it's because I'm bigger? Maybe I'm older?" she suggests. That's not it.

"Okay then. I know what I stand for, and when I say something, I mean it. I don't move from A to B. I am consistent."

That's it.

"Also," she adds, "I really like the kids. It's very important to say how much we get from them as well. Some days, it can feel like too much, then one of the kids will give you a hug and say 'thank you' and it's all worthwhile. We get so many hugs. I missed that in prison. There wasn't so much hugging."

"No."

"And with the bigger kids, you can have a dialogue. They are so kind and funny."

I hear her here. My youngest (by two minutes) is currently indignant that "every Easter, bad guys peg a man called Jesus to a wardrobe!" while my daughter, having learned how we all come from monkeys, is telling everyone that her elder brother has orange hair "because *he* came from an orangutan."

"It's a really good age," says Kitta.

I'm glad to hear her say this, since the twins have a birthday coming up, and I'm about to ask if she wouldn't mind leading a field trip for an hour's cake and chaos. This is the Danish tradition whereby the pedagogue arrives with the class to the home of the birthday girl or boy (or, in my case, both) to go mad for an hour before the teacher takes them away again. There's no hanging around, no small talk, no social one-upmanship, no infringement on evenings or weekends. And the whole thing costs no more than the price of a few snacks. It's an inexpensive, efficient ninja birthday squad: in and out.

"Not like in the US," says American Mom. "There we're talking professional cakes, entertainers, puppeteers, Disney princesses, a creepy snake guy—"

"What?"

"Oh, just this guy who did the party rounds back in the US." She waves a hand in dismissal. "But the point is in Denmark, it's easy! The kid-party production values here are *very low*. As you'll find out."

I can't wait.

The following week, Kitta, two colleagues, and eighteen mini Vikings between the ages of three and five bumble up the road in high-visibility vests for an hour-long game of *du kan ikke fange mig!* (you can't catch me!) before demolishing one kilogram of carrot sticks, twenty-five *pølsehorn* (sausage rolls), twenty sticks of cheese, three red peppers, four cucumbers, and two casserole dishes of popcorn. After what feels like the longest and loudest hour of my life, Kitta claps her hands. The children line up in pairs, pull on their fluorescent-yellow tabards (that my daughter already views as an affront to her personal style), and they are off. As am I: for a lie-down in a darkened room. Give pedagogues a medal. Give them anything they want. They deserve it.

WHAT I'VE LEARNED ABOUT HOW TO RAISE A VIKING IN DAY CARE

- Embrace the chaos. Yes, it's loud, but it's doing them good (probably). Mixing up ages happens in families anyway, with bigger children stepping in to look after smaller ones (or rather, I'm hoping this is what happens).

- Children need boundaries. Denmark is a rule-based society, and Danes tend to follow these in the name of community. No one crosses the road until the green man/woman/ Viking flashes up (Danish pedestrian crossings are more inclusive). And freedom *within* boundaries is something I've come to appreciate. Within a structure, I feel free and secure (oh yeah, and my children do too).

- Danish style children's parties are the way forward. I'm wondering whether I can lower the bar still further next year. Perhaps just "Join us in the park for a play on Saturday morning! No presents please, but bring snacks."

- Small people and their caregivers romp outdoors all year round in Denmark. Regardless of rain, freezing fog, and general end-of-days weather. *What? How? Why? Wait and see...*

NO SUCH THING AS BAD WEATHER

RAIN HAMMERS HARD, AND WATER bubbles up from the drain. It's been wet all week in my town, and the river running through it has churned into a thick stew of swirling sand. Winter comes sooner in Denmark. September 22 to be precise.

In England, I'm sure we had "autumn"...

In Denmark, it's cold and dark within a week. We've only just left the house for a walk, and already my feet are sodden.

Might come back early, I message Lego Man. Rotten out.

Infuriatingly, he sends a smiley face in response and a splash emoji. I make a note to tell him that this doesn't mean what he thinks it means. Especially after he sent that eggplant to a colleague in a restaurant recently. ("What? I wanted baba ghanoush.")

Just as I'm composing a response, my children begin splashing in puddles and ricocheting off wet bushes. *For fun? How are they having a nice time when the weather's so dire?* I wonder, perplexed.

Lucky the kids are dressed for it! Lego Man texts.

Oh yes. That's why.

During my first year of raising Vikings, I sent the miniature redhead to day care in a woolen duffel coat like Paddington Bear. Only with marmalade-colored hair rather than a sandwich under his hat. In my defense, I came from London. Plus I wasn't a Viking yet. Within hours, the woolen coat smelled of wet dog (it drizzles daily), and his toes froze.

"These are no good," one of the pedagogues told me at pickup, gesturing with disdain at my son's stinky Paddington ensemble. "He needs proper outdoor clothes. Otherwise? He will freeze."

In some places, they put up posters to remind parents exactly what children need for each season. In my place, Vikings are just expected to *know*. I did not know. So I threw myself on the mercy of my oldest Danish friend and mother of three, Veteran Viking.

"We'll make a list," she told me. "Come for coffee at 16:00."

Coffee? At 16:00? Danes are hardcore. Still, grateful, I accepted and arrived as instructed, notepad in hand, ready to be schooled.

"Number one, you need a *flyverdragt*," Veteran Viking told me as she marched around the house, dodging cats, picking up stray clothing, and sending texts simultaneously.

"A *flyverdragt*?" My rudimentary Danish had taught me that *flyver* was the verb "to fly" and *dragt* meant "suit." "My son needs a flight suit?" *Were we staging a* Top Gun *prequel?*

"*Flyverdragt* is the all-in-one snowsuit for winter."

"Oh!" I scratched this into my notebook.

"Next, winter boots! Gore-Tex." She banged together two weighty pieces of footwear to illustrate.

Having long evangelized about the virtues of technical outerwear, I knew Lego Man would be thrilled by this.

"Boots they can get on and off easily—no laces." This is because children have to have a good crack at dressing themselves for outside play from the age of two, she told me.

"Two?!"

"Two. Now, you need an *elefanthue*—"

"An...elephant hat?" I stared at Google Translate doubtfully.

"Yes."

"Does it have a trunk?"

She looked at me as if I were an idiot—and not for the first time. A cat slunk past with a similar expression of disdain.

What then? Flappy ears? Tusks?

She rummaged in her youngest son's duffel bag and pulled out...a balaclava. This is the "elephant hat" all Danish children wear much of the year in varying thickness—from cotton in spring to wool in winter.

"He needs *fingervanter*." This translates to "finger gloves." As opposed to toe gloves, obviously. "As well as thermals and in spring and autumn, *termotøj*." She wrenched out a nana-style quilted jacket and matching trousers. "*Termotøj* translates as warm clothes"—Danes like to be literal—"not waterproof but *wind* resistant, so you may hear it called a wind suit."

I tried not to snigger.

"Then there's *regntøj*," she went on. This translates as rain clothes. "Waterproof jackets and trousers for wet but not freezing weather. Used all year round."

"Wet but not freezing weather" all year round? Great.

"From the supermarket is fine. And while you're there, you can also get *gummistøvler*—"

"I know this one! Rubber boots!"

"That's right." She gave me a brief smile, as though congratulating a child who's mastered a knife and fork. "A pair for home and a pair for day care is a good idea."

Some day cares have a drying cupboard—where you can hang up wet clothes between outdoor playtimes for a quick blast with a few dozen built-in hair dryers. Our day care has nothing so fancy: we dry out our clothes with air and Viking spirit.

"Lastly," Veteran Viking told me, "children needed *løbesko*"— running shoes—"for the few days of the year when it's not raining or cold."

"Okay. And what about summer?"

"Just *less* of everything."

"Sun hats?"

She shrugged. "You can send one in, but you can't make kids wear one. Plus pedagogues have a lot going on." She downed the rest of her coffee. "So you're lucky if they get sunscreen."

All these fair-haired children! Prime sunburn candidates! Future melanoma! I made a mental note to slather the redhead in SPF 50 from April to October.

I looked at my list: a mere nine new items to procure and pack for the day care run. It's fortunate secondhand shops rule in Denmark.

Once satisfied that I'd fully absorbed her sartorial schooling, Veteran Viking and her cat waved me off with a parting gift: "We have a saying in Denmark: there's no such thing as bad weather, just the wrong clothes."

I managed a weak smile. Vikings of all nationalities have

variations on this mantra. Calling the Nordics "outdoorsy" is an understatement. In Norway, *friluftsliv*—free air life—is the most popular self-reported leisure activity nationwide, with higher participation than all other sports activities combined. During my last trip, I was alarmed to find Norwegians getting their friluftsliv on in weather so cold my eyelashes froze.

Swedes love being outside so much that 25 percent of the population are members of an official outdoor organization, Friluftsfrämjandet, and many five-year-olds attend Saturday "nature school." Here, mini Swedes learn about life cycles, insect identification, forestry care, and how to stay warm and dry outside in all weathers. "Plus, the more you know about nature, the more you care about the environment," says Per Nilsson from the Swedish Environmental Protection Agency.[1]

Studies have long shown that spending time outdoors can improve mental well-being, reduce stress, help with concentration and cooperation, and even out differences between low-achieving and high-achieving children.[2] "And most kids just do better outside," says Pia at my children's day care. "They get outdoors, and everything is easier for them. They transform."

In the wild, children have to use their imagination to create play, as there are no toys. Researchers in Norway have found improved motor skill development and less conflict when children are out in nature.[3] "Because kids don't have to fight for resources or equipment," says Karen Marie Eid Kaarby from the Faculty of Teacher Education and International Studies at Oslo Metropolitan University. "There are enough stones and twigs to go around for everyone." So children are happier—and grown-ups are too. "Pedagogues are much more relaxed being out in nature," says Karen Marie, "so now we have more and more forest kindergartens, welcomed by parents and taken seriously by academics."[4]

Just as prison guard turned pedagogue Kitta noted how playing in nature helped children learn how to use their bodies, the act of molding and kneading nature's squelch—like mud or sand—can help develop the senses and movement. The Swiss psychologist Jean Piaget called ages 0-2 years "the sensorimotor stage," an essential developmental phase when children predominantly learn through sensory experiences and manipulating objects to develop a sense of self as distinct from the world around them.[5] And then there's the pure unalloyed joy of just getting muddy.

When I was growing up, "Don't get dirty!" was a popular parental catchphrase. Playing in mud or sand, getting grass stains, climbing trees, or anything that might involve "ruining" our clothes was a no-no. I never wore white growing up as it would only get dirty. (I was strongly discouraged from black too, because it "doesn't do our complexion any favors." Instead, I grew up in pastel shades that made me look like a boiled egg.) So I'm determined to let my children get mucky if they want to. And it turns out that mud is good for our immune systems as well as our souls.

Mud-loving researchers in Finland even transplanted soil and vegetation from a forest floor to the playgrounds of four day care centers. A month later, children showed signs of heightened microbial diversity on their skin and in their gut as well as improved immune function.[6] In future, it may be possible to enrich the soil in playgrounds worldwide with beneficial organisms. But for now, parents and teachers work with what they have: the forest and homemade mud kitchens—in our case a few old pots and pans filled with soil and water. Or rather, just soil. The rain comes soon enough in the Nordic countries. But that's okay too.

"Did you know that raindrops release special compounds that combine in the air we breathe?" I geek out at dinner after a day's research into the glories of weather. "And inhaling these compounds improves our mood!"

"Why?" Lego Man is a details man.

I tell him I'll get back to him on this. After dessert and consulting my printout, I announce that "as water and air molecules collide, they create negative air ions."[7]

"What are air ions?" Redhead demands.

Damn...

"Um, well, air ions," I read from the scientific paper with more confidence than I feel, "make a molecule with an extra charge, and this can improve respiratory health and immunity, apparently." The main takeaway, I insist, is that Austrian scientists found walking in heavily ionized air boosted levels of a vital antibody in the lining of the mouth, nose, and gut. "So rain is good. In fact, all weather is pretty good."

"Thanks for that, groundbreaking stuff..." Lego Man comments before loading the dishwasher like a raccoon on meth (i.e., "as normal").

Growing up, my aunt would always send my cousins and I outside to "run in the wind," which all felt rather *Wuthering Heights* on a blustery day. I always suspected this was just to get us all out of her hair, but a 2021 study suggests she may have been a medical visionary. Scientists found that wind actually disperses bugs, so we're all better off being outside on a windy day than cooped up at home. During COVID-19, when we were only allowed to socialize outside, researchers from Stony Brook University had a hunch that slower wind speeds might be associated with increased risk of transmission. They studied COVID cases and average wind speed. And what do you know? It turned out people weren't nearly as susceptible to catching the virus when it was windy out.[8] Wind is nature's air purifier. Fortuitously, it's often windy in Denmark. And wet. And gray. But that's okay.

"You can't wait for a sunny day in life," says Lasse Heimdal, formerly of Norway's Friluftsliv Association.[9] Lasse is now harnessing friluftsliv to help people through the challenges of modern life in Norway's answer to the Samaritans. "When it's snowing and rainy, we still go outside. We had to historically to survive." He tells me how, for hundreds of years, this instinct has been honed. "Those who fell in love with someone strong would survive in nature. Their children would survive in nature. So even today, for example, being super skinny is not the goal in Norway. The goal is to be fit and strong." He looks at me, then adds, "You'd survive!"

"Err, thanks."

"Let's see your arms?"

I flex him the gun show.

"There you go! You could stretch a bow or swing a club if you had to."

This is the strangest compliment I've ever received. But I'll take it.

"Survival in nature, whatever the weather, is a big part of our culture," Lasse goes on. "You learn how to dress, how to handle the cold and dark, how to walk long distances and live in a rough climate. Even kindergartners learn to use a map and compass, light a fire, and be outside, all year round."

From childhood, Nordics develop what Stanford University social psychologist Kari Leibowitz calls a "positive wintertime mindset." "Because if we have this negative idea of winter and feel a sense of dread, we're not only making winter less enjoyable, we're also making the preceding season less enjoyable too," she tells me. A positive wintertime mindset, by contrast, frees up mental energy that might otherwise be spent dreading. Instead of sitting indoors and cranking up the central heating to wish away winter, we'd be better off welcoming it. Because winter's coming—to all of us, every year, whether we want it to or not. Learning to *dress* the part is the first step—for parents as well as their small people, says Kari. "In much of the world when it's cold, people still dress normally to go out, then wonder why they're uncomfortable."[10] But Vikings make no such rooky errors.

Since my first technical outerwear training session with Veteran Viking, I've had two more children. That means two more sets of flight suits, elephant hats, and wool-based products. But I've still been reluctant to walk the walk myself. When I moved from the world of glossy fashion magazines to rural Denmark, I bought rubber boots. This was a big step. Since then, Lego Man has been slowly trying to outfit me appropriate footwear, wet weather wear, and snow gear, but I have resisted, repeatedly. Until now.

Learning more from Lasse and Kari about the importance of dressing the part to truly #goviking and aware that I haven't got a leg to stand on asking my children to wriggle into winter suits while I prance about in a pleather jacket, I submit.

"Will you"—I take a deep breath, addressing Lego Man—"help me to get all the right outdoor gear?"

He looks like it's Christmas.

"I thought you'd never ask!" He swivels his laptop and opens several tabs that appear to have been bookmarked, possibly for years. "Shall we start with outdoor trousers?"

Must we? I look down at my jeans. "Won't these do?"

"No." He clicks Add to Cart. "You want hard wearing, quick drying, and synthetic."

"Aren't there any...nicer-looking ones?" I ask, still hopeful.

"Nothing looks as good as comfortable feels!" he tells me.

I don't think that's what Kate Moss said.

"Now you want an under layer. Not cotton."

"Why?"

"GWSW," he says, not looking up from his screen.

"Sorry?"

He sighs as though I am the most infuriating human that has ever lived. "Gets wet, stays wet! No. What you need is something else—"

"Is it a spa day?" I'm really hoping it's a spa day. Or cake.

It is not.

"Wicking!" says Lego Man. "Something synthetic to take sweat away from the body. Then you need a warming intermediate layer..." He's in his element. "A good outer shell against wind and rain. Then some good hiking socks... You know what they say!"

"No."

"No?"

"No! What do 'they' say?"

"Abrasions are a hiker's worst enemy!"

"I've never heard anyone say that."

He looks at me as if to say "your loss," and the order is placed.

A week later, packages arrive, and I am kitted out with wicking layers, waterproof trousers, a waterproof yet breathable jacket, hat, socks, and walking boots. I look like a ~~nerd~~ walking North Face shop, but my children approve, and I notice there is far less griping over pulling on their own weather-appropriate gear now that I'm wearing it too. Not everything is new—DBA and Reshopper have offered up some prize preloved items, and Vikings can also *rent* technical outerwear. Almost every Norwegian has access to an "outdoor library" to borrow anything from skates to skis, cooking equipment, and tents. Katja in Helsinki tells me that dressing the part is obligatory in Finland too. "One friend has her own sock bar in the hallway, with multiple pairs of wool socks in all sizes on pegs, so everyone can take a pair and be ready to go on a hike. It's part of everyday life!"

I promise to fully commit to the ethos of "no such thing as bad weather" despite crossing my fingers behind my back. This pledge is instantly put to the test when my family unanimously votes on a last-minute road trip to test my new look in the great outdoors.

As a rule, I do not like camping (because camping), but my children love it. So sometimes, there is tent action. This is one of those times. Camping in Denmark is perfectly safe, there are no dangerous animals apart from ticks, and you can often camp for free or stay in one of two thousand wooden shelters dotted around. There are rules attached, naturally, so you can only spend one night in the same spot, must steer clear of roads and buildings, take your litter with you, and when nature calls, you dig a hole. But other than that? You can roam wherever you like. This felt wonderfully liberating when we first began living Danishly. But in the other Nordic countries, this freedom is even more entrenched. "The land belongs to all" isn't just a pithy slogan in Sweden—it's part of the constitution. *Allemansrätten*, the right of public access, allows everyone to roam freely by law, and the Norwegian government has funded a campaign to increase awareness of the right of public access and promote friluftsliv for everyone. "Parents not born into this culture may not be as comfortable getting dressed up to go outside in all weather," says Bente Lier, now general secretary of Norway's Friluftsliv Association, "so we create many initiatives to invite people in, to show how helpful friluftsliv can be and the benefits it can bring for whole families."[11]

Exposure to green space has been shown to lower cholesterol, reduce stress, and spark creativity, while sunlight boosts serotonin and melatonin to improve sleep.[12] Yet three-quarters of UK children spend less time outside than prison inmates.[13]

I was one of those indoor kids. I liked books. And TV. And walls. And sofas. But if I want to raise Vikings, I have to overcome my natural impulse to burrow under a duvet when it's wet and windy out. *But how?*

Lego Man is no help here. "Just strap on your boots and get out there," he tells me in his hearty Yorkshire accent, not saying but strongly implying, "you big southern softy!" He likes to think of himself as an honorary Viking, since "Yorkshire and the River Tees were very significant in the Viking period." Which is great... for him. But it doesn't help me.

Fortunately, Norwegian friends have a better idea: bribery.

"I always recommend chocolate, nuts, and raisins for a hike," says Lasse.

"Food is a big motivation for many," agrees Bente. "When we talk to kids who aren't so keen on the idea of friluftsliv—or people from cultures where this isn't the norm—as soon as food comes into the equation, they're big fans." Several packs of trail mix and emergency "motivational chocolate" later, and we're on our way.

There's a citrusy tang of pine, and the birdsong is louder out here in no-woman's-land. While Lego Man is driving, I look at the scant details available about our destination and read, "What's included: firewood. What's not included: essentials."

Skylarks flutter as we drive. Lego Man, the redhead, the twins, the dog, and I transport about 150 down jackets, wicking layers, a camping stove, several sporks (spoon-forks), pasta, and porridge oats.

We hike for thirty minutes from the car to a place Lego Man decrees is "the perfect spot" to pitch a tent. But blisters? Not one.

Appropriate outerwear: check.

In the forest, the air is clear. The children throw sticks and balance along fallen tree trunks.

Nature's playground: check.

We graze on wild blackberries as we go, stopping to feast on chocolate rations whenever morale is flagging.

Food as friluftsliv motivation: check.

There is an emergency outdoor bathroom break. Once we've dug, buried, wiped, etc., we go on our way.

Call of nature: check.

A child complains of itching. There is an inspection to reveal...a tick. With the aid of a phone flashlight and Swiss Army knife tweezers, I remove a tick from somewhere unmentionable.*

Roughing it contrary to indoor-kid "southern softy" disposition: check.

Since becoming a parent, I've slowly realized that I'm stronger—mentally and physically—than I ever believed I could be growing up. Not only can I push an *actual human being* out of an impossibly small orifice, I can raise one too. I can leave the house without wearing a vest if I want to (though it's Denmark: why would I?). I can get dirty and survive without a shower for twenty-four hours. I can neglect Netflix or my fancy coffee machine for days and no one dies! This has been a self-parenting revelation. Someone hire a blimp! Tell the world: I am tough. I can even handle ticks now. *Fights wave of nausea at the memory***

When we arrive, the twins experience a sudden surge of energy,

---

* A butthole. I had to remove a tick from a kid's butthole. My life is nonstop glamor.

running up and down forest slopes enjoying nature's parkour. Then it rains. We get the tent up. Or rather, I think we do. Only apparently, I've done one of my poles wrong.

"It's structurally unsound!" Lego Man tells me.

"You'll be structurally unsound in a minute," I grumble as rain lashes down.

He fixes the faulty pole. ("It's not the pole that's faulty. It's your assembly," he tells me. Through gritted teeth, I manage, "How's the air up there on your massive high horse?" He flicks mud at me. I fling a whole clod at him. He tells me I'm being unreasonable. I tell him he smells like a teenage boy's car. We call it quits.)

The rain stops. And then there is mud. Lots of mud.

My daughter makes mud pies.

Old friends and health-promoting microorganisms: check.

The rain eases off, we cook over a campfire, wash up in fresh rainwater, and sing, inexplicably, the UB40 hit "Rat in Mi Kitchen."

We sleep like logs and make it home in one piece, loaded with good ions. And possibly roundworm.

But were we cold? Not once.

"Because you dressed the part!" Peter Schmeichel nods approvingly when I recount our adventure. He's a huge admirer of Lego Man's outdoorsy exploits—although we both agree that my husband must never find out, lest he become insufferably smug. "Do you know, we have a saying in Denmark: 'There's no such thing as bad weather, just the wrong clothes.'"

"Yes," I tell him, "a few people *might* have mentioned this."

WHAT I'VE LEARNED ABOUT HOW TO RAISE A VIKING OUTDOORS IN ALL WEATHERS

- The weather's often awful, so we might as well get out there. Hippos were right: mud is marvelous for multiple modern malaises, rain makes magic, and wind blows away bugs as well as cobwebs.

- I might be an indoor girl at heart, but there's plenty of science to show that getting outside is good for us. When in Viking land, I've resolved to do as Vikings do (and even *like* some aspects of it now).

- Dressing the part helps. "You enjoy it so much more and stay out for longer if you're well-prepared and comfortable," says Kari. "Enjoy" is a strong word, but I'm certainly more comfortable. Ordinarily, I run cold. Combine this with wet (see "Danish weather") and bugs, and it's a recipe for misery. But if I'm warm and dry? Turns out I'm a different person. Whole pieces of what I've taken to be my personality jigsaw up until this point are gone. Am I...*hardy* now? Tough? Outdoorsy even? I am Viking. Hear me roar! Turns out Gore-Tex is the new black.

- Still, pack snacks. "It's important to bring food that gives you a lot of calories," Lasse tells me. But what food fuels Vikings? Well, loosen your belt...

6

FORAGING AND FAMILY MEALS

I'M SHELLING PEAS WITH SALTY hands. Sweet and salt combine as I squint in the sunshine to watch five-year-olds—buckets dangling from elbows, ankle-deep in cold Baltic water—scanning for mussels. The eldest has gone up the lane with a twenty-kroner coin to buy a pint of strawberries from the honesty stall, and it occurs to me that this is a far cry from the snacks of my youth.

I grew up in the 1980s and 1990s in a household where the main food groups seemed to be granola bars and All-Bran. No child needs All-Bran. But fiber was king, and what was I going to do? But potato chips were (are) the holy grail. Whenever I could find a classmate to do swapsies ("Who wants a granola bar? Anyone? Anyone?"), chips would be my goal. It was also the era of the Pop-Tart. Squeezy cheese. Bagel Bites. All the processed delights. But not in Denmark. Danes ate real food. And they still do, for the most part.

"We like to think we're pretty healthy," my chatty neighbor tells me, and food is good here. My friend Tracii from Los Angeles calls it "basic with sauce": "Everything is fresh so it tastes so good and goes bad so fast." He's right; it does. All fresh produce in Denmark is like an avocado: delicious for a day, two max. After that? Screwed.

This is because Denmark has the highest per capita consumption of organic food in the world.[1] (Sweden and Norway also make the top ten.)[2] An agricultural nation until a couple of generations ago, there's still a connection with the earth for many. Since 1889, Denmark has celebrated "potato week" every October, when children were kept home to help with the harvest. Although far fewer work on the land today, the tradition persists, and schools shut in week 42 of every year (Danes love a week number).

Once we've survived another Nordic winter and the sun begins warming the land in May, everyone eats Danish strawberries and peas. June means new potatoes, often sold by the roadside (before harvesting the "old potatoes" in autumn). And there's a year-round culture of stick-to-your-ribs food, starting young.

My first lesson in how to feed a Viking came when the miniature redhead started vuggestue. All under-threes are given daily meals that are 90 percent organic. I was never sure what these consisted of, and my son couldn't tell me much, so I usually guessed from the color of his clothes what had been on the menu that day. A weekly food diary looked something like this:

- Monday: brown
- Tuesday: green
- Wednesday: red
- Thursday: pink
- Friday: yellow

Eventually, I asked Pia the pedagogue for the foodie lowdown. "Any child arriving before 7:30 a.m. is offered breakfast or *morgenmad*. Normally oats with milk."

"You mean porridge?"

"No, oats. With milk."

This, I discovered, is a thing in Denmark.

"But there's a technique to it," says Trine Hahnemann, legendary Danish chef and owner of Hahnemanns Køkken bakery and cooking school in Copenhagen. She confides in me the secret to this most hallowed of children's breakfasts: "You make a mountain of oats, and then you sprinkle a little sugar on top to be the snow." [my day care skips this part]. Then you make a river around it with milk and slowly fold in the raw oats. Kids love it."[3]

Midmorning snack is served around 8:30 a.m. (yep, 8:30 is midmorning in Denmark; Vikings have been up for *hours*) and consists of fruit, crudités, and homemade bread rolls or rye bread in neat triangles. Lunch is served around 10:45 ("10:45 *a.m.*?" ask my in-laws, for whom this is too early even for breakfast). This might be fish or meat with potatoes and vegetables, soup, pasta, *frikadeller* (meat balls), or *fiske frikadeller* (fish meatballs—Danish is a direct language). A couple of days a week, it's a more low-key *smørrebrød*, an open sandwich with egg, salmon, mackerel, beets (a.k.a. pink clothes and alarming pee day), or *leverpostej* (liver pâté). Yes, when American kids are having PB&J, Danish children are munching on a thick slab of pork liver and lard.

"Since World War II, liver pâté has been kid food in Denmark," Trine explains. "Pork production industries have had huge advertising behind us all eating the meat in Denmark, and there's a lot of fat and liver left over." Denmark tends to export the more expensive meat, "but Danish Crown paid for advertising to make us think the rest of it was a good idea too," says Trine. Thus the pâté.* The most dedicated Danes make their own. "You grind the liver and add the fat, then you boil this down to make a roux, and bake it in water," Trine tells me. I'll take her word for it.

Trine lived in London when her son was an infant but imported a lot of Nordic customs, "to bring Denmark with me!" Top priority was making her own rye bread. "I couldn't find it in the UK then and felt like rye bread was the core of being Danish, so I baked it." A few years later, Trine moved to the US where she had a daughter. "Suddenly there were these great supermarkets and all this choice, but I still wanted rye bread, so I had to be part of a co-op in Virginia to buy my own cracked rye and make it."

It's impossible to overstate the importance of rye bread in Denmark. It is a staple. It is delicious. It is, in the words of Oprah, "like eating a slice of the earth." Give us this day our daily bread, and let it be rye.

When a child reaches børnehave age in Denmark at around three, many parents enter the dreaded (for me) lunch box territory.

"My parents were very good at packed lunches," says Nanna from the parenting community Momkind. "Dad would make my lunches and put in a little drawing each day. It meant a lot to me. I always had freshly baked bread, but some of my friends would have the same thing every day: *ostehaps* [Danish soft cheese portions],

---

* "Danish Crown also paid for advertising that made us think a rasher of bacon was an essential part of the British breakfast," said Trine.

spegepølse [salami], *leverpostej* [pâté] on rye bread, carrots, peppers, and cucumber."

It's the same in our house. The monotony of daily lunch boxes is a ~~slog, pain in the ass~~ challenge. I can't even make up for my pitiful culinary abilities by slinging in a bag of Doritos in Denmark either. I mention chips as a lunch box staple of my youth only to be met by snorts of derision.

"You British and your potato chips!" Day care dad Peter Schmeichel shakes his head.

What?!

I speak to Line, a Danish mom of three married to a Brit. I ask how the two food cultures compare, and she says, straight off the bat, "English kids get given a lot of snacks on the way home from school, like chips! That is unheard of in Denmark, at least if you want to be a good parent."

Ouch!

I ask my friend Rikke, who has two children, a full-time job, a microbrewery, and a mischievous twinkle in her eye at all times. Rikke also spent a decade in the UK. Her overriding impression of children in the motherland?

"I remember thinking they ate a lot of chips."

What is going on? Can our reputation for salty potato snacks really precede us?

I ask Trine what she noticed about the way UK parents fed their children, and she answers instantly: "Chips! I saw them all eating chips in the playground!" I blush the color of BBQ Pringles. "We don't do that here," she says, breaking it to me gently.

In Denmark, you can't even buy individual bags of chips round my way (believe me, I've tried). This makes it a less easy snacking option. "Because what are you going to do?" asks Peter Schmeichel. "Open a family-size bag and eat them all?"

I took longer than is optimal to say, "No. Of course not..." In truth, my approach to snacking, especially premenstrual, is very much *Everything Everywhere All at Once.* But Danes prefer three solid meals a day.

"For Vikings, lunch has to contain proper filling food," says my friend Andreas, a ridiculously kind and gentle deputy head teacher and scout leader in Denmark who works a lot with exchange students throughout the Nordics. He tells me how American or British children often turn up with a packed lunch of white bread and shiny square cheese sandwiches, "and they can't last the day! There's not enough energy in that to keep going!" White bread is made from refined wheat flour, has a high glycemic index, and can lead to blood sugar spikes, after which we experience a sugar crash and feel awful. Rye bread, on the other hand, has a lower glycemic index, takes longer to digest, and doesn't cause our blood sugar to rise as rapidly. "Despite all the clichés about rye bread and herring, at least Viking kids have fuel," says Andreas, "and children who are well-fed can participate and concentrate."

With this in mind, Sweden and Finland provide free school lunches for all pupils. Sweden introduced daily cooked meals in the 1940s and began charting the impact that this had. Researchers from Lund University found that both boys and girls who received school meals during the entire nine years of compulsory school grew almost one centimeter taller, went to university more often, and even had a 3 percent higher lifetime income—purely because they could concentrate more and so got higher-paying jobs. Children from poorer households benefited the most from the free school meals, achieving a 6 percent higher lifetime income than those without.[4]

"We've got it good in Sweden," agrees Jacob Holmström, father of two and Michelin-starred chef, formerly of Stockholm's Gastrologik. "There's a cooked breakfast at school, a healthy snack, and lunch cooked on the premises, which is really important for me."[5]

Despite shipping and global culinary trends, many Swedes stick to the seasons and eat according to what's growing, something that filters down to school lunches too. "The Swedish approach is about seasonal, local, and organic," explains Uppsala-based food writer and mother of two Liselotte Forslin. "We love to forage, picking nettles and wild garlic in spring, blueberries and cloudberries in summer, and mushrooms and lingonberries in autumn. It's totally normal to spot a family in the woods with plastic buckets picking berries and mushrooms."[6] There's a respect for food, and nothing is wasted. The National Food Agency's website actively dissuades Swedes from throwing away food with thrifty tips that include freezing leftover pasta and using shriveled vegetables in stew.

Mmm...

Finland takes food equally seriously. "Kids get proper hot food every day, *for free*," says Katja, who is now raising her son in Helsinki but grew up in Canada. "You wouldn't get that in North America. But in Finland, it's taken for granted. People still like to complain, but we're talking real first-world problems, like 'oh, my free school lunch isn't as varied as I'd have hoped!' We know we've got it good too!"

What's more, Vikings learn their way around a kitchen from an early age. Once a week, there is "food lab," and the mini redhead can now muster up scrambled eggs and porridge by himself. "Then from around the age of nine or ten, many kids cook once a week at home," says Nanna. "That's what I did growing up, and so did my brother and sister."

This is excellent news. With three children, I might only have to cook twice a week soon. At present, I am the reluctant weekday chef with a selection of underwhelming dishes on rotation. Lego Man bakes (dangerously well) and does occasional weekend dinners when it doesn't matter if we don't eat before midnight. He makes delicious food, but it takes a while and involves a lot of swearing. Something I now blame partly on his schooling.

"Boys all learn to cook properly at school in Sweden," Chef Jacob tells me. "Each classroom had a kitchen outside. It was tiny but built for a purpose. So once a week, we cooked. It was normal. We loved it." A UK study found that getting kids involved in cooking can help encourage healthier eating habits, since 14 percent of British five-year-olds are now obese. By the age of eleven, this rises to 25.5 percent in the UK.[7] In the US, it's one in five across the board.[8] In Denmark? It's 5 percent.[9]

But things may be changing. Researchers from the University of Copenhagen have found that having overweight parents makes children more prone to weight gain, and in Denmark, adult obesity has doubled in the past decade to 18 percent (though for scale, in the US, it's 42 percent).[10] When I moved to Denmark in 2013, there were far fewer prepackaged snacks available, but there's been a rise in ultra-processed foods on Danish shelves in recent years, just as elsewhere. And a diet high in ultra-processed foods has been shown to lead to weight gain.[11] A 2022 study found that 13 percent of Danish children were now overweight (but not obese).[12] There isn't currently World Health Organization data on childhood obesity in Finland or Iceland, but in Norway, 6–7.5 percent of children are obese, and in Sweden, it's 6–10 percent.[13] "It's something we're keeping an eye on," says Peter Schmeichel, who, fittingly, works in fitness. "Though it's more about staying active and eating proper food than dieting or carb-cutting crazes. No Dane would let you take away their rye bread!"

Rye bread makes a second appearance in the daily diet of Danish children as an afternoon snack, provided at around 2:30 p.m., along with crudités and fruit. And then? Everyone goes home to eat dinner together as a family.

"I think this is one thing Denmark really gets right," says Trine Hahnemann. "Everyone goes to kindergarten growing up, there are certain opening hours, and these have defined the way we work in Denmark. So even the CEO of Lego is allowed to say in a meeting at 4:00 p.m., 'I have to leave now to pick up the kids.' And they can just go home, to eat together as a family, every day. In Denmark, we have created family time—between picking up the kids by 4:00 p.m. until around 7:00 p.m. After children have gone to bed, you might do more work then or do sports, but family time is sacred," says Trine.

"Meals are something you have sitting together, to talk about the day," agrees Nanna from Momkind. "We would never, ever eat in front of the TV. We always ate around the table growing up, so I do the same with my kids."

Finns, Icelanders, Norwegians, and Swedes also prioritize family mealtimes. "Having dinner with the whole family is key to the Swedish way of life," confirms Swedish food writer Liselotte. "Men cook too. My husband just opens the fridge and makes something terrific out of leftovers. Whoever has time just *does* it. We share the cooking and eat together around a table. Every day." Unlike back home.

In our old life, Lego Man or I would regularly be shoveling something into our mouth with one hand while clutching the remote or a phone with the other. Dinnertime conversations would run along the lines of "Want food?" "No thanks. I ate earlier. At the fridge." But this won't do in Denmark where "life around the table" is prized.

"At dinnertime, you leave your phones in another room, shut your laptop, and sit down together to eat," says Veteran Viking. She tells me this while confiscating an iPad from her youngest and texting her middle child to lay the table, but the point still stands: Vikings believe it's vital for all children to be part of family mealtimes. And it starts from birth. Most Danish homes are centered around a dining table for the expressed purpose of prioritizing family mealtimes. A large wooden table that fits eight diners is the norm, accompanied by the ubiquitous Stokke chair.

"What's a Stokke?" I hear you ask.

Great question. Take a seat. Pull up a Tripp Trapp in fact.

Tripp Trapp is the high chair designed by Norwegian industrial designer Peter Opsvik back in 1972, now in thirteen million homes worldwide. He wanted something to help his toddler son to sit in a natural way at the grown-ups table. Tricky, since a three-year-old is half the height of an adult. So he created a chair with an adjustable seat and footrest to grow with the child, from eight months to twelve years. Sitting at eye level with adults at the table helps children interact as equals, strengthening connections and a sense of belonging to the family team. Conventional high chairs tend to be fitted with a harness and tray, suggesting children are too messy to share a table with the grown-ups.

"But having a tray is actually less safe," Peter tells me, "since a child has to climb over the tray to get in it." So the Tripp Trapp encourages independence and autonomy, "because why shouldn't children be allowed to get up and down?" This approach is at odds with many parenting practices, and Stokke was forced to make a tray for the US market, where the legislation demands both tray and harness. But Peter isn't a fan. "Safety belts are used in case of a collision or sudden break in speed. Adults do not use a harness when sitting in chairs, so why strap a child into a seat? A child that objects to sitting does not become calmer by a harness."[14]

This much is true. I've witnessed great brutes of three-year-olds being hauled up and placed inside vast plastic contraptions back home, strapped in, kicking and screaming. But in Denmark, everyone opts for the Tripp Trapp instead, with many homes having more than one. "I inherited one and bought one for my kids," Nanna tells me. "They last so long, and they're such high quality that there's no shame in passing one down or buying secondhand."

Traveling around Norway, Sweden, Iceland, and parts of Finland, I see the same trend play out. The design hasn't changed since 1973, and Tripp Trapp chairs are always listed under the "wanted" column in the classified ads. In fact, the greatest competition facing Tripp Trapp in the Nordic countries is sec-ondhand Tripp Trapp chairs. So when I became a parent, there was only one option. And thanks to the hand-me-down culture, I ended up with three Tripp Trapps. There's also a baby unit for newborns now, meaning that my three have been at the dinner table since they were a week old.

As well as making over mealtimes, the Tripp Trapp transformed day care centers. Nurseries and kindergartens used to be furnished with low tables and small chairs, but in Scandinavia, most insti-tutions now have grown-up-size tables and Tripp Trapp chairs. "This improves the relationship between adults and children—of all different sizes," Pia tells me. "And an added benefit is that we don't have to bend down to the level of low tables all the time, so it saves our backs!"

The iconic design—minimalist, angular, and 1970s-cool—also helps mini Vikings develop an early appreciation for aesthetics. "I think in the Nordic countries, children grow up with design liter-acy. It becomes normal," says Nanna.

In Denmark, your average home looks like something out of an interior design magazine with white walls, wooden floors, unclut-tered surfaces, and smart designer touches. (Not mine: mine's a mess.) Furnishings tend to be made from natural materials, tactile to the touch, with lots of wood, leather, wool, and sheepskin, a.k.a. hygge. This is the strange, untranslatable word Danes have been using for centuries that the rest of the world has finally caught on to. Because coziness matters in Denmark. Lighting is a key com-ponent, and Danes burn the highest number of candles per head in Europe. It's always someone's job to light them. "From about the age of three, we got the kids to do it in our house," Veteran Viking tells me casually.

Toddlers and matches. What could go wrong?

Before dinner, someone will light candles, someone else might set the table—napkins, knives and forks, crockery, the lot—and then you'll all come together. Probably on a Tripp Trapp. And everyone's at the table.

"In the UK and the US, so much of food culture is defined by class," says Trine, "but Denmark has been so homogeneous for so long that people eat the same way. Many still have a connection to farms, growing up with grandparents who had two pigs and a cow—a trend that only started disappearing in the 1980s." Meat still rules for modern Vikings with pork and potatoes daily staples in much of Denmark. The Swedes love a meatball (obviously), and there's the running joke that Icelanders drink so much because the food's so bad. Having tried *hákarl* (fermented shark), *hrútspungar* (sour ram testicles), and even *svið* (sheep's head), I can see where they're coming from. Though to be fair, Iceland has a landscape so barren that nothing grows. Finland, Iceland, and Denmark have been ranked third in a global meat-eating table, and in Norway, consumption of meat has doubled in forty years.[15] What's more, Vikings love a hot dog—or *pølse* in Danish.

Wagons selling pølser in presliced white buns or hollowed-out baguettes attract lines of Danes, perusing a menu of sauces, all milked out of dangling rubber teats. These range from your standard ketchup to "klassik brown" and rémoulade, a Danish condiment that Whitestrips-bright American Mom describes as "like mayonnaise but gross." And yes, these are about as appetizing as they sound. But pølser are available at every gas station, every kiosk, every IKEA, and every child's birthday party—grilled outside in summer and cooked inside in winter. There's no time when a hot dog *isn't* appropriate for Vikings. Icelanders like a *pylsur,* or lamb-based version. Swedish children are raised on *falukorv*—a fire-truck-red hyperprocessed mixture of miscellaneous meats. Danes and Norwegians have *ventepølse*—or waiting sausage—eaten around the grill while you wait for the main-event sausage to cook or in line at the *pølsevogne,* or sausage wagon. And Finns even have a special term for the queue to buy their processed meat snack from one of the ubiquitous stalls: the *grillijono,* or grill queue.

Lego Man is delighted by all this.

"Who doesn't love a waiting sausage in the grill queue?"

"Err, cardiologists?"

There have been attempts to wean Danes off their wieners. In 2011, Denmark introduced a tax on saturated fat in foods—the first country in the world to do so—with a planned tax on foods with added sugar. Lego, the bastion of Danishness, even had a "sugar sheriff," purging the company of sweet treats and replacing them with crudités and rye bread. But the company expanded, sugar standards slipped, and *snegle*—delicious snail-shaped Danish pastries—won out.* The fat tax was scrapped and today, Lego has its own in-house *konditori* selling Denmark's world-famous *wienerbrød* (a.k.a. Danish pastries) for all the hygge coffee breaks (or *kaffepauser*).

Coffee with cake is part of daily life in Denmark, and even the

---

* There is still a 'chocolate tax', with cocoa delights as well as marzipan and licorice all weirdly liable. But this hasn't done much to dissuade sweet-toothed Danes.

smallest conurbation in Denmark will have a bakery. Over the past decade, I have selflessly conducted extensive pastry research. In addition to snegle, I can recommend rum balls, made out of all the cakes that bakers haven't sold the day before, and Napoleon's hat—a chocolate-bottomed, marzipan-filled cake that dates back to 1856 when Denmark sided with Napoleon (and so made a marzipan hat to celebrate). But Danes don't just eat a lot of buns. They bake them too.

Sales of yeast and flour continue to grow year on year in Denmark, and while the rest of the world stockpiled toilet paper during the pandemic, Danes went wild in the aisles for yeast. There were no lengths Danes wouldn't go to in search of the gray stuff, and bumper stickers spotted during this time summed up the feelings of a nation: *Keep Calm and Carry on Baking*. Whereas fresh yeast is hard to come by in the US and the UK, in Denmark, it's everywhere—from the biggest supermarket to the tiniest corner shop.

But does it make a difference? Can a squishy gray square that smells like old shoes really make buns taste better?

Lego Man looks affronted. "*Categorically!*"

"How do you know?"

He holds up his favorite book. Forget *The Great Gatsby* or *Catch-22*: Lego Man loves Trine's 2014 classic *Scandinavian Baking*. A more well-thumbed, batter-splattered tome you cannot imagine.

"Just because Trine says so?"

He gasps as though I've suggested selling our firstborn for snegle. "*Just*? You take that back!"

I tell him I won't but that he should bake something, "to prove it..."

Before I've finished the sentence, the oven is on and bags of flour are being slammed on the kitchen counter, sending up puffs of powder. The redhead volunteers to crumble a square of gray old-shoe gunk into a bowl, and I watch as my daughter measures out butter and sugar. The resulting dough is left to rise, and I peek at intervals.

"Is it...*bubbling*?" I ask, perturbed. Is the dough coming to life? It looks like we're about to recreate a scene from *Ghostbusters*. Am I going to be stuck with a Mr. Stay Puft on my hands?

But no, this is normal, I'm told. Once the fresh yeast has worked its magic and the dough has risen, cardamom, cinnamon, and more sugar are combined. The children take turns spreading the brown paste over the dough, the kitchen surfaces, and themselves. The dough is then rolled into a long sausage and sliced into discs, which, I'm assured, in ten minutes will puff into the lightest, most delicious cinnamon buns (*kanelsnegle*) imaginable.

Before we can eat them, Lego Man insists that we go on what he calls a "nice long walk" to "earn" our cake. I'm tasked with cajoling cinnamon-smeared children into rainsuits and miss the final alchemy whereby dough and gunk become buns. But the smell is phenomenal. The children are buzzing, and the dog is beside himself at the prospect of a walk. He starts whimpering, tail wagging, until we can get him out the door, and we walk. Reluctantly (me), striding ahead with purpose (Lego Man), or oscillating between the two (the smalls). After an eternity, we reach the spot that has been designated "snack time." And then, from Lego Man's rucksack, comes a large Tupperware box, fogged up with condensation.

"Ta-da!" My children are near purple with pride as they snap off the lid. And there, with the smell of sunshine after the rain in our nostrils, we feast. And honestly, I'm not sure anything has ever tasted so good. Not even chips…

WHAT I'VE LEARNED ABOUT HOW TO FEED A VIKING

◆ Don't skip carbs. Or protein. Or fruit. Or veg. Danes eat three times a day with a couple of snacks in between. There are still fewer fast-food options available in the Nordic countries than there are back home. Although it's far from one huge Whole Foods Market, my adopted countryfolk have taught me to eat more of the food our grandparents would have recognized rather than ultra-processed fare.

◆ With one caveat: hot dogs. A weird wiener obsession unites all the Nordic countries. The next time I'm peckish pre-BBQ, I'll demand a waiting sausage, explaining that it's a hallowed Nordic tradition.

◆ Eating together and making it *hyggeligt* matters—we're talking candles, place settings, cutlery, crockery, the lot. Living on adrenaline for the first three decades of my life combined with the palate of a toddler means that I've often overlooked the fine art of dining. I viewed refueling as something functional, to be raced through. But since raising Vikings, I've learned the pleasure of lingering over a meal with friends and family. I'm even learning to appreciate the art of tablescaping (though have neither the urge nor the headspace to do it myself just yet). I am, as American Mom observed, "growing up, getting some self-respect, and not eating cereal for dinner." (Who, me?!) Welcome to culinary Valhalla.

SINGING, *SAMFUNDSSIND,* AND THE SOCIAL BRAIN

THE WAVERING SOUNDS OF A piano scale and a lot of throat clearing greet me as I enter the hall. People huddle like penguins, my son among them. His red hair makes him instantly identifiable in any crowd. After a preparatory chord, the pianist gives a nod, and voices start up, of varying ability, tune, and timbre. Little voices blend with bigger ones, and the members of the group exchange occasional smiles across the circle.

"*Now earth and sky are still.*" I can just make out the words. "*Only the croaking of the distant frogs, and…*"

"What are they saying now?"

"*The lowing of the cows*" A woman in a parka helps me out. It's cold in the hall, but fortunately we're warmed by collective good cheer and the three thousand calories we've just consumed at a local bake sale. (It's Denmark. There's always cake.)

"*Thank you for the day,*" they sing on as I attempt to join in, unsure of both tune and words. "*For the days to come and for those that lie behind.*"

I look up to fully appreciate the moment, but everyone's already moved on. This happens a lot with me and Danish. I have little clue what's going on, but group singing is so big in Denmark that locals know all the lyrics by heart. Parka Woman, who turns out to be a history teacher, informs me after the final chord that I did "quite well, for a foreigner." I thank her, and we get talking about why Danes are always breaking into song like they're in a musical (and I mean *always*). She tells me that this is a legacy of the late great Danish poet, politician, and clergyman Nikolai Frederik Severin Grundtvig (N. F. S. Grundtvig to his friends).

At the beginning of the nineteenth century, old NFS decided he wanted to create a feeling of cohesion among Danes by giving public talks. During one of these in 1838, he talked about the Battle of Copenhagen and the heroism of his friend, the naval hero Peter Willemoes. N. F. S. Grundtvig had previously written a poem about Peter (he really liked Peter) called "Kommer hid, I piger små!" or, somewhat creepily, "Come here, you little girls!" The poem was intended to summon ladyfolk to celebrate Peter, who was a "friend of all beautiful girls" (we *all* know a Peter). A composer came up with a melody to accompany the poem, and the crowd got so excited that they jumped off their seats and spontaneously started singing. And the Danish institution of group singing was born.

"Today it's quite common to sing together at schools, offices, community events, voluntary organizations, or sports associations," says Kristian Kongshøj, a political scientist from Aalborg University, when I get in touch to find out more. "We do it as a way to begin a meeting. Or end a meeting. Or both."[1]

Well, this sounds jolly! I think. Many schools still have group singing every morning for ten to fifteen minutes, with parents invited to join in. "My mom and dad would always come for this," says my friend and fellow twin mom, Annika. "It was a lovely way to start the day."

But it serves a purpose too. "When we all sing, we experience a feeling of togetherness," Kristian tells me. "We are involved in something larger than ourselves. We are present, in a flow state, and we feel that the world speaks back to us in some way. This is what singing is—being in tune with others in a social activity that goes beyond ourselves."

All Danes are familiar with the *Højskolesangbogen*, or *High School Songbook*—a collection of 601 total bangers that regularly tops Denmark's bestseller list. Old songs deemed irrelevant are occasionally phased out, with new ones added to reflect modern Denmark. Now in its nineteenth edition, the most recent songbook includes "Ramadan in Copenhagen" by rapper Isam B as well as songs about climate change, existential crises, and divorce.

Less jolly, but still...

"All this helps build community," says Kristian. Joining together in song has been proven to release the bonding hormone oxytocin, which lowers stress, while the synchronicity of breathing together creates feelings of connectedness, according to studies from Oxford Brookes University.[2] Some argue that group singing is also an exercise in democracy, since several voices can express themselves at the same time without conflict. Plus the voice is free, unlike other instruments, so there's no socioeconomic barrier to entry.

The role of community singing in national identity has long been recognized in Denmark, and a study from Aarhus University found that singing not only helped strengthen feelings of community but also *constructs* community and feelings of social cohesion.[3] During the pandemic, Danish choirmaster Phillip Faber led daily sing-alongs on DR TV, the nation's public broadcaster, to boost morale. (I told you choir leaders were all-powerful in Denmark.) In his book *Den danske sang,* Phillip describes how all Danes have a collective repertoire of around one hundred songs and hymns that nearly everyone can sing, even if they haven't sung them in years.[4] So I meet Phillip to find out more. On a rainy afternoon when all I want to do is curl up with a cup of tea. And he is human sunshine.

"I always took it for granted that a group could just start singing in unison," Phillip tells me, "but it's actually a really special thing in Denmark. Neighboring countries don't have this, I discovered." In every choir concert Phillip leads, there is a community sing-along in the middle where everyone joins in. "If I have guests from overseas, they always ask at this part, 'Is this your national hymn?' 'No,' I tell them. Then they'll ask, 'Is it the second-most loved song in the country?' 'Nope, it's just one of many that everyone knows.' The next question they'll ask is, 'Do all Danes read music?'"

Do they?

"No!" Phillip laughs. "It's just that everyone in Denmark can stand up and sing from a pond of one hundred or so songs."

Danes sing all the time—from around the Christmas tree to around the bonfire, at school, at university, at work, and to get children to sleep. "So there's this treasury of melodies that everyone knows, even in kindergarten." Many of these were written by Denmark's national composer, Carl Nielsen, "so they aren't simple children's songs." But they are familiar to all.

This doesn't mean that everyone in Denmark sounds like Adele.

"Many confuse group singing with beautiful-sounding choirs," says Phillip, "but it's the experience rather than the outcome that matters. It doesn't always sound good, but that's okay. It doesn't have to. That's not what it's for."

What is *it for?* I wonder.

"It's about disappearing," he tells me. "In a world where everything is 'me me me,' singing together is like a starry night where you can see the Milky Way. You feel small and insignificant but also not alone and as though you belong. It's the best feeling in the world."

I used to sing in choirs, pre-children. Singing helped me through breakups, bereavements, and the more banal bits of modern life.

There is a tradition of gathering to sing in times of crisis in Denmark, notably during World War II, says Phillip, "so the tradition is there when we need it." Televised *morgensang* (morning song) united Danes with a fifth of the country joining in daily in the pandemic, including the prime minister and Crown Princess Mary. "It was a good fit as group singing is about community spirit, and we were all trying to pull together for the greater good. You didn't wear a mask for yourself; you wore it to protect someone else." And at this most delicate of times, Denmark's prime minister Mette Frederiksen emphasized another linchpin of Danish togetherness: *samfundssind*. A compound noun of *samfund* (society) and *sind* (mind), the term *samfundssind* was first reported in the 1930s but fell out of use until "someone somewhere fascinatingly decided to dig it up again to use in the Prime Minister's speech ahead of the first lockdown," says Kristian. Samfundssind became the corner-stone of Denmark's response to the pandemic, named Word of the Year 2020 by the Danish Language Board.

There have been many discussions about why this term gained so much traction. "It basically means solidarity," says Kristian, "so why didn't we just say that?" He pauses. I hope the question is rhetorical. I am in luck. "Well, solidarity is a bit left-wing. It has socialist overtones, even for Danes, and it suggests common interests, but in the pandemic, old people and young people *didn't* have the same interests. Young people had to stay in to protect old people. Whereas samfundssind or community mindset meant doing something that isn't necessarily best for you but for the sake of others. For the greater good."

And "for the greater good" is the ethos behind another popular Danish institution: the scouts. You may think you know scouts from your youth, your children, or even from books, but Viking scouts are something else (just wait until chapter 10). If the aver-age Dane loves singing and samfundssind, then scouts are sam-fundssind *fundamentalists*.

"There are expectations about what it is to be a good human, and scouts agree to do their best to follow a pledge that includes being a good friend, being considerate, and helping others, both in the family and in the wider society," my friend Andreas the scout leader tells me in the woods the following Wednesday. (After a scout meeting, I should add. This isn't a prerequisite for inter-viewees.) "It's a lot to ask of children as young as six, but kids learn to strive and be aware of other people as well as the world around them."

I've been impressed and surprised by the new badges available for the redhead and his fellow scouts to earn. When I was a Girl Scout, I was encouraged toward badges such as housework (depicted by a broom), cooking (a pan), and hostess (a cup and saucer...kill me now). But my son's patrol can work toward their rights badge (a raised fist) or their comforter badge (a crying eye). "Earned by developing their 'soft skills' presumably," I tell Lego Man.

"As well as their knife skills?" he clarifies.

"The two aren't mutually exclusive in Denmark," I tell him (because this is what Andreas told me). Despite the emphasis on being active, strong Vikings on the outside, on the *inside*, Danes are often *whispers it* soft. Not in a bad way but in a gentle, caring, attuned-to-humanity way.

Danes have a *fri for mobberi* or "free from bullying" program for zero to nine-year-olds, led by a purple bear who teaches tolerance, respect, care, and courage. They learn to stand up for themselves and speak out when they see someone overstepping boundaries. From birth, they're taught to care and be an ally.

Almost every adult Dane I know has been off on stress leave at one point—often as a preventative measure before they hit "the wall." This isn't because work is particularly stressful in comparison to elsewhere (oh hej, thirty-three-hour working week!), but because everyone does it. There's no shame in taking time out and returning after six months. Danes look after themselves (wieners aside), and I discover that the average Dane is in contact with doctors, dentists, and medical specialists eleven times a year.

"Eleven?! That's practically a relationship," Lego Man points out.

So are Vikings just armadillos? A tender heart concealed beneath a rugged exterior?

I call on Marie Helweg-Larsen, a native Dane turned professor of psychology at Dickinson College in the US to find out more. I settle down with a tea and watch swans flying in a V shape out the window as Marie explains to me how Danish culture is governed by predominantly feminine ideals.

"The genders are more equal in Denmark, and Danes in general tend to agree with more feminine ideals, as do people in all the Nordic countries," she says.[5] The Dutch social psychologist Geert Hofstede developed a framework for assessing different cultures and found that whereas countries like the UK and the US tend to rank highly on masculinity as a cultural value and approach to life, Nordics typically...don't. Sweden is ranked as the most feminine society in the world, with Norway a close second.[6] This means that the softer aspects of culture are valued and encouraged, like consensus, cooperation, collaboration, and compromise. Taking care of the environment is also important, as is a good work/life balance.

The welfare safety net and Nordic culture as a whole are considered more caring and feminine (whether we like this definition or not). More caring cultures look out for each other, as seen in the famous wallet study, where researchers dropped seventeen thousand wallets in cities around the world to test how often they were returned.[7] The Nordic countries came out on top. In Denmark, more than 80 percent of wallets with money in them were returned. And more caring countries are also happier, according to the World Happiness Report, with an understanding that we all have to play our part to build social connections.[8]

Samfundssind is baked in to living Danishly. All activities, clubs, and associations rely on the goodwill, time, and effort of the community. Whereas UK or US clubs are often exclusive, Danish clubs are run by volunteers. "Everyone is invested, so children grow up seeing their parents get off their butts and help," explains my friend who looks like Peter Schmeichel at day care pickup. "We don't just *tell* children to contribute. We show it." But he can't hang around chatting. "I've got basketball coaching later today, then toddler trampolining!"

Him too? I can barely keep my head above water, and I'm not doing anything for the local community. The seemingly never-ending list of stuff that needs doing exhausts me on a daily basis. *How do people have the time?*

"They prioritize," Peter Schmeichel tells me, buckling his daughter onto the back of his bike. "Rather than slumping in front of the TV or scrolling their phones, parents make a point of getting out there!"

I'm sure the thirty-three-hour working week helps.

"You'd be surprised," he says. "People do it even if they work longer hours. Even if they have big jobs."

Like Diana.

When I mention to Danish friends that I'm writing about volunteering, they all tell me to talk to Diana. I'm a little intimidated. Am I about to be samfundssind-shamed? (Clue: yes.)

Diana Ringe Krogh is a vice president of social responsibility at a major company. She's also parenting two children, has been on the board of the local gymnastics club, organized annual gymnastics shows, and fundraised for the gymnastics and soccer clubs.

"Then my husband—he's a teacher—coached soccer and gymnastics in his spare time."

Spare time? *Wait one hot minute...* "He was with children all day every day, then he came home to voluntarily help other people's children?"

"It's just what you do," says Diana. "Our grandparents volunteered, our parents volunteered. My dad still does, and he's seventy-three." Diana tells me how she grew up playing soccer "as well as coaching the younger kids and sitting on the board."

As a teenager?

"Sure!"

This isn't unusual. Fellow twin mom Annika volunteers teaching swimming twice a week, runs a movie club, organizes gifts for the soccer coaches each year, and is the class representative at school. "If you want your children to go to an activity and you don't volunteer, then you don't have an activity" is her rationale. Her sons go to swimming, soccer, and something called "esports" (a.k.a. video gaming club). All run by volunteers. Annika tells me that the idea of a community mindset has always been strong in Denmark, "otherwise society wouldn't run." And Annika comes from a long line of volunteers. "My grandma was a scout leader, my dad was a scout leader, then he and my mom founded the scout group in our town." Her parents also led gymnastics classes and started the town's movie club, all while raising four children and working full-time.

"You get a couple of places for free if you're the coach, so it meant that us kids could try out different things." Annika tried handball, tennis, gymnastics, swimming, volleyball, and karate before focusing on playing trumpet in a band. "We practiced three times a week and then played concerts for the community on the weekend."

All unpaid?

"Of course!" She tells me her neighbor, aged seventy-five, organizes board game nights at the nursing home and pushes wheelchairs "for the old people. She doesn't consider herself old. Helping out is *just what you do*."

Studies show that having community-minded parents makes children more likely to volunteer. And research from Arizona State University found that parents who valued kindness and helpfulness above achievements and accomplishments had children with fewer symptoms of depression or low self-esteem.[9] The study concluded that being socially oriented makes for happier children, who in turn are more likely to be socially oriented.

Half of all Danish schools offer *legepatruljen*—or play patrol—where children volunteer to play with younger students during break times. This has been proven to reduce bullying and foster friendships across classes. Children take it seriously too, taking a training course before they can become "play initiators" and arranging cover if they can't make their "shift." Which all sounds very noble.

"But there has been a change in recent years," warns Diana. "We are becoming more individually focused, just like elsewhere. Everyone pays high taxes in Denmark, and there is sometimes the thought process of, 'Isn't that enough?'"

It's not, I learn. A fellow international found this out the hard way when he tried throwing cash at the community mindset conundrum, giving a generous donation to his son's sports club. "I barely got a thank you!" he told me, confounded. Another parent took him aside and told him, "They don't want your money. They want your time." Because time is more precious.

"It's about care and involvement and effort," says Diana, admitting that there's frustration when people from other cultures don't understand this. "But it's never too late to start developing a community mindset, and it's never too early either." Diana's children joined her in fundraising for various charities as soon as they could walk. They also collect litter and help with a Christmas charity drive. "Our kids are growing up in a society where they have everything, so we have to teach them about the importance of giving back. Samfundssind is a big part of being human."

Family therapist and mother of three Sofie Münster chairs the education panel in Denmark's Ministry of Children and Social Affairs and recommends building samfundssind into daily discussions with children. Instead of just saying "Have a good day," she suggests, "Remember to do something good for someone else today!" In the evenings, we should ask "Did you do something nice for someone else today?"[10]

So the next morning, I try it. I tell the redhead, "Remember to do something good for someone else today!"

"Is that the goal?" he asks. "Not no fighting? Or don't just eat raisins for lunch?"

"Err..." Ideally, I'd like him to refrain from both hand-to-hand combat *and* an exclusively raisin diet, but beggars can't be choosers. "Do you think you could maybe not fight *and* do something good?"

He thinks about this.

"I *might* be able to." He nods seriously. "But should I just relax about the raisins?"

"Sure…" *Mother of the Year award, arriving yesterday.*

At pickup, I ask, "How was your day? Did you do something nice for someone else?"

To my delight, he nods.

"Daniel annoyed me, so I turned the other butt cheek," he announces with pride.

"Sorry?" I fear my fleeting explanations of Bible idioms may have been inadequate.

"I didn't fight Daniel, okay?"

For a child uncompromising in his zeal for conflict, I acknowledge that this is a win of sorts. "Okay! Great."

"Anyway, what did you and Dad do for someone else today?" he asks, quite reasonably. I'm tempted to quip something about turning my own butt cheek but realize he's right. If we want to raise Vikings, we need to, in the words of the late great Barry White, practice what we preach.

I used to volunteer before children and life took over, visiting elderly people in my local area for a charity called Age Concern. I played a lot of Scrabble, learned that "tremendous character" was a euphemism for "massive racist," and was once dumbfounded by a lovely lady called Ruby with a fierce competitive streak. In pursuit of a triple word score one Sunday, she began laying down tiles on an available C. She placed first a U, then an N, and I held my breath. She wouldn't, would she? She would. T was carefully tapped into place before Ruby licked the end of her pencil and said, "C, U, N, T. Eighteen points," with all the satisfaction of a job well done. No modern-day volunteering is ever likely to live up to the highs of C-bomb Ruby.

But we can try.

An opportunity presents itself that weekend at the five-year-olds' swimming lesson. This generally consists of one of us attempting not to be drowned (by Twin One, an aquaphobic limpet) and the other front crawling to keep up (with Twin Two, a dolphin), all while being shouted at in Danish by a teenage instructor and scowled at by his sidekick in tiny Speedos. For the past nine months of lessons, Scowling Sidekick has remained completely silent, spending thirty minutes every Sunday hanging on a pool noodle (*slange* in Danish, or snake). All he does is stare moodily into the middle distance, occasionally scratching a love bite. ("Shouty Instructor never has love bites," Lego Man observes. "Maybe that's why he's so shouty.")

Shouty Instructor tells us that he won't be here the following week as he's "going to be ill."

"Wait, what? He knows in advance?" Lego Man rasps, clamped at the neck by Twin One.

"I imagine it's the same way you're going to be under the weather after that bachelor party next month," I wheeze, chasing Twin Two. There's a seal-like plunge as she breaks the surface of the water, reappearing at my side before I can take another stroke.

"So we need volunteers!" Shouty Instructor thunders.

"What's involved?" Lego Man bellows back on reflex.

I know what he's thinking. *Will Love Bite step up? Could there be an opening for a daydreaming deputy dangling on a pool noodle?* Doubtless he'd enjoy that as a welcome break. But alas, they're after a bona fide instructor. A triangular-shaped swimming dad who brings his own nose clip to "splash and play" is selected as a replacement while my husband is thanked for his enthusiasm and put on another important job. Namely, garbage bags.

In Denmark, food waste goes into green bags, supplied by the municipality and delivered by various clubs or associations that are paid by the council for taking the job off their hands. This means that new rolls of green bags can be delivered to your door by anyone from a preschooler to a CEO, helping to raise funds for their various clubs. It's a necessary if unglamorous job. But Lego Man isn't immediately sold.

"*Garbage* bags? I'm on *refuse collection*? I've got a degree! I've got *two* degrees!"

I point out that I've also done my time on trash bags to raise money for my old choir, "and our son has done it for scouts. None of us are too grand for garbage in Denmark. Get on with it!"

With grumbling, he does. That leaves me.

The news that preschooler ballet is canceled due to lack of a teacher (early retirement, dodgy knee) is a blow. I loved ballet as a child and took classes as an adult before having children. My size 6 satin shoes still dangle from their ribbon at the back of my wardrobe. *Could I...perhaps?*

I can plié! I write, fingers dancing over the keyboard. I remember most of the positions! What could possibly go wrong? I mentally prepare for the fact that I may get green bag duty instead, but it feels good to offer.

All neurological research ever shows that we experience a helper's high when we do something for someone else, and while it used to be believed that humans were innately selfish, scientists now agree that we are *wired* for empathy and built for community.[11]

Teacher Louise tells me, "We teach kids about *fællesskab*, or community, and its importance at school too." Teacher training has a curriculum around community, with lesson plans expected to include it. And having a community mindset also means taking care of the natural environment.

Icelanders have a long tradition of activism, with 61 percent taking part in some form of campaigning. In 1975, 90 percent of Icelandic women went on strike to demand equal pay and rights, paving the way for the world's first democratically elected female president.[12] In 2019, Icelanders held a "funeral" for a glacier lost to climate change with a Lorax-like plaque inscribed "A letter to the future."[13] Swedish teenager Greta Thunberg sparked global protests about climate change because she saw that there was work to be done for the greater good. "And becoming an activist gave me the feeling that I was not alone," Greta told Tom Daley on his podcast in 2023.[14] Danes stand up for their eco rights, embracing wind power with a countryside stippled by wind turbines. There are disputes back home about these being a "blot" on the landscape, but in Denmark, they're accepted for the greater good. Wind power is now the country's number one energy source. Okay, so the blustery weather makes me look as though I've emerged from a wind tunnel most days, but it's worth it.

Of course, Vikings aren't immune to the pressures of the modern world. There has been a growing movement toward individualization, and Danish children have a hat trick of near-unlimited freedom, an emphasis on autonomy, and the influence of global culture.

"The decision on life choices has moved from the community to the family to the individual in Denmark," says Rasmus Kjeldahl of Denmark's National Association for Children's Rights. "We say, 'my child has to decide for his or herself.'" This is a challenge, since while some children may be ready, others may not, "so we have to recognize that some children need more support rather than more freedom."[15]

The Nordic countries aren't exempt from economic challenges either. A Boston Consultancy Group report found that 73 percent of people in the Nordic countries were worried about personal finances.[16] One in four households in Norway are now struggling to pay bills, while Swedish food prices are up 25 percent.[17] "People are more vulnerable than before," says Diana, "so some feel like they can't *also* give back to the community."

"We have to be aware that we are living in an extraordinary time," agrees Rasmus, "but Denmark still offers the possibility of one of the best childhoods in the world. I'd still rather be a child in Denmark than anywhere else, because of samfundssind, because of the community."

You're never totally alone as a parent in Denmark. Rather than just keeping an eye on your own children at any social gathering, Danes keep an eye on any children around them. There is a radius of care extending out and around each adult so that all children are looked after. In a group with many circles, there is a Venn diagram of care.

"If there is a kid who needs help—changing, feeding, whatever—you help," Veteran Viking explains. "So you know that your kid is being looked after the same way too."

The overall direction of family in the UK and the US has been to view it as a private unit and children as a private responsibility, encouraging families toward self-sufficiency with minimal state interference. But samfundssind means support for all.

"There is this sense of togetherness," says psychologist Marie Helweg-Larsen of the Danish approach, "of having broader arms, beyond your own child, extending care and concern beyond the immediate circle. And just as you let others look after your children, there is an expectation that you will extend your umbrella to include others too."

This is something I've long been a beneficiary of. The time my toddler climbed into a toilet at a party? He was rescued by another parent. When the redhead scaled a potato display at the supermarket? A fiercely tanned lady all in green hauled him down (older Danes still sunbathe like it's a sport). Then there was the time Lego Man ordered so much lumber during a particularly enthusiastic DIY phase that I couldn't get to the front door with newborn twins. The postman was my hero that bleak Monday. So now it's my turn to extend my umbrella.

The following week, I do not panic (on the outside) when I find myself in loco parentis for eight children ranging from the ages of five to nine (one of whom I have never clapped eyes on before). I am at a popular Lego experience in town with my three children when I spot a mom friend in some distress. She has two children but each of them has a playdate, and then she has taken pity on one of their classmates who was feeling left out. Only a family emergency has arisen, and she needs to pick up an elderly relative from the hospital (nothing life threatening: everyone's okay). I half offer; she half begs, then vanishes. And there I am. Knee-deep in children. I am only in charge of them for an hour or so, but it's a long hour or so, including snacks, toilet incidents, and big questions...

"Is Santa real?" demands a flying child, braids streaming behind her.

"What about God?" A serious-looking boy stares up at me.

"How do you make babies?!" a five-year-old yells.

I'm loosely prepared for these chats with my own children. But with other people's? *What's the etiquette? Who's been told what?* I trot out abstract answers along the lines of "Well, I've never seen him/ her," and "When two people share genetic material..." followed swiftly by "Who'd like a BANANA? Snacks anyone? Nuts? Any allergies?"

Finally, a parent shows up. Then another. I introduce myself, tell them their child is currently playing hide-and-seek somewhere... *and by the way, he now knows how to make babies,* I do not add. We find the missing child, the last parent arrives, and I leave with just my three in tow. I feel, *what is it?* Capable? Competent? Relieved? All of the above?

I was trusted to look after other parents' precious offspring, and we all survived and had a nice time. *I'm practically Kitta now!* I convince myself. Momentarily. Walking to the car, I check my phone. There's a message from my daughter's ballet.

This is it! I think, tapping the message with trembling fingers (though this could just be the excess adrenaline from the previous hour).

Thank you so much for your offer, I read, blah blah blah...won't be needing your services teaching...although we would appreciate help fundraising and might you be available for green bags?

There it is.

Sign me up, I respond.

WHAT I'VE LEARNED ABOUT SINGING LIKE A VIKING AND SAMFUNDSSIND

◆ Singing is good for the soul. Singing together is better still. Being part of something bigger than ourselves is never more important than in the trenches of parenting. The world can feel small, all lunch boxes and laundry. It's good to remember that we're just one of eight billion human beings on a rock travelling around one of one hundred billion stars. When we can't escape or climb a mountain to get some perspective, we need to recalibrate another way. Instead of drinking to forget, let's all try singing to disappear (cheaper and less chance of a hangover). Also, I need to make time to join a choir again.

◆ Building a circle of trust or making a pact to watch each other's children makes for a more relaxing time. Surrounded by other parents, collectively giving each other the look that says "We've got this," helps me be a nicer person. Thinking *we*, not *I*, helps the community, children, and caregivers too.

◆ If all I can do is hand out green bags, I should keep on handing out green bags (unless any sweary octogenarians fancy a game of Scrabble).

◆ But I have a long way to go before I'm Kitta. Or Annika. Or Diana. Or Peter Schmeichel. I still haven't got it all sussed out. At all. As my neighbors are about to discover.

SHOW, DON'T TELL: DISCIPLINE DANISH STYLE

I KNEW I'D HIT AN all-time low when I threw my children's bubble machine out the window. In the morning rush in darkest January, my children were refusing to put their shoes on. Instead, the youngest retrieved a rainbow-maned unicorn to belch soapy spheres all over the kitchen. Blissfully unaware of any urgency, they cackled with glee and leaped about as bubbles grew into shimmering, trembling balls. I got dressed to leave the house in angry, irritated movements, jerking an arm into a jacket. After the third shoe-related request, with the clock ticking toward late, I snapped. Seizing this symbol of pure joy, I opened the kitchen window and hurled it, overhand, into the inky blackness. Then I dropped everyone off and had a long, hard look at my life.

What is wrong with me?

On the street where I live, there are lots of families with young children. In summer, everyone has their doors and windows open. *And I don't hear anyone else losing their mess and screaming into the void.* But on an average morning, I go up and down the stairs so many times that my Fitbit thinks I've done a HIIT workout, and by 7:30 a.m., I am a puree of despair.

Do Vikings just do things differently?

"Yes," says Niki Brantmark in Sweden. Originally from London, Niki relocated to Skåne in 2004 with her Swedish husband. She now has two daughters, a stepson, and an interiors empire (myscandinavianhome.com). "Everyone is just so calm here! They rarely raise their voices!" She sounds baffled. "Swedes often have this very soothing, pedagogical almost, voice. I don't know how they do it. They always reason with children and try to be really fair. I've seen a child slap her father and still no raised voice! Whereas when we grew up... Well, I have memories of being chased up the stairs."[1]

I tell Niki about my morning, and she tells that me her neighbor's daughter locked herself in the shed, making them late for work and school respectively.

"I asked my neighbor, 'Did you lose your shit?' But no, she told me, 'I just kept really *calm*—then I might bring it up the next day with something gentle like, "It wasn't so nice, was it, when *this* happened. How did you feel?"' They always keep their cool."

"And...what about shoes?" I ask. "Don't you have shoe wars in your house?"

"No. We use a horn."

"Sorry?"

"Everyone does in Sweden—schools, day cares, you see them everywhere. It's much easier with a shoehorn. Try it!"

I tell her it's worth a go. "But what about when you're trying to get children to do something they don't want to do?" I ask.

"They just...don't! I've witnessed a couple of instances where if a kid doesn't want to go to school, sometimes they *don't go*." This isn't a daily occurrence "and it's usually among younger kids." But still. "Giving kids a feeling that they are equals and that they get to make decisions is key."

Every Swede I ask about this concurs, and there's a similar approach in Denmark.

"The Danish way isn't to focus on *behavior*, unlike in the UK and US," says family therapist Sofie Münster, who studied in the US. "In Denmark, we focus on what is *behind* that behavior. I'd think, 'What is the child trying to tell me?' So instead of a time-out, we would think, 'This child is really angry.' And then say to the child, 'I can see you're angry with me because I'm saying no, and that is really hard for you.'" By saying this, we "nourish the attachment bond" rather than depleting it. "Because what is the logical conclusion of the alternative? Does the child end up thinking, 'I will only be loved when I'm behaving well'? Or that 'when I am annoying or difficult, I'm going to have to deal with it by myself'? That 'I have to be alone with those hard feelings'? Over time," says Sofie, "this makes a child even more angry."[2]

"We also don't do ultimatums," says my friend Rikke with the twinkly eyes, "since with ultimatums, there has to be a winner and a loser."

"*No ultimatums?*"

"But there *is* always a cause and effect," she adds.

"So if children won't put on shoes...just off the top of my head..."

"I'll tell them, 'If you don't put on your shoes, we'll be late for school,' because that's true. But I also know that when I go over, lay a hand on them, and remind them gently, they may respond better. And if a child is too tired or the fastenings on their shoes are too fiddly, then of course they're going to resist. Also, have you tried a shoehorn?"

Deep exhale

Nordic parenting fosters the notion that the child is essentially good and that there's always a reason for resistant behavior—from hunger to tiredness, boredom, or lack of a shoehorn.

"The Danish way is to reduce the friction for children," says Rikke.

"Isn't that being a helicopter parent?" I ask.

"You mean curling?"

"Do I?"

"Don't you?"

I discover that what the rest of the world refers to as helicopter parenting, Danes call curling, likening the niche sixteenth-century Scottish broom sport to smoothing the way for a child. Obviously.

"I don't see reducing friction as curling," says Rikke. "I think much of kids' *lack* of self-sufficiency is actually because of us— overscheduling so they're tired or putting the stuff they need out of reach or clearing it away unduly. We know by age three that kindergarteners can do a lot themselves. Danish winter clothes are specifically designed so that the kids can put them on unaided."

Another reason my stinky Paddington duffel coat fell at the first hurdle, I think: *too many toggles!*

"If kids aren't being self-sufficient," says Rikke, "we can look for the points of friction and try to be patient." She tells me how until recently, she poured the milk on her eight-year-old son's cereal. "I did it because I couldn't face him doing it, spilling it, then trying to clean it up, not cleaning up right, leaving out a dirty cloth...you get the picture."

I do.

"I would think, 'I don't have a mental capacity for this today.'"

This sounds familiar.

"It became a habit that I would pour the milk for him. But I had to let go—to let him do it, make a mess, and learn. It's the same with many things."

Rikke's husband comes from the UK and can occasionally be exasperated by the Danish way.

"He might say to our son, 'By your age, you should be able to do X, Y, and Z.' Because that's how it is in the UK. But how should kids know if we don't take the time to teach them? Or make sure they understand?"

"In the Danish way, there is a focus on the *process*," family therapist Sofie explains, "so children *have* to learn to do certain things. But we acknowledge that it can be hard for them. And they may not get there as fast as we want or expect them to! So I'm very thoroughly focused on going slow and coaching children through things. You actually save time by *giving* time."

"*Really?*" She can hear the skepticism in my voice.

"Well, I have a three-year-old, so let's talk about her. If you think about it, impatience and conflict actually take longer. So for example, if I'm trying to get my daughter to put her shoes on in the morning—"

"Yes! Thank you!" I feel seen.

"Well, if I give her, say, thirty seconds to get used to the idea of putting her shoes on, I'm also investing in her learning this skill.

I'm being with her in the here and now and helping her regulate a difficult emotion."

The difficult emotion of "I don't want to wear shoes"? *What is it with kids and shoes?*

"The grown-up is taking the lead, telling the child, 'You have to learn it, but I'll be with you until you understand.'"

There's an acceptance in Denmark that when children are pre-occupied, they aren't going to listen. And this is okay, allegedly. We can't get mad at them, say my Danish friends, since when we do, they can't *actually* hear us.

How convenient, I think at first. But there's science here. Brain scans show that getting told off activates the more primitive parts of the brain, causing children to feel threatened and go into a defensive position. In this state, children have no capacity to relate to what parents are demanding.[3]

The late Danish family therapist Jesper Juul popularized Nordic ideas of nonauthoritarian parenting in his 1995 book *Your Competent Child*.[4] He wrote that values like obedience and conformity governing traditional hierarchical families were now outdated, explaining how children parented "the old way" might end up complying but would lose far more in the long term. "To defend punishment by claiming its efficacy is mistaken," he writes, since "children willingly cooperate with any adults they love, trust, and depend on. No matter how the adult behaves."

Earlier theories of parenting were based on the idea that adults had to teach children how to cooperate, adapt, and take others into consideration. But forty years of research into families shows that when children have to choose between preserving their own integrity and cooperating, children choose cooperation 90 percent of the time, according to Jesper. In other words, most children *already* want to fit in and please their parents. What they need help with is learning to be themselves.

When toddlers begin to discover their autonomy in English-speaking countries, they're categorized as "terrible twos" or "threenagers." In Danish, these terms don't exist. Instead, ages two and three are known as *trodsalder,* or the boundary age. Pushing boundaries is normal, not terrible. This makes a difference in how parents respond to toddler behavior.

"We're always in dialogue with our children," adds my friend Camilla (willowy artist, pee-your-pants mothers group Camilla). "A child's voice counts, so we listen to it." And in Denmark, parents tend not to be ventriloquists for their children.

"We don't speak for them or excuse children with a 'she's shy,' because the label can become self-fulfilling," says Rikke.[*]

Instead, Danish children speak out.

"Kids are taught to question—'But why?'—and they're treated as equals," says Rikke, explaining how her own parents treated her like one of them.

"I grew up believing I had cocreated our everyday life, from the food we ate to the clothes I wore," says Rikke. "For a long time, I believed I decided what kitchen we should have. I thought I made the decisions. But looking back, I didn't. How could I? I didn't buy the food. I didn't decide where to put the garden fence. But my

---

[*] Although this isn't universal in the region. "In Sweden, kids are not expected to speak to adults," said Niki. "They're allowed to be shy, and parents don't like to push them. So they may not look you in the eye or shake hands. They may not say 'thanks for supper.' They get there in the end. At around seventeen or eighteen, they're all polite. Somehow, they learn it. But it takes a while!"

parents were very good about autonomy." This can present pitfalls later in life. "It came as a bit of a shock to realize I didn't rule the world." She grins. "I only learned as an adult to be more conscious of my surroundings. But I really want to try and give my children that agency. I let them decide a lot."

What about teaching respect?

"You don't have to teach respect the Danish way. It is assumed," says Rikke.

This is a brain twister for someone raised outside the Nordics. *Respect for each other simply because we exist?* It's all very Mr. Darcy telling Bridget Jones he likes her just the way she is. ("Not thinner? Not cleverer? Not with slightly bigger breasts or a slightly smaller nose?" as Bridget's friend Jude asks in the 2001 film.[5]) Instead, Vikings show each other a basic level of respect, regardless.

"You don't criticize your kids or anyone else's," says Camilla, "so you can never be shitty about your kids' friends. If kids hear you criticizing someone, they start thinking the same thing. They can't help it. It puts ideas in their heads." Danes use their choice of language to teach empathy instead. "We're always trying to find ways to get children to understand another child's behavior without a negative label. So we might say, 'Why do you think she said that?' or 'How does it make you feel when…?' but we're not judging. We might say 'Maybe they were hungry? Or tired? You know how it feels be to be hungry and tired, right?' Helping children understand the feelings *behind* behaviors leads them to be kinder and teaches empathy. And kids mirror us, so the language we use matters. If we are judgmental or critical or shaming, kids copy."

I see this the very next day when a family elder speaks

disparagingly about someone's weight in front of my son. Later that day, he tells me he doesn't want to eat too much as he "doesn't want to get fat." I'm mad at myself for not having spoken up to correct the family elder at the time. Instead, I'd changed the subject and turned on the radio.

Why wasn't I braver?

I tell Rikke about what happened, and she nods knowingly.

"I'm always struck by how much British parents worry about what other people think," says Rikke. "Because really, who cares?"

Family elders! That's who! But I know I need to step up.

"Parents also have to have empathy for themselves," says Malene, another Danish mom and parenting psychologist. "Parenting is hard. We don't always get it right, and that's okay." *Thanks, Malene.* "Being understanding and forgiving of ourselves makes us better at forgiving our kids—and others."

"I think one of the most important jobs for a parent is to show imperfection. To show failure even—to teach your kids that it's okay," says Camilla. And Danes are good on failure. Forget the idea that you buy the drinks after a hole in one on the golf course or a successful business deal. In Denmark, if you've made a mistake, you treat the people who witnessed your failure to a pint. The tradition of *kvajebajer*, or failure beer is a way of celebrating snafus and accepting that they're what make us human and help us learn (hopefully). Then there's the word *pyt*, which means a combination of "oh well" and "stuff happens." Danes bear the slings and arrows of outrageous fortune with *pyt*—letting go of minor frustrations or mistakes. I now have letters spelling out PYT on a shelf above the desk where I work as a constant reminder. (Also, more great tattoo inspiration, not least because *pyt* is nice and short for minimal ouch factor.)

Danish family therapist Jesper Juul encouraged parents to include their own wants, needs, feelings, and failings in everyday exchanges. Instead of saying "What would you like for dinner?" he recommends something like "I'd like fish for dinner today. What would you like?" Rather than "What time should I pick you up?" he advocated saying "I'd like to pick you up at three o'clock. What do you think?"

According to JJ's manifesto, there's nothing wrong with expressing sadness, anger, even irritation as parents, since "children learn that they cannot always get what they want, and that individuals exist within the context of family life."[6]

Head explodes

But wait, there's more. Vikings don't overpraise either. While many cultures adopt the idea that constant praise enhances the development of self-esteem ("Who's my clever boy! That's the best poo I've ever seen!"), Danes just...don't.

"In the UK or the US, you're almost rude if you're not effusive," says Rikke. "But it's not in our culture or language to praise all the time. It's too easy, and it doesn't mean anything if you do it all the time."

Friends from the UK tell tales of noncompetitive school field days where everyone wins and all must have prizes so no children feel left out. But in Denmark, no one wins and none get prizes. Every October, there's a sport day where Danish schoolchildren run around as much as they can, for fun. But no one's getting medals for that. Gutted though I am to be deprived of the opportunity to aggressively heckle my children to victory or take home a rosette for participation, there is method in this madness. Team sports in Denmark are open to all, regardless of ability, so that all children remain active. But they don't expect a medal for it. Which might be a kinder way to prepare children for adult life, where relatively few of us are ever likely to have trophies flung at us for our efforts. The reward is in the doing, not in the praise of others.

Jesper Juul believed that overpraise led to inflated egos and a poor sense of self. And Danes have long lived by the tenets of Jante's law—the fictional Scandinavian set of beliefs immortalized by Danish-Norwegian author Aksel Sandemose in his 1933 satirical novel *A Fugitive Crosses His Tracks*.[7] These are as follows:

- You're not to think you are anything special.
- You're not to think you are as good as us.
- You're not to think you are smarter than us.
- You're not to convince yourself that you are better than us.
- You're not to think you know more than us.
- You're not to think you are more important than us.
- You're not to think you are good at anything.
- You're not to laugh at us.
- You're not to think anyone cares about you.
- You're not to think you can teach us anything.

Intended in jest, Jante's law became shorthand for the egalitarian nature of the Nordic countries. A harsh but fair belief system that persists today.

I gathered early on that Danes didn't go in for gushing. During my first trip to a Danish clothing shop, I emerged from the fitting room only to be told by the sales assistant, "No. That doesn't suit you at all."

"But I'm wearing my own clothes?"

Far from creating a culture of downtrodden dolts, it contributes to a sense that everyone is worthy, just *because*.

"When kids say, 'Look at this!' it's their way of requesting our attention," says family therapist Sofie. "They're not actually asking for praise. So it's better to teach them to evaluate things for themselves. Otherwise they'll spend their lives looking for external validation. We want to raise kids to have a strong inner voice and sense of self." And this is something Danish parents do well.

"You feel like, 'I am all right. I am of value just because I exist,'" says Camilla. "I would never know if my parents thought something I'd done was good," Rikke agrees, "but also, it wasn't *important*. I assumed they loved me. It was taken for granted, not based on achievement."

This feels like a game changer: *To be loved just because? Isn't that what all children want?*

Danes replace praise with interest. I hear a lot of "How did you do that?" or "Tell me more" or "I can see that you have..."

"This shows kids that it is *them* and not their results that we are concerned with," says Rikke. "Plus, when you're honest, it helps kids learn the importance of telling the truth and right from wrong."

Sometimes, I think.

Before my mother's first visit to her grandchildren's Danish kindergarten, I tried to warn her that my newly adopted countryfolk were a tad lax on swearing. But she was so busy admiring the daffodils outside that I wasn't sure she'd heard. We walked in to walls decorated with artwork and "about me" presentations by the new intake of three-year-olds, transcribed by teachers (it'll be a long time before a Viking is writing). The display was all in Danish with a few notable exceptions. I browsed a couple, as did my mother, until I heard her exclamation of "Good gracious!"

My mother's hand fluttered to her heart like a Victorian gentlewoman, and she stood stock-still. I followed her eyeline to one particular three-year-old's "about me" presentation and scanned swiftly.

Favorite food: pancakes.

Favorite sport: soccer.

Unable to see anything amiss, I read on hurriedly.

Funniest word I know...

Oh.

While others had cited "buttocks" and "fart" (*numser* and *prut* respectively—both pretty funny, to be fair), this child had chosen

FUCK!

A word that is, helpfully, the same in Danish and English and so the only word my mother could read. Transcribed by the teacher. Of a three-year-old.

"It's everywhere!" says the head teacher at my eldest's school. "Even the milk commercial uses the f-word here. At some schools, teachers say, 'Get the eff over here!' to kids in the playground! It just doesn't have the same power."

"It does to my mother," I tell her.

"I think we're just a lot freer here," she says. "Kids know the bad words, and they have the responsibility to know when to use them."

What, like in kindergarten presentations? I think.

"Freedom with responsibility" is a guiding principle for parenting throughout the Nordic countries. But trying to be okay with the idea of freedom means letting go of many of the assumptions about parenting that I picked up as a child or from the rhetoric of motherhood. (Most of us start with a manual under our arm nowadays, "but babies don't read them," as Veteran Viking likes to remind me.) Take bedtime. I have been doggedly clinging to my children's 7:00 p.m. bedtime since it's only after that when I feel I can have some evening to myself. But according to Jesper Juul, if a child complains about bedtime and asks, "Why do I have to go to bed so early?" parents should categorically *not* say, "Because you're tired and have to get up in the morning." Apparently, we should just say, "I want you to go to bed now because I want time to myself."

That's it? That's the big idea? Telling the truth? What's the world coming to? Also, how will they ever get up in the morning? *How will I get the ruddy shoes on the ruddy children and get out the door?*

Jesper has thought of that: he recommends alarm clocks, since "children older than five can wake themselves."[8]

Ambitious, I think. But also, *tempting.*

JJ advises sitting the child down and telling them explicitly why an alarm clock is coming their way and even suggests a script for this delicate encounter (buckle up): "Now listen, when you were young, we thought it was nice to wake you up in the morning, so we took the responsibility of making sure that you got up. But we don't think so anymore. In fact, we feel irritated almost every day. So now we've decided to give the responsibility for this back to you. If now and again you go to bed late and worry you won't hear the alarm clock, then you just have to tell us and we'll help you. But otherwise, you'll have to make sure you get up every morning from now on."[9]

Blimey! And this is love? I ask the dog, who rolls over for a tummy rub.

"Yes," is the resounding response from the Danes I poll. It's direct and it's true.

Okay then, I think. *Bring on Operation Alarm Clock!*

That night, I break it to the redhead, then brace myself for a fight.

"So I'm getting an alarm clock?"

I nod.

"Cool." He nods and turns off his light.

A Viking parenting win.

———

I know already about the importance of family meals and food in Danish culture, so I'm surprised to hear about a much more relaxed perspective on dinnertimes than anticipated from the Danes I survey. Like celebrated Danish chef and food writer Trine Hahnemann, who tells me that her policy is "When children are hungry, you feed them."[10]

That's it? No "eat your broccoli first, or you don't get pudding?" No bribery? No blackmail?

"No nothing."

What? So snacks on demand?

But this is another hallowed Jesper Juul-ism. Children, he says, may have an idiosyncratic biological clock so may not be hungry when we are but then develop an appetite half an hour later. The refusal of food at mealtimes can also be a signal that all is not well. Children may lose their appetite when they sit down to eat with the rest of the family if the atmosphere at the table is tense or destructive. When a child can't put this into words, they choose not to eat.

"Because when you're five, you don't have too many other choices," as my dad of two friend Peter Schmeichel says. "You make your power moves where you can."

This makes more sense to me. I'm very aware of the impulse for control around food, having grown up a kid of 1980s and '90s diet culture and working in women's magazines in my twenties. I don't want to pass on any of my own issues here. (I'll just mess my kids up in other ways.) So a liberal approach to meals, I can live with, even if our extended relations remain unconvinced.

But the next Viking parenting policy seems batshit.

According to Jesper's law, we should let children intuitively eat as much candy—*slik* in Danish—as they want. And since the custom is to let Danish children pick themselves a bag every Friday, there's often *slik* knocking around.

Candy on demand? This seems like staggeringly bad parenting. I cast around for an actual grown-up to consult, but finding none, I opt for my usual resort: *What would Mary Poppins do?* I'm pretty sure "unlimited candy" isn't a hallowed Poppins-ism. *Julie Andrews doesn't sing songs about bottomless bonbon bags. Are Vikings quite mad?*

"No" is the response I get from all Nordic parents ever. The logic? If a child is given a bag of candy ("Well, there's your first mistake!" I hear my mother's voice ringing out at this point), then we take it away or tell them to stop eating, we ruin the child's sensible sense of naturally learning how much candy to eat on their own, says Jesper.[11]

At which point I, along with every other non-Viking in the vicinity, roll our eyes in the manner of Dorothy from *The Golden Girls*. It feels like very bad parenting indeed to let a child run off with a vat of glucose syrup. Also, I'm not sure I have an off switch.

"Maybe you would if you'd been raised the Danish way," Veteran Viking tells me.

Touché. Although what about the boundaries that Pia and Kitta talked about?

Veteran Viking sees no contradiction here. "We bring up kids to make their own choices. We don't teach them to place all their trust in external authority—political, religious, or philosophical. It all goes back to our occupation in World War II."

Again? Are we equating my M&M habit with Nazism? This feels harsh. But I take her point: How will they learn if we don't let them?

Jesper believed there were three areas of life that children must be allowed to assume personal responsibility in order to stay healthy: their senses (what tastes good, what doesn't; what feels hot or cold); their feelings (like happiness, friendship, anger, frustration, sorrow, pain); and their needs (hunger, thirst, sleep, nearness, distance).

I ask my Danish parent friends and learn that, for the most part, they agree with Jesper Juul's philosophy and somehow manage to live by it too. Many enjoyed similar freedoms when they were growing up.

"My mom raised me with three rules," says Rikke with the

twinkly eyes. "Treat others like you would want them to treat you. Speak nicely to me: I'm your mother. And you need warm feet and ears. Always."

I tell her I like the sound of her mom and reflect that as well as giving children responsibility, this gives freedom back to parents too.

So could it work?

That night, I tell my son, "I'm going to say good night now because I want to go to bed soon too." This isn't much of an exaggeration: I am a husk by 9:00 p.m.

"Okay." He flicks through *Dog Man* for half an hour, then turns his light off and gets into bed. No fuss. And he's up with the alarm in the morning.

"Does he make his own bed now too?" asks my mother, always eager for the next step.

"Sadly not," I tell her.

"Oh, that's a pity. You do look *very* tired."

I don't know how to tell her that this is just my face now. Or how I can't force my children to make their own beds, according to Viking rules.

"We don't make children do chores," Veteran Viking tells me. "We encourage help so children feel like valuable members of the team."

So mini Vikings won't be obliged to help around the house, and I just have to hope that they want to? Come off it!

This feels far-fetched. I can, however, talk on the phone. When I have to make a call and children are inevitably running wild (see *ramasjang*, or hullabaloo—actively encouraged in Denmark), I should just *say* so. Rather than a polite appeal of, "Mommy would really like to just hear what this person is saying on the phone," JJ has us rephrase our request in an active voice to become something like: "I want you to keep it down while I'm talking to the dentist/ my friend Kate."

When I hear this coming out of my mouth, I feel selfish—not at all the saintly mother figure most of the parenting advice from back home suggests I aim for. But my children? They get it. This is how their brains work, and it makes sense to them. Plus I'm showing them that I have needs too. Needs for a hygienist appointment or a chat with Kate. I'm not asking for things that appear arbitrary and just because I say so. I'm modeling autonomy. And getting clean teeth. And chats. And early nights.

"No, you can't watch more TV," I can legitimately tell my children in Denmark, "because it's finished now."

"Finished? Television is never finished, is it?" asks Lego Man when he hears this. He didn't have a television growing up and so can never be quite sure. But children's TV on Denmark's public broadcaster really does go off at 8:00 p.m. After that, instead of playing reruns or going dark, DR TV shows a continuous loop of its most popular characters—pirates, puppets, artisanal cheesemaker types (just wait until chapter 12)—fast asleep in bed.

"It's easier to get kids to bed when you show them the rest of the world—including TV—has shut down too," Veteran Viking tells me. In other markets, children's programming transitions into youth or adult shows at night, but DR chose not to. Which was kind of them. *And smart*, I can't help thinking, remembering the time I let my kids watch *Winnie the Pooh*—the wholly innocent one-hundred-minute film that I allowed to roll on a fraction too long. They ended up watching the next film alphabetically in our TV's film library: *Withnail and I.* The drink- and drug-fueled comedy that elevated swearing to an art form wasn't *quite* what anyone was ready for. ("Mommy, is Christopher Robin just really angry now he's all grown up?") So Viking TV scheduling, I can handle.

But the final obstacle in the show-don't-tell parenting training course is the hardest yet.

"You have to let kids fight sometimes," says my son's teacher. This isn't what I was expecting. "You have to let them have conflict," she tells me, "so my kids will be fist fighting, and I'll have to let them. I don't always manage this. In the supermarket, for example, I might say, 'Okay stop.' But at home or in a safe environment, with friends or family, we always see if they can solve it themselves. If they can get themselves to the peace table."* I like the idea of a peace table. "The most important experience the child gets when he experiences a clash is that we can disagree but still agree."

Or as my friend Rikke says, "There is still love, no matter what."

Studies show that play fighting is an important part of a child's development, teaching cooperation, building confidence and appropriate judgment. Rats deprived of the opportunity to play fight with their peers (but given socialization and care by older female rats) don't learn when it's appropriate to fight.[12] This means they tend to be a bit touchy as adults and lash out when it's not needed. They haven't learned the rules of society.

---

* FYI, her children are now nice, well-adjusted teenagers. So she may be onto something.

Experts have extrapolated that play fighting helps us learn to socialize. Play fighting is the most common play type across all mammals, but it's also the type of play that parents and teachers are most likely to discourage. In some US institutions, there's even a zero-tolerance policy. But not for Vikings. Throughout the Nordic countries, adults let children handle their own conflicts. "We jump in only when they really start hurting each other," one Icelandic mom told me.

"Like choking," my son's teacher tells me. "We draw the line at choking."

How comforting.

But "it's about self-governance," says Professor Ning de Coninck-Smith, an expert in the history of play and childhood from Aarhus University.[13] And in this self-governing culture for children, they learn about the limits of themselves and other people.

I give this a shot the following day on a dog walk when there is a dispute over who gets to hold the leash (this is standard). The redhead, sensing the exhilaration of battle, insists it's his turn. His brother and sister disagree. They're all needling each other, but instead of intervening as usual, I say nothing. I do nothing. I slow my pace even, the locomotive equivalent of "sitting on my hands" as pedagogue Lise, the Viking from Valhalla, taught me. Soon I hear shrieks of frustration from my daughter (also standard). It takes every ounce of self-control I have not to go to her. I stand still, knowing if I move, I will run to her. I love her. I will not leave her. But I also need to let her win. On her own. There is some jostling. Light shoving even. But she is more evenly matched with her brothers than I have given her credit for.

Good for her.

After what feels like an eternity, there is another sound: *"No!"* My daughter roars at her brothers, *"Min!"* or "mine" in Danish. I'm interested that she reverts to Danish when asserting herself. After some negotiations I can't quite make out, the leash is hers, and she holds it aloft above her head, victorious. Ponytail swishing, arms swinging, she strides home, the dog prancing with projected pride a few paces ahead. I may be imagining it, but I could swear she looks a good inch taller than she did when we set out on this walk.

My daughter arrives home before the rest of us to a package on the doorstep.

"Can I open it?" she calls back to me.

"To the victor, the spoils!"

She tears apart a brown paper package to reveal…

"A shoehorn?"

All hail Viking parenting.

WHAT I'VE LEARNED ABOUT DISCIPLINE, VIKING STYLE

◆ Respect is a given. It doesn't need to be earned. (I know! Madness!) Just imagine how different the world could be had we all been raised this way. In the spirit of self-parenting, I am savoring this gem: We are all worthy. We are enough. Simply because we exist.

◆ Don't curl, but reduce friction where possible. They'll reach the top drawer when they're big enough to reach the top drawer. Until then, I'm putting all the kid stuff in drawers they can actually reach. And I'm trying to be more patient too, allowing them time, coaching them if needed, and making sure they get enough sleep (mine turn into gremlins on fewer than ten hours a night).

- Be nice about other people's children, and don't overpraise your own. Not every picture needs to go on the fridge (or we'll run out of fridge). This feels revolutionary since half of us were raised in the "how wonderful" mode while the other half were dragged up with the old-school idea of "never praise, never apologize." Neither approach works if parents are still making critical comments about other children, because small people internalize this. I did. Vikings play it cool about their children—as well as everyone else's.

- Let them fight it out and see if they can come to "the peace table" by themselves. This way self-governance lies, apparently. I didn't have brothers or sisters growing up. I went to an all-girls Catholic school intended to turn out young ladies. There was no fighting. How different would I be now, I wonder, had I *grappled* a little more? Roughhoused, even? Before having children, I'd never had nonromantic physical contact beyond hugging girlfriends. Then I had babies. Then toddlers. And parenting toddlers is 50 percent hugging and 50 percent WWE wrestling. And I loved it! My children taught me that. They're raising me just as much as I'm raising them, for which I'm eternally grateful.

- If all else fails, buy a shoehorn.

PLAY (WELL)

BIRDS DO IT. BUMBLEBEES DO it. Even bison run onto frozen lakes and slide on all fours to do it. Throughout the animal kingdom, there is play. Macaques make snowballs. Otters prank each other. Hippos do backflips. And my children play with Lego. At every opportunity. At the doctor's office. At the dentist's office. At 7:00 a.m. while I'm ~~yelling telling~~ *coaching* them to "put shoes on!" At the craft fair they begged me to attend (my daughter is such a prolific crafter that glue-gun access is now rationed at kindergarten), they look around for precisely eight minutes before gravitating toward the Lego table (there's always a Lego table).

Why are we here?! How is this still fun?! I wonder, looking longingly at a nearby display of artsy knickknacks. But all my children want to do when they're not wrestling me/each other is play. In an assortment of imaginary worlds (dragons, pirates, cafés, police procedurals, you name it).

I know how much people love Lego. I love people who love Lego. But in truth, I'm agnostic. (Sings "Everything Is Awesome" lest I be struck down by a yellow mini figure with U-shaped hands.) I appreciate that I am in the minority since the clickety plastic bricks are regularly voted the most popular toy in the world. The plastic part may seem surprising in our eco aware age,* but Lego bricks are reusable—often passed down through generations. They're also insanely durable, as anyone who's ever heard alarming clackety noises from the washing machine can testify. It's not advised, but if you *do* end up putting Lego on a spin cycle after a child has forgotten to empty their pockets, you can still click the bricks together afterward. Or so I hear...

The name "Lego" is an abbreviation of the two Danish words *leg godt,* meaning "play well." The company began in 1932 when Ole Kirk Kristiansen—a widowed carpenter struggling to feed his four children—made toys to survive. He started off with yo-yos, until yo-yos weren't cool (who knew?), so he used the ones he couldn't shift as wheels on toy trucks. He made more wooden toys and just about got by until his wood-heavy workshop burned down. Determined to catch a break, he turned to plastic bricks after the war, inspired by the colors of Piet Mondrian and a department store buyer he met on a boat. The Lego mini figure debuted in 1978, designed by Jens Nygaard Knudsen, and it was a hit. When Jens died in 2020, one epitaph read, "He leaves a loving wife, three children, two grandchildren and over eight billion little plastic people infused with life by children's imaginations."[1]

The Lego company passed from Ole Kirk Kristiansen to his son Godtfred, who drew up a set of guidelines, "The Lego Constitution," in 1963 to decree that Lego should offer unlimited

---

* Although they now make some bricks from sugarcane.

play possibilities for girls and for boys, inspire enthusiasm in all ages, foster imagination, creativity, and development, and encourage play all year round. And play is still at the center of it all today, signposted in six-foot-high letters in clicky bricks in the entrance of Lego's Billund HQ. The word "play" is in English, but it's the Nordic versions I'm interested in.

Remember how Lego is made up of the words "play" and "well"? In Danish, "play" is *leg*. But "play" is also *spille*. *Spille* is used when referring to play as in sports, music, or a game—something structured or with rules attached—whereas *leg* is just for fun. And in fact, all the Nordic languages double up on play. Just as Hawaiians have two hundred words for rain, signaling the importance of water in Hawaiian culture, Vikings love to play. The verb forms of "play" in Finnish, Swedish, Icelandic, and Norwegian refer specifically to unstructured, imaginative, enjoyable, and intrinsically motivated activities.** But if you're playing sports, a board game, or a musical instrument, you use *spille* in Danish and Norwegian, *spela* in Swedish, and *spila* in Icelandic. Finns go off script with *pelata*, but the fact remains: play is so big, they named it twice.

So why does play *matter* so much?

To find out, I visit Marc Malmdorf Andersen, a cognitive scientist and play researcher from Aarhus University in Denmark. "Play is a sign of well-being," he tells me. "Among animals who play, it only occurs in the absence of illness, hunger, and stress. After our basic needs are met, we play. So if we're not playing, it can sometimes be a sign that something is wrong."[2]

** *Leikkiä, leka, leika,* and *leka* respectively.

Dr. Stuart Brown from the US National Institute for Play calls play "probably the most important factor in being a fulfilled human being" and says that "when we stop playing, we start dying."[3] *This seems a bit much.* But Marc agrees that play is intrinsic from birth.

I scroll back through my parenting ride, remembering six-week-old babies delightedly scrunching up paper or making faces in a mirror. Toddlers occupying themselves for hours with a cardboard box. Children are nothing if not resourceful, "and they will readily manufacture their own toys and invent their own play," says Marc. Like the two-year-old at my children's day care who gnaws his rye bread into the shape of a gun to shoot with ("pow pow!").

Studies suggest that play makes us happier and healthier and can aid learning, improve problem-solving, and even help with social mobility and reducing inequality.[4] "Some types of play also seem to be able to make us braver and help us learn to deal with adverse emotions," says Marc. In a game, we can "become" someone else, but there's less at stake if things don't go as we'd hoped. "And kids learn a lot from 'just' playing," says Marc, "like taking turns, conflict management, social interaction, negotiation, motor skills, and problem-solving." But play is under threat.

Many US children are so overscheduled with school and extracurricular activities that they have no time to play, according to a report from the American Academy of Pediatrics.[5] Research conducted by Lego found that the toy company's main threat isn't a competitor toy—it's time, or rather children's lack of it. Playtime for UK and US children has decreased by 25 percent in recent years, and unstructured outdoor activity has declined by 50 percent.[6] Some schools in the US are doing away with break times altogether in a rush to catch up with academic work post lock-downs. Yet the enforced isolation without peers to play with has made playtime more important than ever, because children's social and emotional learning "stalled," says Professor Paul Ramchandani from Cambridge University. "Children are increasingly under pressure to 'succeed' and rushed through times when they should be playing," says Paul. "Even the best universities are now admitting that 'smart students' aren't necessarily those with astounding academic grades—they're the ones who can think outside the box, solve problems, try and fail"—i.e., play. In this respect, play is the supreme competitive edge.[7]

Studies show that a play deficit is like a sleep deficit. Animals deprived of play will engage in extra play when it's safe to do so again. So experts want parents to protect and promote children's playtime.

"But some adults fail to see the value of play," says Marc, "and then it can be harder to prioritize as a parent. This is largely because adults become narrow-minded and cognitively inflexible with age." *Speak for yourself...* But Marc explains how "long ago, before we became boring adults, we already thoroughly explored and experimented with how the world works. The more knowledge we amass, the more certain we become that the world works in certain ways." Which means that we rely on our *assumptions* of how everything works rather than testing things out and experimenting, as children do.

This makes sense, but it's a problem, since adults who don't (or won't or *can't*) play become anhedonic—incapable of feeling sustained pleasure. I remember how animals who are stressed won't play.

Is the same true of humans? Are stressed-out parents less likely to play?

"Undoubtedly," says Marc. "So we see in countries like Denmark, where there is a shorter working week, parents should, in theory, be able to play more".

Danes do play more as adults than I had been used to back home, getting together "just for fun" as part of a hobby club or association. Veteran Viking does CrossFit. Peter Schmeichel plays basketball. American Mom is part of an improv choir she keeps asking me to join. Everyone is a part of something in Denmark. The average Dane is a member of 2.8 clubs (fun fact), so everyone gets to play at something outside their day job. This time spent playing doesn't detract from work either. It enhances it, increasing feelings of well-being, belonging, identity, and creativity. Vikings punch above their weight on creativity and innovation, with global companies like IKEA, H&M, Spotify, Volvo, Ericsson, Bang & Olufsen, Electrolux, Pandora, Tetra Pak, *Minecraft*, Lego, Skype, and Nokia all coming out of the tiny clump of countries.

Could a Viking-style shorter working week help the rest of us play more? And keep our mental health on track and allow for more time with family?

Alex Soojung-Kim Pang thinks so. He's a rest researcher and director of 4 Day Week Global, an organization aiming to reshape the way we work. Because outside the Nordic countries, he tells me, "People are reaching the physical limits of their ability to work." Particularly parents. "We all overestimate the degree to which we can handle a heavy workload, especially as our lives change and especially as we become parents. Society dangerously underestimates the importance and difficulty of parenthood." The answer, he believes, is a four-day week. "This has been proven to improve our personal lives by giving us more free time."[8] He wants employers to offer 100 percent pay for a four-day week, promising 100 percent productivity. Because—spoiler alert—it's possible.

Microsoft Japan found that staff productivity increased by 40 percent after a trial of the four-day work week.[9] New Zealand finance company Perpetual Guardian cut the working week to four days and saw a 20 percent rise in productivity.[10] Pilot schemes are now springing up worldwide, with devotees claiming that the four-day week can boost productivity, improve employee mental health, and restore a sense of play.

Throughout the Nordic countries, there is play. All Vikings play for longer before starting school, and studies from Stanford in the US and Aarhus University in Denmark have found huge benefits to starting later. Delaying kindergarten for a year led to a reduction in attention problems and hyperactivity by 73 percent.[11] Some experts now believe a sharp decline in play over the last few decades may be a contributing factor to the overdiagnosis of ADHD. Researchers from Michigan State University claim 20 percent of US children receiving treatment for ADHD are likely to have been misdiagnosed.[12] And a Harvard study of 407,000 children found that the youngest in a class are 35 percent more likely to be diagnosed than their peers, despite the fact that any fidgety behavior is probably because of their relative immaturity.[13] As Finnish educator Pasi Sahlberg put it after a long day explaining to an American psychologist why five-year-olds struggle to sit still:

"In Finland, we have ADHD too, but we have a different name for it: we call it childhood."[14]

There's another important way that Danes embrace play. "Playgrounds are a barometer of development in society's view of childhood," says Professor Ning de Coninck-Smith, "and in Denmark, we take playgrounds very seriously indeed." Ning has studied the cultural history of Danish playgrounds over the past 150 years since Copenhagen philanthropists decided to set aside land in densely populated urban areas for play. These merchants and businessmen could have capitalized on prized land and made a quick buck, but instead, they thought about the future of children growing up there. "It was decided that the areas should not be built on," says Ning. "That was quite unusual, investing in children in this way. The original playgrounds had a focus on physical development, but in time, playgrounds with swings and slides, etc. were joined by junk playgrounds with a focus on construction."

Junk and *playgrounds* aren't words that normally go together, but Ning explains how junk playgrounds came about during Denmark's occupation in the Second World War. Nazi defenses were built across the country, and there were no resources for playgrounds, so kids got used to playing with whatever building materials were lying around. "They built huts and constructions in trees," says Ning, "and also played with ammunition dropped by British airplanes to the resistance movement." Children played with the residual junk of war. In 1943, the first official junk playground (*skrammellegeplads* in Danish) opened in Emdrup, outside Copenhagen. It had no swings, climbing frames, or sand pits, just old wheelbarrows, planks of wood, and, well, junk. "The idea was that children thrive when they have opportunities to unfold creatively," says Ning. Within hours, children transformed the junk into caves, houses, and towers. And the concept spread countrywide. "Junk playgrounds were—and still are—the exception, but they made Denmark famous," says Ning, who wrote the 2022 book *Skrammellegepladsen: The History of Danish Playgrounds* (including a photo of former First Lady Eleanor Roosevelt visiting one). "There are still a few of these around," says Ning, as I watch my children build a den from forklift truck pallets that Lego Man left lying around (our yard is a lot like a junk playground), "but there's been an increasing focus on aesthetics and quality of playgrounds" (unlike our yard).

Today, the playground industry is worth billions, and Denmark is home to the biggest playground maker in the world, Kompan. Founder Tom Lindhardt started out as a sculptor in the 1970s, but seeing how much children loved to play on his art, he decided to make play spaces just for them. Now, the company designs, manufactures, and installs one thousand playgrounds a month across ninety countries—that's one every forty-four minutes. Denmark is also home to the globally renowned Monstrum playground makers. I spend a lot of time with my children at their eponymous whale playground near me as well as the helicopter, rocket, shark, and camel constructions in Billund.

A common criticism leveled at custom-made play spaces is that they are too easy, too sanitized, and that nature is always better. But play historian Ning doesn't buy this. "Some constructions are really challenging." Lego Man still remembers the time he got wedged, Winnie-the-Pooh style, in a twenty-foot-high metal tube rescuing our daughter from a sheer drop at one such adventure play park. "I think our playgrounds reflect a growing creativity when thinking about the needs of children and families living in cities," says Ning. "And play is something Denmark gets really right."

Play is so important that Denmark is home to a global play experiment at a test center for Harvard University's Project Zero, a research organization founded in 1967 with a focus on creative learning.[15]A test school in Jutland is now exploring the pedagogy of play, with every aspect of the school filtered through the prism of play.

So mini Vikings play all day, every day, before they start school, then they're playing in the world's best playgrounds, with the world's biggest toy, Lego. Then once they get to school, they play there too?

I'm feeling pretty good about all this. Surely my parenting work is done?

"No," says Veteran Viking, along with every Nordic parent and researcher ever. "*You* have to play too."

"What?" I deflate, realizing I have some work ahead. I love my children, but there are *three* of them and often three different games going on. I find myself setting a timer for five minutes, "then I'll play with your brother, then I'll play with your sister," until I feel like I'm letting everyone down. ("Is *anyone* having fun?" I ask despairingly as five-year-olds sob and an eight-year-old wrestles me for the sand timer.)

Is this really necessary? Wasn't there something in the wedding vows about putting away childish things?

I grew up in the 1980s and '90s. Parents didn't play with children.

Children *played* and parents *worked*. Or had dinner parties. Or watched *Dallas*. Right?

Wrong, apparently.

"Parents have to play with their kids. It's really important," says Professor Paul from Cambridge University. All the experts I spoke to echoed his view—verified by a barrage of news articles and "shocking new survey results." In one day, I read how one in five parents haven't played with their children in two days and that 54 percent spend "less than four hours a week playing with their children."[16]

I don't mean to be a Grinch, but four hours a week sounds a lot. I don't have four hours a week to do anything else—like exercise or read or see friends.

Or go to the bathroom alone. Or shower in peace.

Another article tells me that 53 percent of parents struggle to find time or energy to play with their children but still manage to spend thirteen hundred hours—the equivalent of fifty-four full days—playing before a child turns five. And in the first five years of a child's life, parents play peekaboo for an average of ninety-five hours.[17]

Ninety-five hours?

The dog yawns in sympathy.

On peekaboo?!

But peekaboo, it turns out, isn't just peekaboo. It's psychological tennis. When a player serves, they know their opponent is ready to return the ball, and that's what children expect too. If a child hides behind their hands, they want us to search for them. If we do the hiding, they search. Researchers from Harvard University found that predictable serves and returns lead to better physical and mental health, empathy, and language in children.[18] Brains change as we learn, and when children do things over and over, this creates new pathways in the brain. So if children serve too often *without* a return, they miss opportunities to create and reinforce valuable connections in their brains.

But ninety-five hours!

That's twelve working days. I could have done a diving course. Or learned to drive a truck. *And I spent it playing peekaboo?* Plus I had small babies twice, with the redhead and twins. I must be nearing two hundred hours of peekaboo by now. *I could have become a commercial pilot in that time, had I not been so exhausted.* I feel weary at the thought that even though I've spent two hundred hours on peekaboo, I *still* may not have played enough.

I speak to numerous experts on this, often older and male, but get the sense that someone else is doing a lot of the parenting. I want advice from a parent still in the trenches. So I ask Sabilah Eboo Alwani from the Faculty of Education at University of Cambridge, the woman leading a project on play today while parenting young daughters.

How are parents supposed to do it all?

"I get it," she tells me. "It's a lot."

Does it only work if one parent stays home? Is she a secret John Bowlby attachment-theory sleeper cell?

Sabilah smiles and tells me, "The ideas around attachment theory are almost a luxury for many parents these days because the decision about whether one parent can or should stay home longer has become more about economic viability than what's best for child development."[19]

So everyone's working now but we're *still* playing peekaboo for ninety-five hours? I mention how no one my age had parents who consistently played with them, "and we turned out all right...ish."

"Ye-es," she hedges diplomatically, "but today, the research has moved on, so surely we could and should act on this?"

I mumble a "s'pose so" then ask why it's so important for parents to play with children.

"Today, we know that the early years period of zero to five is a golden window for a child's development. And the biggest influence on a child at this age is usually their parents. That's why parents have a key role as their child's first teachers and playmates. A parent knows their child more than a teacher or day care worker ever can," says Sabilah. Also, times have changed. "A generation ago, children ran outside to play and came home by dinner. They'd ride off on their bikes and have adventures."

"Like *Stranger Things* but less supernatural?"

"Exactly."

Especially in Denmark. As an agricultural nation until recently, children were routinely left to their own devices. Farmers began work early, then napped at midday, while kids roamed free. Older Danes recall these "wild times" as among the best of their lives.

"But now we know kids are not doing all this," says Sabilah, "and think about what they are doing instead. Big slices of the pie of their time are now spent on devices." Consoles, tablets, smartphones, and Switches have replaced the wild times. Were the film *E.T.* to be set in the 2020s, there'd be no gangs of feral ten-year-olds rampaging on BMX bikes without helmets or adult supervision.

Elliott wouldn't be outside throwing a ball at a toolshed; he'd be inside on an iPad.

And so, Sabilah explains, we can't just expect children to play in a way that they did historically. They need someone to play *with*.

"Aha! But mine have siblings."

Surely siblings are a "get out of jail free" card!

I didn't have siblings growing up. I had Swingball, a game of "hit a ball on a string" that I'd play for hours until callouses formed on my palms from crudely molded plastic paddles. Then came the arrival of Screwball Scramble in 1988, a.k.a. the Christmas that changed everything.* *Good times*, I think back fondly. But actual playmates on tap? Ready and willing and contractually obliged to be linked their whole lives long? That must get me off the hook, surely?

"Sibling play is hugely valuable," Sabilah agrees. "It's customized one-to-one peer play, ticking many of the boxes. But playing with a parent is still important."

Urgh. "Why?"

"Bonding."

"Oh."

According to a Lego "Play Well" study, 84 percent of children wish they could play more with their parents.[20]

The guilt of parenting never ends.

"I'm not saying it's easy," says Sabilah. "I get my kids home by maybe 4:15 p.m., and I have to get dinner on the table by 5:00 p.m. They're exhausted. It's nobody's best time of day..." She trails off,

---

* A much-loved game that you could play solo.

and we both take a moment to wish we were on a silent retreat in Tuscany. (Then again, I could just be projecting.)

"So when are parents supposed to find this mythical rainbow playtime?" I ask.

"Well, these days, I try to do something in the morning, like read a story or two at breakfast. Or I pick and choose my moments throughout the week so that by the end of the week, hand on heart, I can think, 'Did I actually sit on the floor with them and play? Did I host that teddy bears' tea party? Did we do that puzzle together? Were they happy? In their eyes, how was I this week? Did they feel Mom and Dad were there for them?' Because they don't care about chores. They don't care how dirty the house is or whether the laundry gets done. They want you."

But it's not just about putting in the hours either. The type of play parents engage in matters too. *Jesus wept...* There are different ways of playing—all important and all essential to help children learn different life skills. (I know: it's a lot. Make tea/ have a power nap, then come back if you can't take this next part right now.)

Ready?

Okay.

There's a lot of research on play. I've read it, and it's frankly tough going (unfortunate for play research). So to explain it in ways that won't make anyone's eyes bleed, there are four different types of play that I now think of in terms of decorating a cake.[21] First up, there's free play—giving a child bowls of icing, sprinkles, and other toppings and leaving them to create whatever they like. Then there's guided play—saying "Hey! Who can decorate the most colorful cake?" or "Can you make your cake look like a narwhal?" Then there's gamification—racing a child to see who can decorate their cake the fastest. And last but not least, instruction—sitting down with step-by-step directions for decorating the cake and encouraging small people to follow them. (Good luck with this one. Best attempted after a really good night's sleep.)

Et voilà! Cake.

"But now you just need to do it," says Sabilah.

So I do.

The next time all three children are about to pulverize each other, I declare that I am all in: ready and willing to be part of whatever play they choose for the rest of the afternoon. *Beanie Babies–Hot Wheels mash-up, here I come!*

There follows the most surreal hour of my life.

"Emergency, emergency! There's been a car crash! In the rabbit's face!" my son announces, somewhat disturbingly, as we begin our free play.

Wait, what? Okay, play along. "Oh no! What shall we do?"

"Quick: cookies!" My daughter's recommendation.

Cookies?

"Now!" my youngest son chimes in.

Okay...how about guided play? "Does the rabbit need any medical attention?"

Youngest son: "Yes! Susan needs a sleepover!"

"Susan"? No one has been christened Susan since approximately 1983. "Her name is Susan?"

Daughter: "Their name!"

"Susan uses *they*?"

Daughter: "Yes!"

I apologize to Susan for making such binary presumptions and decide to bring on the gamification. "Who can help Susan the fastest?"

"Me! Susan needs a sleepover and cookies, stat!" my youngest son announces.

"Okay. Right. Well. Err, here's a cookie!"

Daughter goes for the jugular: "Susan doesn't like your cookie."

What the @$%&? Say that to my face, Susan!

The redhead changes tack and takes on instruction mode: "I'm directing a movie. Out of my way. This is a raid!"

A raid? Do their brains work faster than mine? Why can't I keep up?!

Daughter: "You better say sorry, or you're not coming to my birthday party!"

What? Why? What am I sorry for?

Youngest son, shaking his head: "Susan is really mad now!"

No arguments there. Susan appears completely bananas.

Daughter: "It's the village party and rabbit's birthday."

Redhead: "And they've won the World Cup."

Who? Susan?

All shout in unison "Yes!"

Then the raid gets underway, youngest son announces he's changed *his* name to "Frank the Tank," and the Hot Wheels cars do stunts over the Beanie Babies birthday party as my daughter shouts at the world, "Susan hates your cookies!"

Ah, the magic of child's play.

WHAT I'VE LEARNED ABOUT
HOW TO PLAY LIKE A VIKING

* We all need to play to stay happy and healthy, regardless of our age. Or whether or not we grew up a bookish only child in the 1980s.

* Playmates matter. Friends and siblings are good, but parents need to step up too.

* We should make space for games (*spille*) and just-for-the-heck-of-it play (*leg*). I find this hard on both counts. As an adult, I barely remember what it even feels like to (a) have free time and (b) know what to do with it. I'm not always sure I can remember what fun is, let alone how to do it, guilt-free. And this isn't because I'm any sort of martyr-like domestic goddess—it's because I'm exhausted. But if it's going to make me a better parent and human, I'll prioritize fun (and let my domestic standards slip still further...oh well #selfparenting).

* Remember the cake analogy? Embrace free play ("You know where Mommy keeps the Friday *slik*? Go wild."), guided play ("Who can decorate the most colorful cake?"), games ("Who can eat their cake first? Mommy can!"), and instruction ("Here's a recipe. Make Mommy a cake?"). Then eat the cake.

* Parenting is officially insane. But at least Susan and the Beanie Babies were relatively low stakes. The next aspect of Danish play is likely to result in far more gray hairs, if not plaster casts. *Strap in.*

RISK (A.K.A. VIKING HEALTH AND SAFETY)

10

IN EIGHT HOURS' TIME, I'LL be in the hospital. I don't know this as I begin the day shoveling snow. Not unusual in Denmark in December, where it's your civic duty to clear the sidewalk outside your home before 8:00 a.m. so that passersby don't do a Bambi. It's 23°F, snowing hard, and the world is muffled in a thick white blanket. Driving carefully, I drop the twins at day care and the redhead at school where I gather that today's gym class is sledding. It's breathtakingly cold and barely light, but I presume the teachers know what they're doing. With a few minutes to spare before work, I stand and watch, in an attempt to be more present and savor the magical moments of childhood people are always telling me about.

Snow glistens in the dawn, and I wave to my son as he reaches the top of the hill adjacent to the school. He waves back a gloved hand while the other clutches a bum sled. Various children I vaguely recognize are already bombing downhill (it's tough to tell who's who when everyone's wearing a balaclava and the same navy-blue, maroon, or green snowsuit). I pull my collar a little higher around my neck as I follow the figure I'm assuming is my child.

There must be a knack to sledding, I think. I'm not a huge fan of a cold behind, so I can't be sure he's doing it right. *But he's with the school. They wouldn't let him do anything daft, would they?*

I notice he's going quite fast.

*He'll definitely slow down at some point. Or turn. Won't he? He'll probably turn…*He does not.

I notice he is going *very* fast now.

Aren't you supposed to throw yourself off the sled? Abort mission if it feels out of control? I make waving motions to indicate "abandon ship."

He does not.

And then I notice that he's running out of hill.

There's a rudimentary fence made up of two wires at the bottom, but we're in farmer country here, and I'm not entirely sure if it's electric or not.

If he doesn't get electrocuted, I calculate, *he will almost certainly be garroted.*

A sickening feeling spreads in my stomach, and I begin a run toward the careering figure. But moving in Moon Boots (see 23°F) is akin to trudging through molasses. The sled is hurtling at an alarming velocity. I'm running/trudging. Other people are shouting. The child is leaning back, screaming.

Or is it more of a whoop?

The figure reclines flat against the snow. The fence looms closer, and the child…passes underneath the lowest wire.

He hasn't been electrocuted or garroted! Hallelujah!

But still the sled does not stop.

It keeps going, leaving the field, and skidding into the adjacent *road.*

Oh god...

My Moon Boots and I move in slow motion as the sled sails across the first lane of traffic, coming to a stop at the broken center line. Time stands still as cars screech. The figure on the bum sled slowly scrambles up, pulls off the balaclava to reveal a beaming smile and...a shock of red hair. The driver of a blue Volvo (welcome to Scandinavia) gets out, and I wonder whether he's going to give my son a telling off. But instead, he crouches, puts a hand on his shoulder, then gives him a high five before leaving with a wave of "*God tur!*" ("Good trip!").

My son, seeing my stricken face approaching, asks, "Are you okay?"

To which I respond, "*?!?!?!?!*$?*"

I'm relieved when his teacher appears and announces it's time to go inside. But nothing more is said. There is no "bump report." No apology. No drama—except from me, it seems. And then my phone rings. With a sinking feeling, I see that it's day care calling. This never means good news.

"Your daughter hit her head," the pedagogue tells me calmly.

Sweet Jesus.

"She was playing and tripped over—"

"I'm on my way."

My daughter has not simply hit her head. She has, it emerges, gashed her face from eyebrow to eyebrow.

"On an IKEA table," the pedagogue adds.

"An *IKEA* table?" *What are Scandinavians doing to me today?*

"It was a Lack," the teacher nods, as though the Swedish furniture maker's most basic design has let us all down today and is wholly responsible.

We see a doctor who confirms that the cut is "pretty bad" and needs stitches. Immediately. We're sent to emergency to wait, but my daughter is, understandably, distraught. Eventually we're told she needs to go under general anesthetic to be sewn up again and has she eaten in the last four hours?

I check with day care.

"Oh yes. I gave her carrots as soon as she fell."

Carrots?! Is this an approved Viking cure? Root vegetables?

We sit and wait until she has an empty stomach for the general anesthetic. Several hours and twelve stitches later, I'm watching my daughter's oxygen monitor go up and down like a roller coaster. This is the third time I've seen one of my children go under general anesthetic, and it doesn't get any easier. My thumping heart feels too big for my chest.

Am I a terrible mother? Am I doing this parenting thing all wrong?

"No!" fellow day care dad Peter Schmeichel tells me. He drops by to pick up house keys and let the dog out for a pee in my hour of need. "This is why we pay taxes!" Peter Schmeichel insists. "We have healthcare so you can live how you like. You can take risks."

I'm not sure I want to take risks. At least, not with my children.

"You have to," he says, suddenly serious. "Otherwise you really are doing it wrong."

Wait, what?

He shrugs. "That's how I was raised."

———

Our daughter is allowed home later that night. I put her to bed and stroke her hair, spread out like a fan on the pillow. Everyone else in the house is asleep, but the adrenaline is still surging through my veins. So I do exactly what the experts warn against: I google. By the blue light of my phone at my daughter's bedside, I begin investigating the Danish attitude to risk and learn that it isn't just Denmark where there's a relaxed slant on health and safety.

Norwegian professor and former rector of the Norwegian Sports Academy Gunnar Breivik believes that "children have the right to freeze from time to time." He says we have "failed as parents" if our children haven't broken any bones by the time they turn eighteen.[1] He also thinks we should let them "be hungry once in a while, to get scratches...and to bleed a little."[2]

So I'm...winning? I watch minutes flick by on the clock. *Because this really doesn't feel like winning.*

Once it was a decent enough hour, I call Marc, the play researcher. He's been exploring the importance of fear and risk in play to help with growth and resilience. I tell him *my* fear, and he tells me, "Sure, in the *short term*, risk could in principle increase your chance of dying."

Not the pep talk I'd been hoping for, Marc.

"But in the long term, it increases your chance of survival!"

Okay, tell me more.

"Think about it: children are curious because curiosity helps them learn effectively," says Marc. "It's crucial. Compared to adults, children have a low certainty of the consequences of their actions. They wonder, 'What does this grill do?' 'Is fire hot?' 'If I jump off this table, what will happen?' The brain wants to increase certainty in its predictions by seeking out uncertainty."

My brow furrows as I try to follow. "So children are pro-grammed to seek risk?"

"In a way, yes! For a child, risky play can be very rewarding and fun because it allows the child to transform the uncertainty of a situation into something more certain and predictable, which in turn feels good," he says.

Not for parents, it doesn't. I reflect on recent brushes with elec-trocution, garroting, and IKEA tables.

Marc tells me how many modern parents discourage children from activities like tree climbing and unsupervised outdoor play. "They're afraid kids will get hurt. And due to urbanization and heavier traffic, they also keep kids indoors more."

And this is...*a bad thing?*

Marc understands the reluctance of some parents to embrace so-called risky play. "It's actually undergoing something of a rebrand with many preferring to refer to it as 'adventurous play.' Partly to stop parents getting scared by it and partly because often it isn't really risky at all, yet the child might perceive it to be, and that's the point! For children, risky or adventurous play is an important way of gathering information about the world and about themselves."

Professor Ellen Beate Hansen Sandseter explores risky play, well-being, and outdoor education in early childhood at Queen Maud University College in Trondheim, Norway. As well as Marc's information-gathering theory, Ellen believes our desire for danger is a necessary part of our psychological development.

"The way children approach risky play is a way of getting rid of some innate fear they may have when they're born," she tells me.[3] "From birth, children will have these instinctive fears—like fear of separation from caregivers or fear of heights," said Ellen. These make sense in evolutionary terms: staying close to our caregivers was more likely to keep us alive. Dangling from a tall tree? Less so. "During play, children test this—climbing a tree branch by branch, working on their motor and physical skills until they can handle it, then building up courage until they can get all the way up." This is what psychologists call "exposure therapy"—exposing us to the things we may be afraid of in incremental steps. "We learn that this is something we can manage, and we develop mastery," says Ellen. Studies following kids from birth show that it's not the ones who climb a tree, fall, and break a leg who have a fear of heights—it's the ones who never climbed a tree. "Play in this way has an antiphobic effect." Ellen supports Gunnar's theory that we fail as caregivers if we *don't* provide opportunities for risky play.

But I find this hard. Really hard.

Losing my sister at an early age, years of infertility, then finally having babies who all spent time in special care with tubes up their tiny noses, my natural inclination is to cocoon them in Bubble Wrap *at all times*. I assume the risk researchers I speak to are natural thrill seekers, so I'm surprised to learn that Marc has a similar story to my own. His sister died when he was young, and his parents were understandably vigilant from then on. "They wrapped me in cotton wool, so I get it." He tells me how risky play is regularly repressed for those who grow up as only children. "My colleagues tell me this is something they see a lot in China, following years of the one-child policy. If you only have one child, you tend to shield them even more from any type of potential danger, big or small."

I wonder how he copes now, as a father. "How do you manage not to be a helicopter parent?" Or rather, in Denmark, a curling one?

"I don't!" he tells me. "Luckily, I married someone who reminds me to let my kids experience risk: to let them climb a tree, to let them run off on their own. I find it hard. But I'm really happy my wife is different from me on this, because I definitely need it."

This is something else we have in common. My children are saved from my own cotton wool tendencies by a father who is far more outdoorsy, gung ho, and a power tool devotee. (This isn't a euphemism: our local DIY outlet sent Lego Man a "loyalty dagger" for his generous patronage. Peter Schmeichel was livid: "I've been going there for years and nothing!")

So are some people just naturally more comfortable with risk?

Ellen studies risk-seeking personalities and found that these can be loosely divided into two categories. "There's negative risk seeking, like criminal behavior or drug abuse, behavior that doesn't quite follow the law or is not socially acceptable," she says, "and then there are positive risk-taking tendencies, toward things like extreme sports." But here's the thing: there's only a paper-thin gap between the two. Risk-seeking personalities deprived of peril in childhood can often face difficulties in adolescence and adulthood. "High sensation-seeking personalities who *don't* have the chance in school or family life to get their thrills through positive experiences are *more inclined* to seek them out via negative experiences in later life."

This seems self-evident, but it's something I've never considered before. Is it just me? Am I a total idiot? (Probably.) Why don't more of us know about this?

"Ethically, it's challenging to get hard data," Ellen says. "By now, we have a lot of literature indicating that risk in childhood has a positive effect later on. But you can't just throw kids into something risky. And if you have a hunch that experiencing physical risk is good for children, you can't then ethically deprive children of risky play!"

Fortunately, these ideas are spreading organically. In Germany, insurers recently demanded that playgrounds build in risk to make children more resilient.[4] Swedish children in the Sollentuna municipality take part in *isvaksovning*—a hole-in-the-ice exercise where they jump into a frozen lake to test their mettle and make sure they know what to do if they fall in by accident.[5] In the UK, David Ball at Middlesex University and Tim Gill, former director of the Children's Play Council (now Play England), are working to turn around the British approach to health and safety. Instead of just doing a risk assessment or a risk analysis for all potentially thrilling play, they are demanding a "risk and benefit" assessment.[6]

"Of course, having a tax-funded healthcare system helps," says Ellen. "No family is going to be bankrupt if a child breaks a leg, whereas in the US, this could be a catastrophe. If there is no safety net, this will impact children's play." It's easier to have a Viking attitude to risk when you know you'll be taken care of and a broken leg is "just" (just!) a broken leg rather than medical bankruptcy. "In some countries, litigation is a real problem," adds Ellen, as we talk about parents suing local authorities in the US.[7] "This isn't the case in the Nordic countries, but we still have to work at it." She tells me how even in Norway, "parents who aren't as familiar with being outside and challenging environments are more cautious.

Plus, media is all around us now, with rolling news and smartphones. People get the idea that there are more accidents. No one wants to be on the front page of a newspaper if something terrible happens," says Ellen.

Or at the top of Google, I think, *or trending on the app formerly known as Twitter.*

"There is often a different approach to risk generationally too," says Ellen.

Bente from Norway's *friluftsliv* association tells me how the fifty-plus generation consider taking risks to be a cultural competence. "We grew up believing children should learn to feel their own limits," she says, "to make sound decisions, and be responsible." But this belief is under threat. "We see in schools that younger teachers in their forties don't feel so comfortable taking risks in the outdoors."

While delighted to hear fortysomethings described as "younger," I'm sorry to hear that my generation is less confident.

"There is an increasing tendency among younger teachers to want professional guides on school trips to avoid accidents," Bente adds, "but this is not how we've done things historically. You can't blame others if something goes wrong. You have to take risks and take responsibility. So it's something we're working on now. We can make a change, but *now* is the moment."[8]

Finns seem to have their risk-o-meter in a good place, with an emphasis on *sisu* (grit) meaning that things can be hard—even scary at times—but you keep going, said *Everyday Sisu* author Katja Pantzar.

Icelandic children are all allowed to roam free until their

state-sanctioned curfew. During the school year, children under the age of twelve can be outside until 8:00 p.m., while thirteen- to sixteen-year-olds have to be home by 10:00 p.m. "It's quite useful as a parent," says psychologist Hrund Þrándardóttir from Reykjavík, "because you can defer on any curfew negotiations and say to kids, 'sorry: it's the law!'"[9] In the summer holidays, when Iceland enjoys twenty-four-hour sun, thirteen- to sixteen-year-olds are allowed to run wild until midnight, while children up to the age of twelve have to be home by 10:00 p.m.

"Wait, so children as young as six or seven are actually out till 10:00 p.m. in the summer?"

"Yes!" she tells me. "What helps is that it's pretty safe and we have a small population," said Hrund. In fact, Iceland is ranked the safest country in the world (for the fourteenth year in a row, according to the Global Peace Index).[10] The rest of the Nordic countries don't do too badly either with the region considered the safest in the world, whereas the UK comes in at thirty-fourth while the United States ranks 129th.

So is it really fair to expect the rest of the world to embrace risk in countries where healthcare isn't so accessible and streets may not be so safe?

Marc and Ellen recognize the challenges here. "But we still owe it to parents to share research about what risky play seems to do," says Marc. "And we see the evidence that encouraging children to use their bodies is beneficial wherever they are," says Ellen, "so that's what we have to aim for."

Just up the road from where I live is a treetop wonderland bringing risky play to those who may not be so comfortable with the concept. Like me. Walking through a forest of seven thousand trees, I meet Jacob Hindhede, ostensibly to chat risk but in reality to foster a blossoming bromance between our two dogs. (Mine is a lamb who thinks he's a lion. Jacob's is an enormous woolly creature who thinks he's a kitten.) Jacob is a tall, tanned, rangy Viking who screams "health" and exudes "hearty outdoor living" from every pore. He and his brother grew up the children of tenth-generation farmers. "It was a tough life. My parents would be up at 4:00 a.m. working," Jacob tells me. "Then, in common with much of that generation of farmers, they would sleep at midday, working more later on. As kids, we were on our own a lot. I spent hours a day out in the forest, building tree houses, rigging rope swings, digging tunnels, and building campfires." Growing up, his brother continued in the family business while Jacob left to train as a physical therapist but becoming parents, both brothers wanted to give their children a taste of the wild magic they'd enjoyed growing up ("and keep them off screens for as long as possible"). So they bought a patch of woodland the size of forty soccer pitches and lashed together suspension bridges, giant Tarzan swings, and treehouses. Wow Park Billund opened in 2020 with a rough-and-ready, hand-whittled feel. There are no harnesses (unlike at Go Ape in the UK), and accidents happen. "There are some sprains," Jacob admits, "some twists, some breaks..."[11]

Isn't that terrifying?

Jacob is thoughtful. "It's more that bodily risk is so important. If you don't take risks, it's not only that you're not as good at using your body, but you're not as *confident* either. By using your body in the natural environment, you develop yourself. You can transfer what you learn to other areas," he says. "If a kid develops mastery of something? That's a really good feeling."

We passed cloud-scraping A-frame rope swings, and Jacob tells me how his eight-year-old daughter can hang on them with one arm.

One arm? I can't manage with two!

"She's lighter than adults, but she's also strong. And she takes the risk that she will fall. I think that's something we're really good at in Denmark—getting kids into risk and physical activity."

I bring my children to the park, and the redhead, who's harbored a fear of heights since toddlerdom, takes precisely ten minutes to acclimatize before heading fourteen meters up a tree and down a zip line, whooping all the way. The twins take to it like monkeys, scrambling to the tops of conifers and down again for an hour, then announcing "low blood sugar." The park has fire pits and plenty of wood, so we build a fire, sharpen sticks with the eight-year-old's dagger, and toast the marshmallows I just happen to have in my backpack (see "food bribery"). And just like that, we have an outdoor feast. As well as every conceivable danger you could probably cram into one of those "What's wrong with this picture?" hazard identification images where you have to circle all the risks.

This is all good preparation for the ultimate Viking challenge: scouts. Yes, as well as *samfundssind,* Danish scouts are grand masters of risk.

"Scouts here is about fun but also about *bøvl,*" says Andreas, the scout leader with the kindest face in Denmark. *Bøvl* is a Danish word that basically means "trouble." And rather than telling children to "keep out of trouble," Vikings *lean in to it.*

"Bøvl builds you up as a person," says Andreas. His Finnish wife and fellow scout leader, Emilia, a petite brunette with big blue eyes, puts it in a more pragmatic way, in line with the Finnish idea of *sisu* (grit): "We are raising their tolerance for discomfort. When they have managed to do a hard thing, they feel good. They feel mastery."

There it is again, I think. *Mastery*. That singular sensation that makes you feel as though you can take on the world.

Emilia tells me about an early scouting trip where she got lost, aged seven. "It was raining, it was late, and we were miserable. But looking back on it now, it was a really great experience."

"You didn't panic?" I ask.

"No. I just got lost."

I get lost in the town where I've lived for eight years. And I panic. *How do I *not* panic?*

"It's about perspective," she says.

"Of course we are *aware* of safety," adds Andreas, "but not too much. You get lost? You get lost. You break your arm? Then you broke your arm. That's not our *aim*. But children have to get experiences on their own. For us as scout leaders and parents, it is important to find out—and discuss—how much and what kind of risk you are willing to take."

Andreas and his fellow scout leaders aim to give children two things: "responsibility for what seems appropriate at that time and the competencies to handle this responsibility." Take the knife badge. "Once they've been introduced thoroughly to how to use a knife, if they try hard, they should be able to succeed. Some things can go wrong...but it's important to give children the possibility to explore their physical limits."

So now, every Wednesday, the redhead goes marauding with

his knife (as I murmur, "You'd get four years for that in London."). His siblings go to family scouts for under six-year-olds. It's pretty much the same, but their blade use is supervised by adults since they haven't yet earned their knife skills badge.

"Scouts earn badges for knife skills, sewing, axe skills," Andreas tells me, as though these are all on a par, "but badges can also be taken away if they're not safe. It doesn't happen very often, but it can. It's important for children to learn that sometimes there are hard outcomes, and sometimes it hurts."

It hurts all right: I used to sit between the twins at family scouts to prevent bickering. I'd help hold sticks as they whittled with borrowed blades to make kindling. Until one day, a twin muddled up the direction of attack and confused the stick with my hand. As I turned to assess the damage of the cut on my right hand, the other twin sliced into my left.

"*Fuuuc-goodness sake!* Daddy's turn to take you next time..." I managed to wince.

This year, the redhead has his first jamboree where forty thousand scouts descend on Roskilde, near Copenhagen, for the largest camp in the Nordics. I was already apprehensive when I received the letter home that read: "Dear Scouts, pack light. No one is changing their underwear every day. ;)"

The instructions were to let children pack for themselves with assistance if absolutely necessary. So obviously, I ignored this and laid out everything I thought he might need. *Pajamas, T-shirts, toothbrush and charger, socks, shorts...* Somehow, I managed to fit all this in his backpack, and off he went, into the unknown. Free from all the trappings of modern life and his mother for five whole days.

I miss him terribly while he's away but try to keep it together.

The day before pickup, I mention to my day care dad friend who looks like Peter Schmeichel that I'll be getting off the train at Roskilde in the morning. His face contorts and he snorts slightly.

"What?"

Roskilde is the penultimate stop on the train from Jutland to Copenhagen. "So if you're getting off just before the big attraction, you're...you know!"

I stare blankly. He raises an eyebrow.

I continue to stare blankly until he explains that "getting off at Roskilde" is a euphemism for the withdrawal method, or coitus interruptus, in Denmark.

"Aren't you Catholic? I'd have thought you'd know that!"

"I'm lapsed," I tell him and decide to drive instead to avoid lugging an enormous rucksack on the train. That way, Lego Man can come for the ride to relive his Scouting youth and we can show the twins what they've got to look forward to next year.

As it happens, the extra manpower proves advantageous. The camp is immense and I feel instantly overwhelmed. A red alert above my head projects a Bubble Wrap bat signal that I am sure must be visible for miles around.

Lego Man and I take a twin each and head in opposite directions, looking for a feral child among forty thousand other feral children. It's as though they've escaped the twenty-first century to live as their Viking ancestors did. We pass a few leathery-looking grown-ups in shorts, legs like knotted rope, but none of the scout leaders seem to know the whereabouts of my son's patrol.

No sign yet, I message Lego Man. How's it going your end?

Like Woodstock for kids! is all he responds.

My daughter points out a strong smell of burning in the air but also...could it be...pizza? I spot flatbread cooking in pans and see someone kneading in wild garlic. Another opens a tin of tomatoes while a third grates a gnarled hunk of cheese for an ad hoc margherita. I'm impressed.

We're still sidetracked by pizza when the redhead, grinning from ear to ear with approximately ten thousand new freckles, rambles into view. He has grown at least a foot and has a swagger of independence I haven't seen before. But still he runs and flings his arms around me. I squeeze and don't let go.

"It's so good to see you! How did it go? Are you okay?"

"Ye-es," he says, a slight wobble in his voice.

"What is it?"

"I haven't exactly brushed my teeth like you said."

"Oh, okay. Um, why?"

"My scout leader said he wasn't quite sure where to charge the electric toothbrush."

Oh crap.

"Everyone else had a normal one."

"Sorry!"

"Maybe I should pack next time?"

"I think that might be a good idea." I ruffle his hair and inhale woodsmoke. "Wait, so there's going to be a next time? You want to come again next year?"

"Definitely!"

WHAT I'VE LEARNED ABOUT RISKY PLAY

- Let them climb; let them fall; let them maraud. I'm learning to turn off the Bubble Wrap bat signal (or rather ignore it occasionally). I'll never stop worrying, but I'm trying to let my children grow and face challenges on their own, taking incremental steps so that they build up Viking-style mastery.

- I'm attempting this in my own life too. As a self-parenting experiment, I'm approaching daunting tasks with an uncharacteristically can-do attitude, safe in the knowledge that if I do something, anything, I'll have made a start. I'll be moving in the right direction. In the words of Anna from *Frozen II*, I'll do "The Next Right Thing."

- If the world around us doesn't allow for risky play, we're going to have to seek it out. Or make like Jacob and create it from scratch. What scary thing should we all do this month?

- With fresh air in my lungs, no children in the hospital for at least a week, and something approaching muscle definition on my upper arms, I feel like a bona fide, North-Face-and-Patagonia-clad, double-dorking outdoorsy type. A Viking even! Then hubris deals me a massive blow. Because it turns out that there's a third way Danes play. A mighty game on a vast web to threaten the very foundation of our Danish-style parenting efforts to date. *Cracks knuckles* Shoulders back, head up, let's go...

DIGITAL BLIND SPOT

IN A DARKENED ROOM, BLINDS drawn, a dozen bodies lie, lit only by the glow of iPads. Slim fluorescent cans of a particularly pungent energy drink are dotted about. There's a stack of pizza boxes in one corner, next to a mound of sleeping bags. Because this is a sleepover. For nine-year-olds.

"It was meant to be a party," says my American Mom friend with the Whitestrips smile and great hair, "but no one was talking to each other, and the parents told me the kids normally play online—until around 2:00 a.m."

I tell her that's crazy.

She tells me that's nothing: her son's friends play *Minecraft* for seven hours on the weekend. "And I mean seven hours a *day*."

"Is that...normal?" I can't help asking. "Is that even fun?"

"It is for boys," says science journalist and technology researcher Søren Hebsgaard, who works with Danish schools.[1] I call him up to find out more on a day when the air is filled with a hopeless damp and I am filled with a horrible head cold. Between honks on Kleenex and sips of honey and hot lemon (Danes don't do NyQuil), Søren brings me up to speed on Denmark's digital climate. He explains that a gender divide begins to emerge "around age ten," with girls becoming interested in the social side and boys getting more into gaming. Half of all Danish children are now daily gamers, according to Denmark's Media Council for Children and Young People.[2] For Danish parents, this is the new normal, I learn, as somewhere in the distance, a dog howls dismally. Danes may play more and take risks, but they're just as susceptible to the lure of screens as the rest of us. And digital gaming is huge.

Full confession: I never so much as played *Pac-Man* growing up. Friends spent hours with a boxy Pierce Brosnan playing *Goldeneye* as I looked on, nonplussed. Lego Man is no help here either. Deprived of even a TV growing up, he took to improvising the plot of *The A-Team* to keep up with his peers ("it never ended well"). He's grateful for many aspects of his ye-olden-days upbringing but still swears that missing out on "all cultural references ever" put him at a social disadvantage. So as the redhead begins to express an interest in *Minecraft*—the modern gaming gateway drug—I realize we may have to visit this brave new world.

Although aren't we supposed to spend less time on screens, not more? Aren't grown-ups always in trouble for being on their phones too much? How is giving a child a screen going to help?

A Common Sense Media study from 2020 found that by the age of eight, most American children have spent a year, alone, in front of screens—more time than on any other activity.[3] The majority of children in the US now own a smartphone by the age of eleven.[4] But in Denmark, it's *nine*. At a school near me, six-year-olds have "game day" every Wednesday where they're asked to bring in either a phone, a Switch, or a tablet to play with. All day.

I watch my eight-year-old play on the family iPad, hunched over, legs tucked under him. After thirty minutes, I tell him his time is up. (What can I say? I'm mean.) He attempts to move, legs rubbery from having sat still for so long. I think of something former physical therapist Jacob from Wow Park told me recently: "It's not just that spending time in front of a screen leaves less time for physical activity. It's that being stationary for so long may be actively harming their bodies."[5]

Researchers from the University of Copenhagen found that the more time children spend in front of a screen, the greater their risk of developing neck or back pain—as early as eleven years old.[6] And a US study found that when children spend more than two hours a day in front of the screen, it damages their concentration, language skills, memory, and sleep.[7]

The redhead starts "dreaming in *Minecraft*." He complains of headaches and has trouble concentrating. This could just be being an eight-year-old, but Lego Man is a lifelong glasses wearer, and in recent years, I've succumbed. So could screen time be damaging his eyes too?

I take him for an eye test, and he gets drops to make his pupils dilate until he looks as though he's on mind-altering substances. He has to wear my outsize sunglasses for the next five hours like a 1970s Elton John. The redhead's eyes are deemed "fine for now," but I'm told to have him checked annually. The typical age for a child to develop myopia used to be between eight and twelve years old, but there's growing concern for the eyesight of children as young as four, since excess screen time can increase the risk of shortsightedness by up to 80 percent, according to a study published in the *Lancet*.[8] And Danish children spend among the most time playing digital games *globally*, according to research conducted by Lego.[9] A 2022 survey of fifty-five thousand parents and children worldwide found that Danish children came fifth in terms of most screen time. Children in the UK and the US came in at third and second respectively, with Brazil topping the charts for digital play. But the Danish findings still come as a surprise after the Enid Blyton–style upbringing my children have experienced so far. The idea that digital devices are about to encroach on the outdoorsy idyll, thrusting my mini Vikings into the twenty-first century, is unsettling.

So why is it happening?

"In Denmark, there is a social codex to give kids freedom," says Jacob, physical therapist turned outdoor living evangelist. This is thought to be because of the legacy of trust and freedom post-WWII. Remember the farmers' children running wild? Well, today's young Danes are being allowed to do the same, *online*.

"But screens are addictive. The mechanisms have been carefully designed to override what might feel 'right' to a child—or any of us," says Jacob. He rubs his forehead at the mere thought. "No matter how much we try, this is something we can never beat. The best minds in the world, the best psychologists, have all thought, 'How can we fuck up as many minds as possible?' And it's working."

I'm a grown-up and I struggle to stop scrolling on Instagram. *What hope does a child have?*

I think about this as I stand under the shower for far too long the next morning, like someone waiting for a bus in the rain. I think about it in the night when I wake and check my phone on autopilot. I think about it when I get up the next morning to surly weather and a melancholic mood, no clearer on what to do.

"It's addictive," Søren commiserates. "Even as an adult whose job it is to know all the research, all the dangers, it can still get you."

After trying and failing to become a parent for so long, when it finally happened, I had lofty goals that my children would never see my face lit up by a screen. Then came 2020 when lockdowns thrust all of us into the digital space, whether we wanted it or not.

"Parents allowed children to be at home and on their devices for the first time," says Bente Lier from Norway's Friluftsliv Association. "Norway has always had such an active culture, but in the pandemic, people took to their sofas. Now, it's a challenge to get them off again."[10] The number of Norwegian children who played outside after school daily has dropped from 41 percent in 2015 to 18 percent in 2022.[11] "We're seeing now that the consequences for mental health are very negative." And in countries with particularly pronounced outdoor lifestyles, like Norway, a dramatic increase in myopia rates is expected thanks to screen time during lockdowns.[12]

Many now believe that the benefits of technology in education have been grossly overstated. Naomi Schaefer Riley, visiting fellow at the American Enterprise Institute, told the *New York Times* that "the real digital divide...is not between children who have access to the Internet and those who don't. It's between children whose parents know that they have to restrict screen time and those whose parents have been sold a bill of goods by schools and politicians that more screens are key to success."[13]

So how much screen time is too much?

The World Health Organization (WHO) published screen time recommendations for under-fives in 2019. For children under the age of three, it's zero, while those aged three and four should not have more than an hour a day.[14] The American Academy of Pediatrics, Canadian Pediatric Society, Norwegian Health Authorities, and Icelandic parents' associations all followed suit with similar guidelines. China went further, clamping down on "spiritual opium" and limiting video gaming for under-eighteens to an hour on Fridays, weekends, and holidays.[15] The UK keeps things vague, the Royal College of Pediatrics and Child Health suggesting families negotiate with their children based on the individual child (thanks for that).[16] But for parents in Sweden, Finland, and Denmark, there has been no advice historically.

In 2023, a digital task force for the Danish government recommended placing a time limit on children's use of social media and raising the age of consent for the processing of personal data from thirteen to sixteen years.[17] At the time of writing, the government has agreed to raise the age limit for consent to share data with companies like Meta and Snapchat.[18] But in terms of social media use and screen time? Nothing. Denmark's minister for children and education, Mattias Tesfaye, called for a change in the legislation so that children aged zero to six use screens as little as possible "to protect children from potential negative consequences."[19] But so far the law has not changed.

"I'm determined to wait for hard evidence," says Stine Liv Johansen from the Center for Children's Literature and Media at Aarhus University. Stine helped advise the Danish health authorities on their current legislation. We met in her plant-filled office at the university, and she wears an olive-green jumpsuit that I instantly covet. The overall effect is one of pastoral bliss rather than advocate for a digital age. But Stine insists that the threat of screens has been overplayed: "Many of the studies WHO have taken into account are based on data from Asia, where there is a very different culture." Stine is currently taking part in a Danish research project exploring zero- to eight-year-olds' use of digital media in everyday life and says: "If all the basics are in place for a child—good sleep, a good experience at school, good parents, etc.—then the time a child spends with digital devices shouldn't make much difference. The screen time itself is not the problem."[20]

Isn't this a bit "guns don't kill people, bullets do"?

"It's more about the idea of a one-size-fits-all rule," says Stine, who said of the global screen time restrictions in one interview on Denmark's TV2, "It's like saying that all children must wear rubber boots in October."[21]

Not a bad idea, I think. *It does rain most days.*

"The WHO data is just so black and white," says Stine. "They say a one-year-old can never see a screen, but imagine you're waiting at a doctor's office with a ten-month-old screaming its head off. Why not show them a video on your phone? Instead of focusing on X number of minutes on screen, the conversation should be about the three Cs: content, context, and connections." She points out that it's not the first time "older generations" (*thanks*) have been suspicious of new technology. "Before we were afraid of the iPad and the internet, we were afraid of cartoons, considered lowbrow, killing books and stunting children's development. Then came VHS. There's always been something people liked to worry about."[22]

Video killed the radio star back in 1980. Are screens really so different? *Am I just a dinosaur? Or worse, a snob?*

Stine has a novel argument in praise of screen time too. "The digital world is a bit like a schoolyard," she tells me. "You meet risks, and children should experience risk, learn coping skills, and so grow. In this way, the risks of a digital life for a child have some benefit," she believes—to survive in the modern world.

So how can we keep children safe? Allowing them to take risks without going too far?

"By being with them" is Stine's answer. Denmark's National Board of Health officially encourages parents to get gaming and "take an interest in your child's online life."[23] "Just as we take our children to soccer and school events, we should help our children with digital media," says Stine.

I struggle with a value judgment here. Isn't soccer fractionally more improving? And I say this as someone who gives no hoots about balls.

But Stine calls me out. "Parents need to stop condemning—stop standing with raised eyebrows and expressing that you think what young people are preoccupied with is stupid or a waste of time. Then you definitely shut down the dialogue."

That's me told.

"If you don't understand what they're doing, ask—and listen!" Stine reads my mind as she continues, "Many parents feel like they don't have the time, the energy, or the will. But think of it like soccer again—I don't have to learn the rules of soccer to be able to talk to my son about it, about the team, how he feels, when he wins, when he loses, to bake for the team, wash the gear, be a taxi to games, etc."

Well, this sounds exhausting...

"The point is I'm supporting him and inviting him to tell me about the experience," says Stine, "even though I don't personally care about soccer."

So now I have to pretend I care about soccer and Minecraft*?* I experience a wave of weariness. But Lego Man is coming around to the idea.

"You know what they say..."

"No? What do 'they' say?"

"It's better to be inside the tent pissing *out* than on the outside pissing in."

"Sorry?"

"We're all sorry. I'm just saying that with this gaming stuff, we may as well be in it to see what's going on."

I'm not sure who's the tent, who's the urinator, or who's the urine in this analogy, but I catch his drift.

"Children will come into contact with gaming or social media with or without parental permission," says Stine. "And if they use it without their parents, they'll be alone if they get into trouble." She wants parents to roll their sleeves up and get involved. "If your child expresses an interest in YouTube or other social media, see it as an opportunity to start researching the media yourself and get involved together with the child. Like the Münster family."

Naja Münster is a thirteen-year-old Danish YouTuber with 232,000 subscribers who's been online from the age of three ("and she and her family are all still very nice and normal!" Stine assures me).

I get in touch with Naja who does, indeed, come across as fairly grounded.

"I make one video a week for my channel, and that can take between one and three hours," she tells me, "so I use my phone a lot, but not more than my friends. And it doesn't take up any more of my time than my friends' sport clubs do. I go to YouTube while others go to gymnastics. Being on social media is also entertainment for me—like watching something funny on TV," says Naja. "Plus you're creative when you make videos for YouTube. There are some parents who think it's dangerous to be on social media. I think it's because they haven't familiarized themselves with what social media contains. You don't have to sit still for hours behind a screen because you are active on social media. You can actually be creative and active at the same time."[24]

This is a drum that Stine in the olive jumpsuit likes to bang too. "Screens aren't in opposition to an outdoorsy life. They're 'as well as,' because kids can bring the iPads outdoors, filming nature and being creative."[25]

But who are these mini Vikings making nature documentaries? Mine have never once done this. It's an expensive piece of equipment for starters. On the odd day when it's not raining or snowing in Denmark, the sun may deign to shine, in which case, one word: glare. Yet the chair of Denmark's teacher union, BUPL, is another champion of screens in nature. Elisa Rimpler recently told public service broadcaster DR TV that when children "meet an animal and want to find out more about it...today, it is natural to use an app and not look up a book."[26]

Orders book on animals and bug identification immediately

As well as "pro-digital" Stine and her supporters, there's also the "we've got it so may as well like it" gang. This includes the historian of play, Ning de Coninck-Smith, who takes a more pragmatic position: "A lot of people say everything is worse these days. But actually combining gaming with physical play is a smart move, and a good answer to the constantly complaining."[27] Because Luddites like me may be fighting a losing battle.

The Danish government has made a commitment to be digital by default, with paper used only as a last resort, so if you need to pay taxes or make an appointment with the doctor, you do it from a screen. The government's vision is that Denmark should be a digital front-runner globally, and many schools are now predominantly digital. "My kids went to school in Odder," says Stine, "the first municipality in Denmark to give iPads to all children in schools in 2010."

In Sweden, Malmö Council gave every child a laptop to bring home and work on. Most children get their own phones by the age of eight or nine, when they go to school by themselves, and Sweden has long been a cashless society. "So kids need their phones for everything from their bus pass to their Swish—the app-based payment method in Sweden," says Niki Brantmark, mother of daughters in Malmö. "It's not like it was when we grew up!"[28]

And perhaps this is it.

"The challenge must be to be able to keep up and accept the developments," says YouTuber Naja's mom Hanne. "Denmark is a very open country. And we are also very open when it comes to raising our children. Another positive about social media is that it creates contacts and friendships. Back then, the child who had no friends at school went home and was alone. Today, the same child goes home and is with his online friends."[29] Because online, everyone can find a community somewhere.

But don't we all have to learn to respect and work with all sorts of people? Isn't the Nordic way about getting along with everyone? Even when we may not agree with them?

Research from the University of Michigan found that empathy levels have decreased by 40 percent in recent years.[30] The authors of the study fear we have become desensitized because of the technological world. Having online friends is easy as we can tune out when things feel hard, but this approach is trickling down into real life. According to Danish neuroscientist Albert Gjedde, "being on the iPad, computer, or PlayStation a lot prevents children from meeting in reality and using all their senses. We can find it difficult to be together socially if our brain is not trained for it while we are children."[31] (Although I checked, and he plays a lot of Wordle then posts about it on the app formally known as Twitter. So none of us are immune.)

Adults are often subpar digital role models, taking emails from work on their phone around the house or scrolling Facebook, Instagram—even Tinder. A third of Danish children told Nordic parenting group NOPA that their parents spend more time on the screen than on them. Rasmus Kjeldahl from Denmark's National Association for Children's Rights hears this a lot. "Now when kids are seven or eight, they realize that their parents are less interested in them than they are in their iPhones."[32]

"Which is just so sad!" I try telling Veteran Viking, but she's playing chess on her smartphone.

"Which is just so sad!" I try again to American Mom, who puts down her iPad and lays her hands on my shoulders.

"Listen, grasshopper." She uses her no-nonsense voice. "We *all* wish it was the good old days when kids played with Rubik's Cubes, but we live in the *real* world. Your kids are still small, but mine are older. I've seen the future. And all this"—she lets go of me to gesture around her at an iPad, iPhone, Apple TV, and three children, all engaged in different screen-based pursuits—"isn't going anywhere. This generation will *never* use a watch to tell the time unless they get rich and buy a Rolex! They'll *never* order pizza from a big book! They'll never go to Blockbuster, even! Times change. We move on. Suck it up."

I sniff slightly and blow my nose. *No Rubik's Cubes? She'll tell me kids don't play marbles next...*

"Anyway, I'd *rather* my kids were gaming than watching conspiracy theorists on TikTok."

Oh god, I hadn't thought about this.

"So, and I say this with love, stop being a big baby."

"You say this with love?!"

"I do." She nods. "Now let it go."

I know I need to live in the real world, but as I scroll through my phone in bed that night (like I said: hypocrite), I see a post from psychologist Adam Grant saying that the earlier kids get smartphones, the worse their mental health as adults.[33] He references a Sapien Labs study of more than twenty-seven thousand volunteers showing that owning a smartphone at a younger age predicts lower self-worth, motivation, and resilience. It's also associated with an increase in sadness, anxiety, and aggression—especially for girls.[34] The takeaway? Smartphones should wait until children are thirteen.[35]

"There should be regulation and a real age limit on social media," agrees technology researcher Søren. "Parents often feel very alone in their decisions, but we know enough now that the health department and schools could all say to parents, 'This is our advice.' It would be easy for schools to tell all the parents of first graders, age six, not to give them a smartphone until they are, say, ten. And not to be on social media until at least thirteen. Because at present, social media is actually rewiring the whole idea of friendship, and kids' brains aren't ready for it."

Silicon Valley leaders typically shield their own children from digital devices until they're in their teens. Bill Gates didn't let his kids have phones until they turned fourteen. "The people who work with this stuff don't want their kids to be around it," Søren points out. His own daughter asked if she could go on Snapchat, aged twelve. "And my answer was no," he tells me, "because there is an obvious business model for Snapchat, and I don't feel my daughter should be helping them to profit from this."

Rasmus from Denmark's National Association for Children's Rights goes further: "I would compare it to the tobacco industry. The tech industry has spent billions lobbying for their market, which, by the way, is kids' attention. It has been disseminating information along the lines of 'Is it really so bad?' But it is. It really is. And we have the balance completely wrong at present."

At this, the neighborhood dogs start up again, setting one another off in a chorus of elegiac yowls as though sensing my growing despair. I hang up the phone and stare at my laptop. If we decide to push back against screen time for our own children, it's unlikely they'll thank us. *Or even like us.* Being among the holdout parents won't be easy. Isn't it the duty of the state to regulate technology that's harmful to its population? What happened to Denmark being a rules-based society? Where are the boundaries? I need boundaries!

My laptop doesn't respond so I seek out the Vicks VapoRub and hide from the world under a tea towel over a basin of hot water to inhale steam and attempt to shift my cold. The radio is on, and I hear something that lifts my spirits. A UCLA study of eleven- to thirteen-year-olds found that after just five days at an outdoor camp with no devices, children were able to read facial expressions and emotion significantly better.[36] *After just five days!* So can I perhaps match my son's lust for gaming or balance it out with other things? Keep him busy? With improving, outdoorsy hobbies? In the spirit of *samfundssind*?!

I stand at the window doom scrolling (#hypocrite) as an invitation arrives for a ten-kilometer hike with the scouts. It's on Sunday—the day the redhead is normally allowed to play *Minecraft*. I ask him whether he'd like to go. He thinks about this, weighing his options.

"If I go, will there be snacks?" the redhead asks slowly.

"Loads," I tell him.

"I'm in."

Lego Man exhales.

One day at a time. Just take things one day at a time. Filling up his days with enough other stuff that screen time is minimized for now.

Full of ardent if vague and snotty purpose, I sally forth and sign him up.

WHAT I'VE LEARNED ABOUT DENMARK'S DIGITAL BLIND SPOT

- Fucked. We're all fucked. No, but really, I need rules. Ideally from the government. Or the health authorities. Or schools (or prison guard turned pedagogue Kitta?!). Otherwise, it's up to parents, and many of us are addicted too. The evidence is clear: even if children under fourteen need phones for communication, they don't need smartphones or social media. I would love for parents to align on waiting so there aren't just a few children who feel left out of the phone arms race.

- I've realized how much I rely on parents of older children for wisdom on what's to come. Self-parenting 101: find good role models who can offer advice and interventions where necessary.

- The redhead now has his hiker badge and insists on telling everyone, just casually, "Oh hey, just done a 10K, no biggie." Keeping kids busy with other things helps balance out the digital/analog diet.

- I've fallen a little out of love with the Nordic dream. So I do what I always do when I'm sad: I read. Buried in a book and cocooned in a comforter, things start to feel better. And after three chapters and two cups of tea, I get one marvelous idea to lift the spirits: an adventure.

THE NEW NORSE SAGAS

THERE'S A SCENT OF HONEYSUCKLE in the air, and the rolling hills look a lot like home were it not for the fact that they're dotted with pink and white...marshmallows?

"Why are there *massive marshmallows* in the fields?" the youngest (by two minutes) asks.

"For the horses," Lego Man tells him.

A firework display goes off in his tiny head. "They feed horses *marshmallows* here?"

"*Yes, son. Yes, they do,*" I very much want to reply, but the eldest butts in. (Age eight, he *knows* stuff and wants you to *know* he knows stuff.)

"No, they wrap hay in pink and white plastic here," the redhead informs his brother with a world-weary sigh. "I know because my teacher told me."

We're driving to Sweden in pursuit of another redhead—the ultimate Nordic hero. No, not Erik the Red or even Thor but a nine-year-old girl.

Pippi Longstocking is the red-haired, freckled, superhumanly strong, rebel girl who lives alone with her trusty horse and a monkey named Mr. Nilsson. Leader of the plucky redhead troop that includes orphan Annie and Anne with an *e*, Pippi is the GOAT.* She befriends Tommy and Annika, the more conventional children next door, and all manner of scrapes ensue. Written in 1944 by the grandmother of Swedish literature, Astrid Lindgren, *Pippi Longstocking* became a bestseller. Five more Pippi books followed, and Astrid Lindgren sold 165 million copies worldwide, translated into 107 different languages. A TV show based on Pippi ran for just thirteen episodes in 1969 but is still one of the most popular programs on TV in the Nordics today. "It's always in the top five," says Kajsa Peters, executive producer at Swedish national public television broadcaster SVT.[1] Morten Skov, head of the children's division at Danish public service broadcaster DR TV, agrees: "Pippi has a huge influence."[2] So, to understand modern Vikings, I must get to grips with Pippi.

Old Norse literature emphasized self-reliance, loyalty, modesty, hospitality, compassion, courage, and wisdom through experience, and the modern equivalents encourage similar qualities. The original sagas of the ninth century were oral histories of heroes, passed down from fathers to sons and mothers to daughters in Iceland, only written down in the thirteenth century. Then there were the Eddas, very much the soap operas of Viking times. Together, they inspired generations of writers (oh hi, Tolkien). And the *new* Norse sagas continue to influence mini Vikings today.

---

* Greatest of all time.

School refusenik Pippi is the OG *Home Alone*, who holds no truck with societal norms. When told that children should be seen and not heard, Pippi retorts, "People have got both eyes and ears, I would hope. And even though I'm an absolute treat to look at, I definitely think ears benefit from a little exercise."[3]

As well as one-handed horse lifting and besting strongmen, Pippi stops local boys beating up a smaller child and is a fierce defender of the underdog, since "If you are very strong, you must also be very kind."[4]

Astrid Lindgren's books—and Pippi in particular—are so influential in Europe that they were used after World War II to help "de-Nazify" German youth, according to Astrid's great-grandson Johan Palmberg. Johan told the BBC that her rebellious, free-thinking approach to life combined with an inherent kindness and generosity was deemed "the perfect thing" for children growing up in a war-ravaged Germany. And her books were an easy sell, since "she had this understanding of what a child might be interested in," said Johan. "She would be the first one to climb the trees and have the children follow her up."[5]

So now I'm following her up the metaphorical tree. And I'm taking my children with me. We're making a pilgrimage to Astrid Lindgren's World in her hometown of Vimmerby, Sweden—a seven-hour drive from home through meadows of marshmallows to learn more about the gospel according to Pippi. While most theme parks are heavy on plastic swag and marketing opportunities, Astrid Lindgren's World is built on a one-to-three scale from predominantly natural materials, mesmeric in its attention to detail. It's raining (because Scandinavia), but this doesn't stop flocks of fans from scaling Pippi's house, clambering on her roof, meeting her horse, and trying their hand at sailing her boat. The universe of Astrid's imagination is brought to life at the park, and we learn that Pippi isn't the only role model Vikings can thank Astrid Lindgren for. In her Emil stories, the eponymous hero runs away from home, steals a horse, and tries to join the army, aged five. In *Nothing But Fun in Noisy Village*, the perpetually fidgeting Lasse is sent home from school by his remarkably farsighted teacher until the following year because, she senses, "he had more playing to do" first.[6] In Astrid's Lotta books, a kindergartener decides to move in with her elderly neighbor. Lotta is only four, but she's already an independent thinker. And this was important to her creator.

Born in 1907, Astrid Lindgren was a rebel from the start. She was the first girl in her town to cut her hair short, causing quite a stir (passersby would ask her to remove her hat for a look). Aged eighteen, she became pregnant after a relationship with a married man who already had seven children. The scandal forced Astrid to leave Vimmerby. Her son, Lars, was born at Rigshospitalet in Copenhagen, where women were allowed to give birth without having to reveal the father's name. She left Lars in the care of a foster mother for three years to work in Stockholm. Astrid worked as a typist and stenographer, saving whatever she could to travel and be with Lars. Eventually, she could afford to raise him herself. But Astrid's early struggles had a huge impact on her work. She was a lifelong activist and helped ban corporal punishment of children in Sweden—the first country to do so in 1979. Throughout her books, strength of body and spirit is matched by kindness, generosity, and independent thinking. Her creations continue to move Vikings today. (Pippi Longstocking is still a popular costume for adults and children alike.)

"Pippi taught us never to underestimate children," says Kim Fupz Aakeson, an award-winning contemporary children's writer in Denmark. "She taught us that everyone should be valued as individuals—and we all get to find our way in the world." This is a red thread in Astrid's books. "Kids can do more than we believe as grown-ups," says Kim, "so nothing should be off-limits. And I think there's more fluidity in Denmark about what is appropriate for kids." As well as children's books, Kim writes for adults, including gritty Nordic noir and even a Dogme 95 film, following the principles of the decidedly un-child-friendly Lars von Trier. But changing his audience doesn't mean as much of a gear shift as it might elsewhere. "I deal with big themes in all my work, death, alcoholism—you name it. If we talk about life's highs and lows and normalize them from an early age, children will be more resilient in the long run. And books are a great way to teach empathy."[7]

Researchers from Oxford Brookes University have found that books let children try on situations and feelings for themselves and help promote empathy for those who are different from us.[8] "So why wouldn't we write about everything?" Kim asks. "We also go further in Denmark. We feel we can write about more, and we write about the kind of kids you'd meet on the street."

More so than in the other Nordic countries?

"Oh yes! In Sweden and Norway, there's a shit show if I use the language I hear on the street here. My approach is that if I hear it in the schoolyard, I can use it in my books. I don't want to *teach* kids 'bad' words, but we have to be realistic. We have to dare to tell them the truth. I don't clean things up."

Kim is currently working on a prison drama, followed by a retelling of Norse mythology. "The Norse gods feel very human," he observes. "They're good at fucking each other up!" Last year, he wrote a children's Bible. "It's striking the difference in approach between the two. It says a lot about our cultures."

How so?

"Shame and guilt are not so much of an issue in Norse mythology as they are in Christianity. You just have to be strong and brave in the Nordic tradition."

Rather than a hierarchical deity who can smite you for eating the wrong type of fruit?

Kim laughs. "There's a darkness to the Nordic approach too. But then, life can be dark." So can the weather.

"I think there's a link between the two," says Morten from DR TV, and most Vikings agree that the climate encourages Nordics to develop a strong interior life.

"When it's dark all the time, you're driven to tell stories," says my Icelandic friend Birna in Reykjavík. "It engages the imagination."

Books have a special place in Icelanders' hearts, and Iceland has more writers, more books published, and more books read per capita than anywhere else in the world. Birna's husband, Siggi, tells me that there's a running joke that one day they'll erect a statue in

Reykjavík "to honor the only Icelander who never wrote a book." Because stories matter.

Denmark's most famous storyteller, Hans Christian Andersen, was a master of darkness. The original Little Mermaid doesn't get the guy: instead, her tongue is cut out and her new legs feel like knives, slicing her with every step. The prince makes her sleep on a cushion outside his door like a dog and marries someone else, and our heroine turns to sea foam in a "fairy-tale ending." Then there's the Tin Soldier who only has one leg and ends up in a drain, then a fish, then a fire. Your typical rom-com. In "The Red Shoes," a girl named Karen gets her feet chopped off. In "The Storks," a boy who teases birds is given a dead baby brother as punishment. Weirdly, this hasn't been snatched up by Disney yet.

My youngest is still having flashbacks after our last visit to the Hans Christian Andersen Museum in Odense, the storyteller's home town, where all his tales are brought to life. "The Tinder Box" had already driven him to the brink when the audio narration of "The Little Match Girl" ended abruptly with "I am dead. The story is over. Do you want to see me die again?"

Bottom lip quivering, my son pointed nervously at the next exhibit. "Is that another one where they all die?"

"Um...it *might* be."

It was.

"We do darkness well," agrees Morten from DR, "but it's how kids feel. They have big feelings, even from very young, and we should respect that. Nordic storytelling is good at helping children feel less alone."

In the classic Finnish Moomin tales by Tove Jansson, the presence of deeper philosophical thoughts is normalized. Finland's most successful writer and illustrator introduced the world to the Moomin family in 1945 with the release of *The Moomins and the Great Flood*. Seven decades later, her white hippo-like animals with long, rounded snouts are more popular than ever. They go on adventures, meeting new friends and mysterious strangers, from the Groke, who freezes everything she encounters, to the small but fierce Little My and the harmonica playing Snuffkin. They confront obstacles in the natural world (comets, floods) as well as personal hurdles. In one of her most loved tales, *Moominpappa at Sea* (1965), Tove maps out midlife malaise in one of the most poignant descriptions of what it feels like to experience an episode of depression I've ever encountered. From gray-sky thinking ("the sea's just a weak character you can't rely on") to despair ("it takes a long time sometimes...a terrible long time before things sort themselves out") to a day when the sun finally comes out again and they can "live and lead a wonderful life, full of troubles."[9]

Tove Jansson's niece Sophia Jansson believes the secret behind her aunt's success is that "people find themselves in what she writes—it's personal but also universal." And Tove was always interested in other people and the world around her. Sophia remembers that her aunt never treated her as a child growing up, but "as interesting as anyone else in the room. It didn't matter who you were, she fixed her eyes on you and was interested."[10] Tove started writing seriously after World War II, a period she describes as "utterly hellish." She felt a strong wish to write about a better world—and chose strange hippo creatures as the vehicle to do so.

"Moomins are very 'human,' but they're *not* human, so Tove had that extra freedom," says Sophia. "There is room for imagination that things might be different and hence better. This has always been a solace for readers."

In her 1960 book *Who Will Comfort Toffle?* the hero "doesn't notice quite how lonely he has grown," and Tove notes, "if all you do is hide away, you'll never find a friend." Toffle eventually finds a purpose when a smaller creature needs his help: "Both had seen the end of fear and fright and long, dark night, now each has found a friend."[11] (No, *you're* crying.)

In the warmth of the Moomin House, all are welcome and safe. Tove always believed in equality regardless of sex, gender, or race. "The soul behind the outer shell was what was important to her," says Sophia, who has fond memories of summers spent with Tove and her partner, artist Tuulikki Pietilä. As a high-profile lesbian, Tove has long been an icon in the LGBTQ+ community—"and many of her characters in the Moomin books are nonbinary or non-gender-specific," Sophia tells me.

I think about this. Okay, so the Hemulen "always wore a dress he inherited from his aunt."[12] But aren't the core family of Moominmamma, Moominpappa, Moomintroll, and the Snork Maiden fairly...traditional?

"Yes and no," says Sophia. "They are gifted with personality traits that are not necessarily stereotypical."

What about Moominmamma's apron?

"Oh, that was for syndication," she tells me. "They felt they needed to distinguish characters. That was why Pappa got a cane and Mamma got an apron. But that came later. Her original stories were much less stereotypical. These gender stereotypes were not Tove's intentions. It was society putting constraints on the Moomins."

Society, messing things up for everyone...

Changes like this may seem small, but they have an impact on receptive young minds. Global headlines roared that it was political correctness gone mad in 2015 when Sweden added the gender-neutral pronoun *hen* into the official dictionary. There was predictable outrage in some quarters, but as my Swedish friend and mom of two Maria tells me, "*hen* is very useful if it's unclear who's involved or it doesn't matter what gender someone is. I think it's smart. In children's books, when it doesn't matter if they are male or female animal characters, they'll use *hen*." A Florida State University sociologist led a comprehensive study of twentieth-century children's books and found that heroes were more than twice as likely to be male.[13] Books featuring animals have even more of a gender bias, with heroic male animals outnumbering females three to one. So it might be high time we all embraced *hen*. "It's fairer and it's important for children to see that girls and boys can be the key player in a story," agrees Maria.

I am forever editing children's books as I read them aloud. I don't want my small people getting the idea that only boys go on adventures and that girls are always the sensible ones (or "fun killers" as Lego Man puts it).

"We've got all these history books filled with men and written by men, so it's a helpful way of redressing this and understanding that when you're writing about a character, it doesn't always matter whether they're a boy or a girl," says Maria. "It's not that Swedish children don't say 'he' or 'she' in kindergarten. It's just that we use *hen* when it doesn't matter."

My children have known and understood when to use they/them pronouns since starting kindergarten in Denmark. A fuss-free, openhearted approach of inclusivity has meant that by the time they're talking, it's second nature for mini Vikings. Two children in the year above my son at school are nonbinary. Some parents and teachers are still getting their heads around this, but the kids are all right: their classmates are just their classmates.

Sophia describes the Nordic perspective in children's literature as "very humanistic," adding, "Tove always recognized that everyone should have a voice and everyone should be seen." Like in "The Invisible Child" story in *Tales from Moominvalley* (1962) where a small, scared girl called Ninny has been so neglected, she disappears. Ninny is welcomed into the Moomin family and treated with care and respect. As she gets her confidence back, she becomes visible, bit by bit. Tove knew how much a child could be damaged by not being loved. And unqualified love is fundamental in the new Norse sagas.

You don't have to win or be the best or even behave well to be loved as a child. "It's unconditional," says Morten. "We're not afraid of kids being unfair or hurting themselves or losing, because that's part of life. They are still loved."

Pippi Longstocking is a prolific liar, but Tommy and Annika's friendship is given freely with no strings attached. Another of Astrid's protagonists, Emil, is described as "a dreadful little boy" who "got up to more mischief than there were days in the year."[14] He annoys the people of his town so much that they collect money to send him away to America. His mother, horrified, announces that they will do no such thing, saying, "We love him just as he is."[15] (To which the housemaid adds, "We ought to think about those Americans too. They haven't done us any harm, so why should we dump Emil on them?")[16]

"I like this approach, because it's real," says chef Trine Hahnemann, who raised her children in the US and the UK. "In some countries, it can all get so sickly sweet in books and TV for children." She tells me how when her children were small, they would watch things like Barney, the big purple dinosaur. "I just remember thinking it was so fake! One character would hold the door open for the other, and they would say 'thank you' and I just thought, 'no child is like that!' Children can annoy each other, and they can be selfish. That's what kids do. And that's okay."[17] It's even expected in the Nordic countries.

Take Bamse, the big, yellow teddy bear who has been the star of Denmark's most popular children's series *Bamses Billedbog* (*Teddy Bear's Picture Book*) for the past forty years. And he's a little shit.

"It comes naturally to Bamse to believe that he is the center of the world, and he can be a little despotic now and then," reads the official character breakdown for Denmark's most famous bear.[18] But he is still loved. "Children identify with him because he is spontaneous and selfish," says Morten from DR TV, home to Bamse's show. "He's a universal character in whom children can recognize themselves." Bamse lives in the woods, bossing around his friend Kylling, or Chicken,who plays a younger sibling role. "This mirrors kids' reality," says Morten. "They get used to being in relationships that are difficult and where there is conflict, but you can still be friends. That's a powerful message."

So the fluffy tyrant is actually teaching us all a valuable lesson? Huh...

I'm not sure it's one I ever learned during a childhood where eyebrows were often raised but never voices. Conflict, I surmised, was bad and to be avoided at all costs. But that's not life. And it's not how Vikings are raised. "There is huge value in not only talking about the good and easy things. We should train our kids in talking about and accepting more complex emotions too," says Morten, because "there are no wrong feelings." Bamse's show is so big in Denmark that when the man who plays Kylling had his fiftieth birthday party and guests traveled from all over, Danish border guards happily waived one merrymaker through despite the fact that she'd forgotten her passport. Apparently, any friend of "Chicken" was a friend of Denmark.

———

Since the original Norse sagas were told rather than read, I'm interested in what the modern "talkies"—a.k.a. kids' TV—can teach me about raising Vikings. Danish anthropologist Christian Groes describes watching Danish children's television as a lot like taking LSD (and he's Danish).[19] So in the name of research and the pursuit of a natural high, I tune in. On day one of this experiment, my children and I are greeted with an animated series aimed at four- to eight-year-olds about John Dillermand, a man who overcomes hardships with his record-breaking genitals. Danish slang for penis is *diller*, while *mand* means man. So John Dillermand directly translates as "John Penis-man." He wears a woolen hat and a knee-length red-and-white-striped bathing suit, like an X-rated Where's Waldo. There's also Onkel Reje—or Uncle Prawn—a sweary Satanist in a heavy metal band who we first encounter wearing a black leather thong and a studded bra, scratching his bare behind before farting as my children hoot with laughter.

Do my children have terrible taste? Or do all children have terrible taste? I wonder. Out loud. To Morten at DR TV, who programs these shows.

"These stories work because in all of us, there is rebellion," says Morten. "Parents don't always like this, but then it's not important that parents love it. They show kids it's okay to be different." Uncle Prawn and John Dillermand are anarchists in the Pippi Longstocking mold. But there's also an attempt to represent other outlooks in Nordic children's culture too.

"We can't all lift a horse is the way I look at it," says Hr. Skæg (or Mr. Beard), a six-foot-five giant of a man with a floor-skimming beard who looks like he makes artisanal cheese but is basically Beyoncé in Denmark. Real name Mikkel Lomborg, he fronts a TV show about letters and numbers and is swamped by fans wherever he goes. Curious to find out more, I arrange to meet him and he tells me how he too is inspired by the Pippi Longstocking stories. "But Hr. Skæg isn't a rebel. He represents Tommy and Annika, because they are the identification figures for many. Hr.

Skæg normalizes failure and the underdog. He teaches kids that this is okay."

Interesting, I think. And then: *you wouldn't get that back home...*

We take a photo together in the hope that it might give me some street cred with my own children, but when I get home, they have other plans. My daughter is staggering around with a puzzled dog while my son is dressed as a monkey. It's hard to know where to start.

"What are you doing with the dog?" I try.

"It's not a dog. It's a horse and I'm Pippi. So strong I can lift a horse. That's Tommy, and he's Mr. Nilsson, the monkey," she says as she points at her brothers. Apparently, there weren't any takers for Annika. "We're making a new book, so if you don't mind?" She proceeds to dictate a fanciful array of dark twists involving pancakes, pirates, and several secondary characters, all called Susan.

Anarchy: check.

Empowered female leads: check.

Love and tolerance no matter what? Pending...

"Come on!" my daughter continues from behind armfuls of dog. "We haven't got all day! We're trying to find hidden treasure. Or *leverpostej* sandwiches. Whichever we find first. Ready? Let's go."

The redhead and his brother follow along as best they can, and a new Norse saga begins.

WHAT I'VE LEARNED ABOUT THE NEW NORSE SAGAS

- Never underestimate. Even very young children can surprise us in their abilities and understanding. The fact that my smalls have been able to talk about life, the universe, and everything in age-appropriate language since toddlerhood has astounded me (and their grandparents). The modern world can get gritty, but honesty might actually be a pretty good policy. I once interviewed a child psychotherapist who told me that if we don't tell children the truth, they make it up. They invent their own version of what's happened, and often, what children imagine is worse than the reality. So from a really young age, Vikings are told the truth.

- We shouldn't shy away from the dark side. We don't have to go full-on *Little Mermaid*, but life isn't a series of Disney dance-to-credits endings. Life won't always be fair. We don't always win, and that's okay. Children can handle this. A few smaller "practice hurts" in childhood mean they'll cope better with the bigger hurts that can blindside us in adulthood.

- All are worthy, no matter what. And everyone deserves love. (Even if they're behaving like a little shit. I'm looking at you, Bamse.) Being around these stories and TV shows as an adult has helped me shake off decades of social conditioning and realize that I am enough. Even on days when my parenting is suboptimal (hi, unicorn bubble machine day!), even on days when my children are feral (hi, every day!), I have hope that we'll be okay. Probably.

SCHOOLTIME (BARELY)

IT CAME WITHOUT WARNING. NO heads-up. No disclaimer to sign ("Tick here if you're happy for your child to turn temporarily vegan!"). In the spring of the year my eldest started school, he emerged one afternoon white as a sheet. Which is saying something when you already have red hair and pale skin and live in Mordor.

"Are you okay?"

"Mmm…" was all he would mumble.

On the way home, past tractors trundling manure and carpets of yellow rapeseed flowers, he barely spoke. Turning off onto side streets lined with trees, heavy with pink blossoms, he asked what was for dinner.

"Pasta," I told him, and his shoulders lowered slightly.

Back at my house, I FaceTimed my fellow fish-out-of-water friend, American Mom, to ask if she had any intel, and she informed me that it had been "spontaneous dissection day" for some classes. Teachers invited a parent who also happens to be an emergency room doctor to come in with a cow's heart and a pig's liver for the most visceral biology lesson ever.

WTF? I did biology in secondary school without so much as holding a scalpel. But in Denmark, they let six-year-olds loose with a surgeon's knife? He's only just started school. Shouldn't reading, writing, and the number stuff come first? What's with the Tarantino scenes?

American Mom shook her blow-dry and said that was nothing: her eldest dissected an eyeball last year. "And you still have the school trip to look forward to!"

Oh god.

I learned about these "educational" excursions when I first arrived in Denmark. Peter Sandøe, professor of bioethics at the University of Copenhagen, explained how dissections were an old Danish tradition going back four hundred years. He assured me that taking a trip to see a dissection was "a typical thing to do" in Denmark to "open children's eyes to the world of science."[1] Dissections are carried out countrywide, on creatures from snakes to seals, whales to wolves, lions to lizards. Every Dane remembers their first dissection trip, and animal autopsies are so popular in Denmark that there are often two a day during school holidays to meet demand.

"Danes just aren't squeamish about animals," local teacher Louise Lingaard told me. "We were an agricultural nation for so long that we're still pretty used to the circle of life and all that. Take horses..."

Okay...

"We're huge horse lovers in our family, but sometimes a horse has to be put down and fed to the lions," she added, just casually. "I think my daughter was around the same age as your son when we watched a horse autopsy together."

Ahh, mother-daughter bonding.

"At one point, the intestine sprang out at her, and I was worried she would freak out." Horse guts are huge, I'm told. "But she was fine! There's an understanding that you can be a horse lover *and* be interested in the way an animal's body works. That you can be a meat eater *and* you can know that animals are part of the food chain. It's all part of a child's education."

And don't worry. The veganism doesn't last long! American Mom messaged with a thumbs-up emoji.

Two days later, my son made himself a liver pâté sandwich, and I overheard him telling his then three-year-old siblings with some authority how the left ventricle of the heart was "the powerhouse of the whole body."

Is it? I was amazed. *He knows things! He can't read, but he already knows things! Beyond his parents' knowledge pay grade! How did that happen?*

"School," said Veteran Viking, who has a tendency to take things literally.

"Yes, thank you."

"I mean *Danish* school. We do things differently." She can say that again.

All children in Denmark have access to tuition-free government *folkeskole* from the age of six until they turn sixteen. There's no scramble to secure a place or move house to a good catchment zone.

"You just go to the local school," says my willowy artist friend Camilla, whose daughters go to the same school as she did ("with many of the same teachers!").

Some parents choose a private school, or *friskole,* because they're smaller or have a particular educational stance or specialization. "But in Denmark, a private school is not very private," says Veteran Viking. Three-quarters of the fees are paid by the government, so private schools in Denmark often cost no more than day care.

"It's very different from the situation in the UK," says Professor Ning de Coninck-Smith. Parents might pay around 3,000 DKK a month ($429) for private school education, from breakfast club at 6:30 a.m. to after-school club until 5:00 p.m. "So if you have that money accounted for in your budget from day care, it's quite normal for parents to send their children to a friskole," says Ning. "In Copenhagen and other big cities, I'd say around 50 percent of parents do this."[2] As one friskole dad says, "The Danish government is prepared to subsidize a very good education. It's an investment in our children." Because for every 3,000 DKK a parent pays for a private school education each month, the government contributes 9,000 DKK ($1,290) from the communal pot, replenished via taxes.

Either way, a child will show up at school aged six in Denmark, Sweden, Iceland, and Norway or aged seven in Finland.

"And once they start, I imagine they get down to work, right?" every friend and relation from back home asks (regularly). "I suppose they really knuckle down, catch up on all they've missed by starting school so late?"

"Err, not so much."

Because it's still pretty relaxed compared to other cultures. The current Danish system can be traced back to our old friend and founder of Denmark's group singing tradition, N. F. S. Grundtvig. The nineteenth-century clergyman, politician, and poet advocated a new outlook on education: teaching according to children's interests and inspiring them to learn rather than forcing them to. More carrot, less stick.

After WWII, Danes added another layer to their promise for future generations: prioritizing free thinking above all else. There was a movement to emphasize democracy in schools, to catch children early, in the hope that something like a Nazi occupation could never happen again. And free thinking plus an antiauthoritarian streak have been championed ever since. Teachers are addressed by their first name, there is no uniform, and schools remain unlocked, because "there is trust that students won't run off!" says Mette Bay Velling, a teacher from Mariager in Jutland who I met at a Schools Democracy Festival (Danes love democracy). "There's still respect for teachers, but the relationship between child and teacher is equal," says Mette. "A teacher may have a lot of knowledge, but children should also be respected as individuals."

This way of thinking has been widespread in Denmark for generations. "I would always argue with my teachers and my parents," says teacher Louise. "If I could argue that something was reasonable, that it was important, then I would be heard. It's healthy when kids are so secure that they dare to tell us what they'd do differently." Vikings are encouraged to be free thinkers. "We ask kids their opinion and encourage them to consider: 'What do I like? What do I want to do? How do I feel? How can I solve this problem?' They're taught to think, not just pass exams."

From the start of school in Denmark, children learn to question, debate, and stand up for what they believe in. Literally. "Kids do show-and-tell or sing a song—anything really. We normalize standing up and opening our mouths very early," says Louise.

I wonder how this fits with Jante's law, where no one is to think they're special and showing off is frowned on.

"Ah, but they're not showing off. They're speaking out. There's a difference," says Louise. "You have to stand up for what you want or argue your case in Denmark." Whether you like it or not. "Many aren't so confident, but they know that there's no way out!"

The redhead hated speaking out at school when he started. Two years on and he still doesn't love it, but he knows that it's important to have a voice. He's accepted public speaking as part of school life, and his nervousness has lessened. Primary school assembly has become another form of exposure therapy, and his confidence is growing.

I love this, since public speaking is seldom taught at state schools in the UK. The Oracy campaign is fighting to change this, with speaking now part of the curriculum in Scotland and Wales. But few places elsewhere prioritize public speaking. Denmark is an outlier among the Nordic countries in oracy skills. "We don't do that so much in Finland," says Emilia, the Finnish scout leader with the big blue eyes married to my Danish friend Andreas. "I always see how comfortable Andreas is when he has to speak at an event or give a toast at a family gathering or anything like that, and I think it's a great skill to teach children. I definitely missed out on that in Finland. I'm glad our boys are going to school in Denmark where they'll learn public speaking as part of their education. Eventually."

Eventually is the word.

"Oh, but I love the fact that there's not a lot of pressure on kids here," says Niki in Sweden. "I remember visiting the UK when my kids were in kindergarten, and all the other kids that age could write. Parents would say to their children, 'Why don't you read this out loud to us?' Showing off. And I'd think, 'Oh God! I'm failing them!' But back in Sweden, this was no problem. I asked the pedagogues, 'Should I be helping them learn to read?' And they told me, 'No! You be the parent; we'll be the teachers. When they're ready, they'll do it.' And they did." Niki has seen firsthand how all her children got the hang of reading when they were ready, "in a way that was less stressful for kids and for parents." She's grateful now that Swedes take things slower. "Friends in the UK have kids who spend hours each night doing homework, so they do too. And then everyone's miserable!"

Homework in the Nordic countries is minimal. Sabilah Eboo Alwani from the Faculty of Education at the University of Cambridge thinks this is a good thing, since "the early onset of lots of homework erodes quality time from a developmental point of view."[3] I'll just let that sink in, for any policymakers reading.

"Until you reach the age of ten, there is no homework at all where we are," says Niki. "Even after that, they're not allowed homework on Fridays for the weekend or over the holidays, because they don't want to stress kids out." Niki tells me how her twelve-year-old has only just started getting grades. "And there's no competition at school either. I'm really pleased and protective of this. It means children are much more creative as they have opportunity to just *play*."

Johannes, photographer and father of three in Helsinki, says that there isn't a culture of pushing children to excel in Finland either. He explains how his eleven-year-old and thirteen-year-old sons have been deemed "high achievers" at school, "so we're actually encouraging them to do less. We don't want them to push themselves too hard. We keep telling them, 'It's okay! It's enough! You are enough.'"

Astonishing, I think. But also: *smart*. Since confidence, motivation, resilience, and communication have been found to be "as or more important than academic qualifications," according to education charity Sutton Trust.[4]

The Danish school system largely avoids class rankings and formal tests until the end of "gymnasium" school, aged eighteen or nineteen (more in chapter 16). This is the equivalent of A-levels in the UK and high school in the US. In Denmark, graduating teens get a score from -3 all the way up to 12. Local teacher Louise tells me that when her daughter graduated, she thought she'd get a double zero. "We call this 'the glasses grade,'" she says, making two circle shapes with her fingers and holding them up to her eyes to make glasses. "So I sat her down and I told her, 'You know what? It doesn't matter. I didn't get high grades at school, neither did your dad, and we turned out just fine. We have great jobs, and we have a great life!' Most kids born today will live for one hundred years. Your life is not over as a teenager if you don't get top grades."

She's right, I know. But still. We're all thinking it: *How did her daughter do?*

Louise makes the glasses sign. "She got a double zero. But that's okay! She's gone on to get a good job as a police officer. She has a great life. I'm incredibly proud of her!"

This attitude sounds outlandish to many of us. I was drilled to succeed at school, encouraged to grasp for exceptionalism. Yet I'm now parenting an eight-year-old who's only just learning to read. A sentence that still makes me a little queasy.

"But, darling, you were on Point Horror books by the time you were eight!" my mother tells me.

"Well, that's not how they do things here," I tell her.

"Oh dear." She shakes her head. "You do look tired. Hollow eyes."

"Thank you."

"Dark circles."

"This is actually quite confronting." I don't know if I mean the unspoken criticism of my son's reading ability or my increasingly ragged complexion. Both, probably. The truth is my eight-year-old is still sounding out sentences, one at a time. But he is sounding out Richard Dawkins (the YA one, but still). Mini Vikings may not be able to read by the time their UK and US peers can, but they *are* taking in the world around them at an astounding pace. This means that by the time they can read, they can tackle far more interesting books than early readers elsewhere. There is no *One Fish Two Fish* in the land of Nord. I'm trying hard to be okay with this (rather than a dirty bomb of cynicism) because science.

Research now shows that pressuring children to read too early can cause stress and anxiety.[5] A study from the University of Regensburg in Germany found that later readers easily catch up with and even surpass early readers.[6] Learning later allows children to match their knowledge of the world to the words they learn, as "they've got to unlock the ideas," says Professor Sebastian Suggate, who led the study. He also found that learning to read early has "no discernible benefits" by the time a child turns fifteen.[7]

The latest Program for International Student Assessment data on students' proficiency in reading ranks all the Nordic countries above the OECD average, with Denmark and Finland ahead of both the UK and the US.[8] By age fifteen, Danish students are also ahead of the OECD average in mathematics and science.[9] UNICEF's latest global league table of children's overall academic and social skills ranks Norway at number one. Denmark comes seventh, Finland ninth, and Sweden fourteenth. The UK and the US? Number twenty-six and thirty-two respectively.[10] The Cambridge Primary Review concluded, "there is no evidence that a child who spends more time learning through lessons—as opposed to learning through play—will 'do better' in the long run."[11] So children in the Nordic countries play for longer, learn later, but still do better than children in the US and the UK—and they're happier too.[12]

I look out at the smalls currently gamboling in the garden at a time when their contemporaries in the UK and US would be knuckling down to homework and think perhaps my Viking neighbors are onto something.

I still worry that children learning to read so late will miss out on the full canon of children's literature. *How can they possibly cram it all in?* I ask my son's teacher, who assures me that mini Vikings don't miss out. "We recommend parents read to children for twenty to thirty minutes a day until they reach around the age of twelve. Even when they *can* read, it's a *hyggelig* bonding activity between parent and child." Reading bedtime stories is one of the lovelier parts of parenting, and I remember how mother of two and play researcher Sabilah Eboo Alwani from the University of Cambridge told me that reading to children counted as play too.

Two birds with one book… But still: until they're twelve?

Reading aloud for thirty minutes a day, every day, for twelve years clocks in at 2,190 hours. That's 292 working days. More than a year's work.

I could do an MBA in that time! Train to be a phlebotomist!

"Yes, but would your children be happier?" says Veteran Viking. "Err…"

She looks around her before divulging, "You can cheat a little. We do half reading, half audiobooks." Veteran Viking plugs her youngest into an iPhone, and I thank her for her honesty.

But that doesn't mean parents get to kick back until their children turn fifteen. Since the 1970s in Denmark, parents have been mandated by law to be "collaborators" with their children's education. "It doesn't matter whether you're a CEO or a stay-at-home parent [rare in Denmark]. You will be expected to be involved in school life," says Professor Ning.

"It's a lot, but it's understood by employers that you just take the time off for your kids," says Nadine, the Dane who spent ten years in Silicon Valley. "In the US, I was a 'reading mom,' reading two hours a week to kids because teachers didn't have time. It felt like a civic duty, and I wanted to be supportive, but it was optional. In Denmark, it's expected to a far greater extent—that you'll just take the morning off to be at your kids' craft day or leave work early to help with a class event."

I get daily updates from my son's school via not one, not two, but three different forms of intranet (why?) informing me of parent participation days, annual meetings, and events. Then there are the in-theory-optional-but-in-practice-obligatory committees and social groups. I currently see my children's classmates more than I see my closest friends. As Nadine said, this isn't exclusive to Denmark. But parents in Denmark are expected to do all this on top of a full-time job.

Which is fine if your Danish employers are on board. But for friends who work remotely for British or US employers, it's not so easy. As a freelancer, I can usually be flexible, but there are times of the year when it all gets too much, and I wonder whether the sheer organization required to parent a child in Denmark—let alone three—is beyond me.

How do I do this? I wail. To anyone who will listen.

American Mom flashes me her Whitestrips-bright smile and tells me she manages it with "a whiteboard and caffeine."

I tell her I might need something stronger. Especially since schools also encourage playgroups outside school. Class representatives organize a rotation so that once a month, parents invite five or six children over for *spise-lege* (or "eat-play") after school. "It's a different mix of children at a different house every time, so everyone participates. It's really *hyggeligt*," says Lise, the Viking from Valhalla, "and it fosters trust and community."

"There's a lot of focus on making all kids feel welcome," agrees my friend Camilla, "with open doors between classrooms and hygge hour every Friday. Children take it in turns to bake, then they have an hour a week where it's more relaxed."

More relaxed? As in horizontal?

"They can just socialize—something Danish schools do very well and that helps the children learn to be a good person," says

Camilla. In fact, tolerance and social skills appear to be major parts of the curriculum.

This feels important since many schools around my way aren't exactly diverse. We've been lucky where my children have ended up, but I've been to events at friends' schools where there's a sea of flaxen-haired children, so similar looking that often no one's quite sure whose offspring is whose. I don't want my children growing up thinking this is normal.

"We absolutely teach kids that you have to get along with different people, from different backgrounds, who experience life differently," teacher Mette tells me. Although because Denmark is still more homogeneous than the US or the UK, this is often focused on different age groups in lieu of any *actual* diversity in class. "We have a special bonding session each week where seventh graders [age twelve to thirteen in Denmark] have 'friendship class' with second graders [seven- to eight-year-olds] for example. The little ones learn a lot from the big kids, and the bigger kids remember what it was like to be small and so develop their empathy. There's a team coordinator there if needed, but mostly we see that kids manage themselves in friendship class. It has a really positive impact."

This is like Lise's "sit on your hands" tactic in *vuggestue* or even the alloparent idea in *børnehave*. "We get a child to where we want them but at their own pace," agrees teacher and head of Denmark's Playful Learning program Tobias Heiberg. "It's a deliberate tactic to just lean back. Shut your mouth. *Wait.* Raising Vikings has a lot to do with ninja skills."[13]

Isn't this disingenuous? Aren't we all supposed to be equal? Or, in the words of George Orwell (almost), are some Vikings more equal than others?

"I think we have to remember that we are the grown-ups," Tobias offers as justification. "We can think ahead. We can be flexible. And tactical. And sensitive. The Nordic countries are all pretty similar in this respect. And it's an approach that we see works."

Even though it's sneaky?

"It's tactical," Tobias corrects me.

Mette agrees. "In Denmark, we always believe in the good of the kids, that they always want to do the right thing. If kids are acting out of the ordinary, it's a sign that something is out of whack. And *then* we help. If they can't fulfil what we want them to do, it's not on them," says Mette. "Teachers here never talk about kids being 'bad.' Instead, it's the adults' responsibility to change their behavior and meet the child where they are."

Goodness, I think, *this sounds like hard work.* I'm very glad my homeschooling days are over. Teachers are a special kind of saint.

In Denmark, there's been a policy of including all students in mainstream public schooling where possible, whether they have ADHD or dyslexia or other challenges that may impact learning. "But more and more have a diagnosis of one kind or another nowadays," says my friend Anne, a teacher of sixteen years' standing who I met at choir in my child-free days. Anne attributes the hike in diagnoses in Danish classrooms to better detection but also fears that with greater awareness may have come overdiagnosis ("We talk about it so much now"). Either way, it makes teaching trickier. "There may be a few in each class taking up all of the teachers' attention." And class sizes have stretched. "We're supposed to have twenty-four to twenty-eight students per class, but many classes exceed this," says Anne.

Just like at home, I think, disheartened.

Denmark's school system is far from perfect. In 2022, a TV2 documentary exposed accusations of abuse, bullying, and violence at an elite Danish boarding school attended by royalty. Crown Prince Frederik of Denmark and Princess Mary immediately pulled their son from Herlufsholm School, saying they were "deeply shaken by the reports."[14] But the exposé showed that within the walls of Europe's exclusive boarding schools, things look much the same as elsewhere: with social privilege outweighing cultural norms.

There's a common misconception that private schools don't exist in Finland, although around 2 percent of schools are private, according to the Finnish Ministry of Education and Culture.[15] But *profiting* from education is prohibited, and the goal of the public education system since the 1970s has been to equalize Finnish society. There's no school selection, and because everyone attends the same state schools, even the wealthiest and most educated members of society are invested in making these great. And they are great. Since the 2000s, Finland has been a global leader in education. To understand why, I get a quick history recap from Finnish friends.

When Finland emerged from years of war against the Soviet Union in the late 1940s, it was poor with few natural resources. Finns felt that educating children was the best way for the next generation to get ahead. But Finns also value childhood, so school doesn't start until children turn seven, and school days are short—8:00 a.m. until noon or 2:00 p.m., depending on the day and group. Lessons last forty-five minutes with a fifteen-minute break after each one for play. After-school care is usually offered until 4:00 p.m. when parents leave work to pick children up. So in Finland, students spend only six hundred hours in school each year. While in the US? The average time spent at school each year in many states is eleven hundred hours—almost double that of Finnish children.[16]

Finns see the goal of education as not to prepare children for tests but for life. Finns of both sexes study carpentry, sewing, and cooking. Oh and "teaching to test" is an alien concept. Finland spends ten times more on teacher training and career development than it does on testing. Teachers are trusted as professionals and enjoy significant leeway in classrooms—sensible, since research suggests that teacher autonomy is linked with happier classrooms.[17] Teachers working with seven- to thirteen-year-olds must have a master's in education, while those working with older children must have a master's degree in their subject.

"I've been very impressed and pleased with the school system," says Katja in Helsinki. "The Finnish approach is inclusive, and they'll work with the students, so they'll vote on what they're going to be eating, what activity to do. Schools work with a child to find out what they need and their specialist interests. My son is into coding, so he gets a free after-school coding program. The teachers have said 'he knows more than we do!' but they still do all they can to help him. In North America when I was growing up, you'd get less encouragement for individual skills. You had to fit a mold, and you'd only get extra help in something if the school knew how to manage it. In Finland, you get help and support regardless. And we all work better when we're able to use our strengths."

"We always feel supported as parents too," says Johannes in Helsinki. His daughter is nonverbal and attends a school for children with special needs. "The head teacher told us on day one, 'Your role is to be parents. Nothing else.' And this was so refreshing. Because when you have a child with special needs, it feels like the list of things that you *could* or *should* be doing is endless. But all that her teachers want us to do is love her. I'm really satisfied with the system here."

I think perhaps I might be too—eyeing my eight-year-old who has just built a fighter jet out of Lego, freestyle, and is now explaining life cycles to one twin and the D-Day landing to the other. *Extraordinary...*

Trine Hahnemann schooled her children in the UK and US as well as in Denmark and reflects on how the educations systems compare. "We pay high taxes in Denmark, but I think we get a lot back." As Denmark's most beloved baker who has been running her own businesses for years, it's safe to say Trine contributes a lot in Danish tax—more than she would in the UK or US. "But a friend from the UK who sent her kids to private school and I sat down and looked at everything—from the amount of tax we've both paid over the course of our children's education, to uniform and school fees. And honestly? When it all adds up? We both paid about the same. But I said to her, 'You only put your kids through school with that amount. I put other people's kids through school too. Those who didn't have high-earning parents got a better education as a result. So I got better value for money as I helped other children too.' I feel proud of that."[18]

She should feel proud. All Vikings should. Remember the tax math my US friend and I did after we left the hospital, post birth? How Danes pay high taxes but actually end up with more disposable income than the average American or Brit? How they're happier? And less stressed? Well, most of the Vikings I speak to take this for granted. It's only internationals who see this as oddly eccentric. And it's only Nordic nationals who've spent time overseas and experienced the alternative—like Trine—who are quite so grateful to have been born Viking. Getting children through school in a way that doesn't break their spirit or put them under undue pressure feels like a goal worth fighting for. Rather than viewing the school years as hurried, intense preparation for adulthood, what if we saw them as an opportunity to encourage a love of learning?

Now there's a crazy idea.

WHAT I'VE LEARNED ABOUT SCHOOLING VIKINGS

- Nordics take...their...time. As the alumna of a school where pushy parents were the norm,* this has been hard to swallow. But I'm trying to have *tillid*—trust and faith—that my children will get there in the end.

- Danes teach children *how* to think, not *what* to think. Which, in our fast-paced, digital world, where AI is likely to make much of what we currently know redundant, might be a good move.

- Vikings don't test, they don't do homework, and they let

---

* Half were aging rock stars or light entertainers, the other half were stage parents shuttling offspring to perform in the West End several nights a week. It was a lot. #jazzhands

teachers do their job of inspiring the next generation. Teacher autonomy makes for happier classrooms, so everyone benefits.

◆ Children are encouraged to find their voice and use it. I love this. Especially for girls, who are often told to be quiet, to live small. Well, not me. Not my kids. Public speaking skills shouldn't be the preserve of the privately educated, as is often the case back home. Oracy is for everyone.

◆ It feels really good to finally get at least one of my mini Vikings something approaching an education. I share my sunny outlook with Veteran Viking, who promptly squashes it. "Not for much longer." "Sorry?" "Nearly vacation time. They'll be home again before you know it." She's right. They will.

GOD FERIE! HOLIDAYING LIKE A VIKING

DUST MOTES DANCE IN SUNBEAMS as the dog dozes. It's a lazy Saturday, and all is momentarily peaceful before my daughter flops dramatically back in her chair and announces, "I need a holiday!"

"You're five!"

"Yes?"

"So what do you need a holiday from?" I ask.

She gestures with a glue gun at the mountain of craft she's already made this morning. "Everything! I'm exhausted!"

"It's not the worst idea," says Lego Man, already on his third coffee. He's gone Viking on caffeine, even ordering an after-dinner espresso recently (like a *lunatic*).

We're approaching July or "tumbleweed time," when schools and offices shut, the streets empty, and traffic lights turn green to red and back again without any cars coming near. The air is close, heavy with jasmine. And the country powers down as the entire nation takes their summer holiday en masse. Try contacting a Viking any time in July, and you'll be lucky to get a response. In the UK, we were always encouraged to stagger holidays with colleagues so that work could carry on as normal, and I never took more than two weeks off at a time. But Danes have a whole month off to *hav en god ferie* or "have a good holiday."

Studies from Sweden show that this "collective restoration," as it's called, increases levels of well-being and contentment because everyone's off at the same time, doing the same thing, so there's none of the pressure of feeling like you should be working or that you must check your email.[1] Everyone's off together, so you're guaranteed quality time with friends and family. Then when everyone comes back, they are rested and restored.

For Nordics, holiday time is a treasured opportunity to switch off from work, digital devices, and whirring brains. To be with family (even more), celebrating simple pleasures. And what Vikings love best is doing all this in a hut somewhere. Norwegians call it a *hytte*, Icelandics have *sumarbústaður* or *sumarhús*. Finns favor a *kesämökki*, while Swedes love a traditional red-and-white hut or *sommarstuga*. In Sweden, there are around 610,000 of these countrywide, and 51 percent of Swedes have access to a summer cabin through extended family or friends.[2]

Danish *sommerhuse* or summerhouses are a core part of Danish culture, going back four hundred years. The government began offering plots to industrial workers to give them a place to grow fresh produce and have a smog-free getaway (the olden days were grubby in Denmark too).

Today, there are more than 180,000 summerhouses in Denmark, but many are pretty basic. We're talking ancient plumbing, mismatched crockery, and no Wi-Fi so you have to talk, like it's the '90s. I know this because around 40 percent of Danish summerhouses are rented out on Airbnb for those of us not fortunate enough to have been born Viking. By July, the archipelago waters are a bearable temperature for swimming, so smart Vikings take a holiday within the country—when the weather has a chance of being decent.

The forecast may be unpredictable and facilities may be minimal, but the point of a summerhouse is not to replicate home comforts. It's to strip everything back, slacken the pace of "normal life," and find serenity.

"We eat pretty simply when at the summerhouse," says Esben from Copenhagen, who still takes his three children to the cabin his grandfather built in the 1950s. "We might pick up some salad leaves, new potatoes, or fruit from the produce stands with honesty boxes along the roads. And there's a small fishing hut where a fisherman and his son smoke fish and sell great seafood." Esben's summerhouse is on the Helgenæs peninsula, "known locally as the 'snot drip' of Jutland" (there's a bump on the east coast that looks a little like a nose). The house was built with two tiny bedrooms, a kitchen, a living room, and a toilet. "There was no bath. You just washed in the sea, one hundred meters away," Esben says. He spent three weeks there every summer growing up. "We swam, ate strawberries, and the sun was always shining. At least that's how I remember it." Now, he takes his wife and children there every summer to spend time with extended family. "My dad built another small house on the same plot to fit everyone in, but there's usually still someone sleeping on the sofa or the floor." Not a lot goes on here, but that's part of the attraction. To get to the house, you have to go down an overgrown track, and there's hardly any phone signal. "We spend our time swimming, talking, walking, and barbecuing. If we're ever in need of fancier attractions, we go to Ebletoft, an old port town thirty minutes' drive away."

What can you do there?

"Um," he says, "well…there's a glass museum?"

It's not exactly Ibiza.

"Or there's a brewery. They do a nice IPA. And really, what more do you need?" The place isn't anything fancy ("although we did install an indoor shower in the 1990s") but Esben loves it. "My wife and I even got married there."

Swedish summerhouses take simplicity to a whole other level. Most have rudimentary cooking facilities and perhaps running water in the kitchen, but that's it. Showers are considered an unnecessary extravagance, so most Swedish families will walk from their summerhouse to a nearby lake or the sea for a morning bath. Lack of plumbing is a running theme, and many Swedish cabins have a dry outdoor toilet, or *utedass*, in a separate wooden hut a stone's throw from the house.

"What is *that*?" the redhead asked, mystified, when we first encountered a plank of wood and a bucket in lieu of an *actual* loo.

"That, son, is our toilet," Lego Man assured him with all the confidence of a seasoned camper, used to even more primitive facilities (cut him and he bleeds canvas).

In case you're unfamiliar with the delights of a Swedish summerhouse bathroom, you perch over a hole and then throw a handful of dry earth or sawdust over your "output." This is intended to aid rapid composting and prevent odors. Although in a hot July, odors triumph. Composting toilets may be eco-friendly, but they still smell. Bad. When waste buckets are full, they're emptied into a composting area (not by me). But what Swedish summerhouse bathrooms lack in water, they make up for in vistas. With a traditional heart-shaped hole in the door, there's nothing like a smallest room with a view. "And if you haven't seen a shooting star while taking a midnight dump, have you really lived?" as my friend Peter Schmeichel says.

"No" appears to be the answer.

The low-key *lagom* living of Swedish summerhouses attracts an array of luminaries, from ABBA's Björn and Benny, who wrote floor filler "Dancing Queen" from their cottage on the island of Viggsö, to Will Ferrell and his Swedish wife, actor Viveca Paulin, in Gnesta, south of Stockholm. And then there's Ingmar Bergman, who had a cottage on the islet of Fårö off Gotland. Writing about Sweden's Vikings for a UK newspaper, I meet Lars Kruthof of the Gotland Museum, who grew up on Fårö. He tells me how the filmmaker would teach local children photography, even letting them be in his movies. "We looked out for him in return," Lars remembers. "When American tourists would flood in every summer asking 'Where's Ingmar Bergman's house?' we'd send them in the wrong direction."[3]

Forget the Hamptons or a Nordic Lake Como. Here, simplicity is the measure of happiness.

"You get to a summerhouse and your daily life and habits are totally different," says Veteran Viking, stepping over a cat and removing an iPad from her youngest. "Instead of looking at screens, you look at each other."

After all I've learned about Denmark's digital blind spot, this appeals.

"Then when you get sick of each other," she adds, ever the pragmatist, "you look at the view. Or trees. You slow down."

She looks at me, and we try not to laugh. Both of us are bad at this, and we know it. *But I'm working on it,* I think. And so is she.

"As soon as I turn down the dirt track where we go, I feel the stress leaving my shoulders." She rotates them to illustrate. "I become twenty percent more relaxed."

"Twenty percent?"

"I know: 'have some ambition.' I'm trying for thirty percent this year."

I'm not sure relaxation works like that. *But then, what do I know?*

"The great thing is you can just throw a few things in the car and drive there," she adds. Considering the hassle of holidaying abroad post Brexit, I'm surprised more of my countryfolk don't do this.

"It sounds lovely," I tell her.

But just packing up the car won't suffice for Lego Man this time.

"I want to feel like I'm going somewhere," he tells me.

"You are going somewhere: to a summerhouse. Via road."

"I don't want roads."

"What do you want?"

"Sea!"

Denmark is made up of 406 islands (more, even, than Greece) and 5,437 miles of coastline, so you're never more than thirty miles from the sea. Aside from Jutland's forty-two-mile boundary with Germany, Denmark is entirely surrounded by water, a lot like the UK. But Vikings seem to have a special affinity with the sea—the great unknown that's always there but never the same. On the west coast of Jutland, waves roar as the North Sea brings an icy slap to the air and sand blasts old bunkers from WWII. Of the eight thousand bunkers in Denmark built by Germans during the occupation, seven thousand of them are on the west coast.

Further north, Klitmøller is known as "Cold Hawaii" thanks to seven-foot high waves and a wicked wind from the west. Camper vans stacked high with surfboards rumble along coastal roads where everything that might get blown away has to be lashed down. "There's a strong history of fear around the water here—and respect for it too," says Casper Steinfath, a Klitmøller local and world champion stand-up paddle surfer who I interview for a magazine. He tells me about a tradition of going swimming with a rope tied around your waist for fear of being pulled under. I shudder. Lego Man dislocated his shoulder swimming on the west coast and very nearly didn't make it back. Casper nods and says, "We have a west coast saying that we're 'born against the wind'—but it makes us stronger."[4]

At the northernmost tip of Jutland is Skagen, where the Baltic Sea meets the North Sea and you can stand in the shallows to feel currents converge. Skagen used to be a fishing hub, but now it's famed for otherworldly sand dunes and a luminous light that's inspired everyone from the Skagen painters in the nineteenth century to artists today. "Salt crystals found in the air from the sea are reflected in the sand, so we have a special light," local artist Niels Poplens tells me. "In Skagen, even the shadows are bright."[5] He's right; they are. I visited while pregnant with the redhead, waddling the beach at dusk, or "blue hour"—when sea and sky appear to merge. It was a transcendent experience, in spite of the fact that I was completely sober and wearing compression socks for varicose veins. It was *that* good.

All this water was perfect in Viking times, when sailing was the best way to get around, but today, water means leisure for most Danes. "We take it for granted. It's a way of life," says Rikke Johansen, curator at Denmark's Viking Ship Museum. "For many, looking out at water every day is key."[6]

But Lego Man doesn't just want to look at water. He wants to be in it, surrounded by it. He wants an island.

We've already ticked off a fair few of these in our Ø-PAS, or island passport—from Samsø to Strynø and Fanø (ø means island). Every island ferry has a brass plate that you can take a rubbing of in your "passport" to mark off those you've visited (a solid five minutes of entertainment for the smalls on each boat trip). A few favorites include Bornholm, where you can walk barefoot in sand so fine it was used in sand timers until recently. Or Anholt, the bird-shaped island a three-hour ferry ride from both Jutland and Sweden. Or Møns Klint, the dramatic chalk cliff on the island of Møn, famed for its dark skies and lack of light pollution where you're supposed to be able to see the Milky Way (I didn't). And then there's Ærø, the island off the southeast coast of Denmark famed for its beer and beach huts, including the yellow beach hut from the cover of my first book. Also, it's beautiful, all low timbered houses on cobbled streets, flanked by hollyhocks. It's one of the leading renewable-energy islands in the world, on track to be carbon neutral and self-sufficient by 2025, with an electric ferry and free buses with bicycle racks, so you can go there car-free. So we have. Twice.

Yet he wants more islands? Jeez.

"What do you actually do on these 'holidays'?" Deep V bachelor friend asks, making air quotes around the word "holidays."

He's just back from two weeks in Barbados and has the tan lines to show it.

"Um…chat?" I suggest.

He looks skeptical.

"Eat? Play cards? Uno?"

He recoils with a look that says: "You do *you*."

It's fair to say that when it comes to island life, there's not much going on. Perhaps a seasonal café or a *kro*—the closest thing Danes have to pubs. Then every second street has an honesty box selling salad leaves, potatoes, or honey. You'll never run short of honey on a Danish island. And for everything else, there's usually a co-op.

Aware that my children are getting older and the delights of "Ooh look! More artisanal honey!" may be wearing thin, I ask Veteran Viking for further inspiration. She's making coffee while messaging her daughter to empty the cats' litter tray, but she manages to share, "If kids start complaining, send them out to collect rocks."

Rocks? Did she say rocks? Rocks aren't fun, are they?

"Yes, they are," says Veteran Viking and every other Dane I meet. On the west coast, lucky beachcombers come across fist-size pieces of amber, just there for the taking. And all over Denmark, there are *hulsten* or "hole stones," formed on beaches where currents collide. Small pebbles come crashing down on larger stones, eventually wearing through them. "It's tradition to collect the stones for good luck, hanging them from twine in your doorway or just keeping them," says Veteran Viking. She hands me one from a tastefully arranged jar of pebbles on her otherwise minimalist shelf. It's surprisingly soothing to feel the smooth, sun-warmed stone. "And if they get tired of stone collecting," she tells me, "send them out on the water."

Denmark has thirteen hundred beaches and a population of just 5.8 million so, often, we have a beach to ourselves. I learn that there are all manner of sea-based leisure activities available to the intrepid Viking in summer, with its long, light days—from paddleboarding to sailing, rowing, kayaking, and wild swimming. "Though there isn't much waterskiing or wakeboarding," I mention to Veteran Viking, "and you don't see a Jet Ski in Jutland."

She winces at such ostentation. "Jante's law and Jet Skis don't mix. Anything that needs an engine is a little…showy." Her nose wrinkles. "Plus we're all meant to be relaxing. Remember?"

"I remember."

Being around a large expanse of water has been shown to help with relaxation.[7] Experiencing nature on holiday has been found to improve our well-being, and spending time by the water may even help us sleep better.[8] Researchers from Northwestern University found that those who fell asleep listening to water slept more deeply,[9] and a National Trust study found that participants slept forty-seven minutes longer, on average, after a seaside hike.[10]

I point out to Lego Man that we live just ten minutes from the sea by car, but apparently a seaside hike near home won't cut it. So despite the extra step of adding a ferry to an otherwise relatively easy summerhouse break, we're going.

A week later, we set off for an hour's drive followed by a ferry to Avernakø, an island south of Funen that's just two kilometers by one kilometer with a population of 106. (If you think that's small, neighboring Hjortø has a population of just seven. *Seven!*)

An expanse of open water separates "real life" from pancakes-for-breakfast holiday mode, offering mental and physical distance from all that has gone before. The water's choppy, and the air has a chill to it, so we head inside to nose around and spot cupboards marked "toys for the ferry children," "books for the ferry children," and "craft supplies." I'm wondering whether my smalls count as "ferry children," so I ask the steward, who tells me "No." She explains that there's no kindergarten or school on the island of Avernakø, so children going to børnehave must travel to the mainland. That meant an hour's round trip on a ferry for parents, twice a day. Which was a *pain in the ass*. So the local council put their heads together and came up with a plan, appointing a dedicated boat chaperone to escort under-sixes home on the ferry each day. Lest they miss out on precious play time on their commute, the ferry is equipped with entertainment to continue the børnehave experience at sea.

My five-year-old son is near giddy with envy. ("They get to *play* on a *boat*? Every day? Twice? With no parents?! Luck-y!") I have to agree it is pretty "luck-y" (pronounced with the emphasis on the y, always). The chaperone system encourages families to live on these remote islands, and when children get bigger and start school, they take the ferry on their own.

Lightheaded with excitement about their new surroundings and wobbly of leg after time on the boat, we make it to the Airbnb and settle in. The redhead is permitted to stay up past his bedtime, and we sit out on wicker chairs, having big chats. Like this one:

The redhead: "Are you scared about dying or getting old?"

Me: "Not in that order."

Him: "Should we burn you?"

Me: "Do you mean cremate?"

Him: "Yes."

Me, thinking for a minute while staring at stars: "Sure, cremate me."

Him: "Cool."

Lego Man: "I've just realized when Gollum talks about 'my precious,' he means a ring."

The redhead and I both turn to look at him.

"What did you *think* he meant?"

"I thought it was just that he had a really nice wife or something."

"*Extraordinary.*"

Eventually, we relax. Properly. Possibly up to Veteran Viking's 30 percent. There's a cadence to island life that's largely dictated by the ferry—from the times new people arrive to when the supermarket gets fresh deliveries. "Rush hour" is twice a day, when the four cars on the island (four!) head to or from the ferry. (And we're not talking cross-channel here; the boat has space for six cars "to accommodate tourists.") So we manage to fill days with...nothing.

"It's like we're turning into our retired parents!" I say with disbelief, checking my watch and realizing I have managed to sit still for... eight minutes and fifty-three seconds. *A new record!* Days are spent at the beach, and once the five-year-olds overcome their indignation at not being able to watch TV, collecting *hulsten* becomes a favorite hobby. Evenings are spent barbecuing, a.k.a. spying on what the neighbors are having for dinner. "He made a seafood platter!" I stage-whisper to Lego Man as he turns a charred sausage. Still, everything tastes better eaten alfresco while watching Aperol spritz sunsets. Slowly, we fall into a rhythm, and I feel a pressure valve loosening.

The smalls play with toys left behind in the house, long out-grown by the mini Vikings who once loved them. My son goes a whole morning without asking for the iPad. My daughter takes a shine to a stuffed lemur with a long stripy tail, carrying it around with her from morning until night.

"It's Lemur's birthday," she tells me.

"How old is Lemur?"

"Susan."

"Sorry?"

"Her name is Susan, and she's one hundred."

"Goodness…she looks good for it."

Susan celebrates her centenary with a bear named Nigel and a one-armed action figure called Cutie-Pie. Only it turns out it's Susan's birthday the next day too. And the one after that. On day three of "happy birthday, dear Susan," Lego Man stands and announces that he is going to "be alone with his thoughts." After ten minutes of being alone with his thoughts, he decides that's quite enough of that. He proclaims he's "finished relaxing" and leaves the summerhouse. A few minutes (hours? days?) later, he hurtles back, falling through the door like a marathon runner at the end of a race. There is a reckless air about him, and I feel a constriction where my Zen had been.

"What have you done?"

"Why would you say that?"

"Because I know you. What is it?"

"We're going sailing!" he tells me, triumphant.

"Are we? Why?" I tend to associate sailing with spongy-nosed men sporting luxurious bouffants and women with skin like a satchel.

"For fun! Tomorrow!"

I rather had tomorrow down as "chill, snack, repeat," not sailing. But the mini Vikings are now primed for adventure and I am outnumbered. So this is happening.

A man who looks like a greyhound tells us he'll be our guide and all we have to do is "exactly what he tells us." The Greyhound equips us with life jackets and even a health and safety briefing (not guaranteed in Denmark). Where sand trails down to the sea, we're led to a wooden, almond-shaped boat and told to "carry it into the water."

"Carry? A whole boat?" I appear to be the only one with reservations about this since my children are already midheave. I lay my hands on the boat and am surprised to find it's hot to the touch, heated by the sun.

"First, we row until we're clear of the shore." The Greyhound takes up an oar and hands me the other.

Me? Not Lego Man? Damn Nordic egalitarianism... My daughter stares at me, unblinking, watching how I'll react. It's like Elsa from *Frozen* watching me scale a tree all over again. I can't let either of them down. *Must. Channel. Inner. Viking. Am not an English rose. Am strong shield-maiden...*

It's hard going, but I remember what Lasse in Norway told me about having the arms of a survivor. *I can do this,* I tell myself, pulling harder.

Lego Man is stationed by the tall pole thingy in the middle that

I'm reliably informed is the mast. He is charged with "undoing a bow" on the Greyhound's command.

That's his job? Undoing a bow? And I have to row? Unbelievable.

The Greyhound tilts his head, feeling the wind. Then, wordlessly, he gives the nod: *do it now*. Lego Man unties the knot that binds a ream of white fabric to our mast, and with a swift, violent unraveling, the sail lashes outward. It whips and cracks as it fills with air, and we lurch forward, wind blasting my face. I can taste sea. The twins are yelping with joy, and the redhead is waggling his limbs like one of those inflatables with waving arms outside a car showroom.

"Hold on!" I yell. Remarkably, he does, grabbing a rail wet with sea spray.

The Greyhound secures the sail and tells us how even children can "read" the waves.

About all they can read, I can't help thinking.

"You just have to think, 'Are the waves still at the same angle to the boat as they were?' 'Is the wind blowing in the same direction?'" says the Greyhound. "When we're near shore, we look at the water and judge how flat it is to work out how shallow the sea is. Then there are swans."

"Swans?"

"Swans. Their necks are about this long"—he holds his hands just over a foot apart—"so if they have their butts in the air, you know the water's deep enough for a boat like this. If swans are just poking their heads under to fish, it's too shallow, and you'll get grounded."

This is my new favorite swan fact. (*Everyone* knows the break-your-arm one.)

"All birds can help you in a boat," says the Greyhound, "since most fly toward land. And ravens are a sailor's best friend."

At this, Lego Man starts humming "Diamonds Are a Girl's Best Friend" from *Gentlemen Prefer Blondes*.

The Greyhound ignores the musical interlude and explains how the blue-black birds fly higher than most. "It means they can see land sooner. They'll head straight for it, and you can follow."

The redhead nods gravely, storing this raven data for future scout escapades.

"You can also use clouds. There are always more clouds over land than there are at sea," says the Greyhound. "And you need to *listen*."

Lego Man stops humming "Diamonds Are a Girl's Best Friend."

"You can actually *hear* land. Traffic, sirens, dogs."

All I can hear is the wind, whistling around my ears. But this is useful too, he tells me, as we soar through the surf.

"Move your head until you feel the wind blowing evenly on both ears. Then you know you're facing into the wind."

I move slightly until I can feel the wind whipping around each ear, and it works! We fly through water as the Greyhound wrenches ropes stiffened by salt. It is...invigorating. I'm having a...what is this feeling? Oh! I know: a nice time!

The boat grates on sand as we reach shore again and disembark, with sea legs and silly smiles. I thank the Greyhound. And then I thank Lego Man. "For making me do the scary thing I didn't want to do."

He looks pleased. Smug even. With notes of "I told you so." I bring him back down to earth by telling him: "But we have to crack on with the packing and cleaning now." I'm fun like that.

Everyone knows that packing to go home is the worst part of any holiday. But leaving a rented summerhouse entails an added undertaking: the cleanup. From emptying bins and eco-toilets (grim) to mopping, scrubbing, vacuuming ("floors and beds" as one recent Airbnb demanded). Most significantly in our case: going home means saying goodbye to Susan the lemur.

After tears (some) and protestations (many), we load the car and make a dash for the ferry. We are late. We are always late since having children. We arrive just as our loading lane is closing, and it takes all my powers of persuasion and Danglish, but we make it. After a tight game of car *Tetris*, we head up on deck to wave goodbye to "our island." And it's then that I notice our daughter looking suspiciously bulky.

"What have you got up your sweater?"

"Nothing."

"I can see a stripy tail sticking out."

"No."

"Is Susan the lemur up your sweater?"

She shakes her head.

She continues to style this one out until Lego Man appears and immediately spots the offending article. Over the wind, I hear "not yours," and a bottom lip begins to quiver as she looks down, tracing the outline of the deck slats with her foot. I let Lego Man handle this one and compose a message to the owners of the summerhouse.

I'm so sorry...now on the ferry... I'll send it to you asap.

I'm just walking back when my phone pings.

Cry laughing emoji. Heart emoji. Lemur emoji.

Okay...

Don't worry. Our son used to do the same. He's 27 now. Tell your daughter she can keep lemur as long as she promises to give it plenty of kram [hugs in Danish]. Winking emoji.

Oh my.

There follows a parental debate in hushed tones. "How's she supposed to learn if she gets the lemur anyway?" and "Got any better ideas?!" We compromise on a teachable moment about not taking other people's property and a thank-you letter since it's now *technically* a gift.

But I wish there was a grown-up on board to tell us what to do. Like Kitta. *If she can handle prison, she can handle lemur larceny. Stuff Mary Poppins: What would Kitta do?* WWKD? (Another top-drawer tattoo inspiration...* makes note*.) Increasingly convinced that this is the Rosetta stone of raising Vikings, I return below deck in search of snacks. I see another message on my phone, this time from Veteran Viking. It says simply, 30 percent.

I write back immediately: Congratulations! Relaxation: crushed it.

WHAT I'VE LEARNED ABOUT HOW TO HOLIDAY LIKE A VIKING

- ◆ Keep it simple. No running water? No problem when it comes to Viking holidays (but not for emptying the eco-toilet). We don't have to spend a lot to have a memorable family holiday. Children don't care how many stars somewhere has or what angry men named Clive say about it on Tripadvisor. I hear from friends back home who've shelled out for trips to Dubai or the Maldives with small children, and now think: *why?* I'd much rather save to go somewhere long-haul once they're old enough to appreciate it. Or better still, get away solo once my children are teenagers and have decided that going on holiday with mom and dad is officially uncool.

• Going offline, if not off grid, helps. I *can* relax, I've discovered, but there really need to be no other options. I will happily busy myself with *anything* before sitting down and doing nothing (parent: know thyself).

• Stones are acceptable kids' entertainment. And contrary to American Mom's assertion, an old Rubik's Cube in the summerhouse proved remarkably absorbing for my children once they realized that there were no iPads available. Perhaps that's what all the play research is getting at: given the time and the space, humans will just play. With pretty much anything.

• We're all stronger than we think. Especially if there are impressionable small people watching. Children make us braver, and this is a good thing. Update: I can row a Viking boat now. Tell *everyone*.

LET'S GET PHYSICAL

SWEAT POOLS ABOVE THE COLLARBONE. My cheeks feel like they're melting. And...*could my eyeballs be sweating?* I'm in a sauna with my daughter, my mother-in-law, and two moms from school. And we are all stark naked. I am trying very hard to be nonchalant about this but feeling, heat aside, distinctly *chalant.*

Chalant I shall remain, I think, until I get out of here and get a bra on.

I know, logically, that the body is just a body. That it's healthy to be relaxed about nudity. And oddly, I'm okay about it in front of strangers. I've been naked in front of enough of them in Danish communal changing rooms by now. But naked in front of people I *know*? And am neither biblically acquainted with nor have given birth to? In a municipal swimming pool sauna? Like I said: *chalant.*

It's safe to say that Nordics don't go in for prudishness. In swimming pools, gyms, and sports centers throughout Denmark, changing rooms, showers, and saunas are separated by gender. But within those? Nudity is the norm. Swimming pools all require a nude full body soaping in a public shower room before entry. And helpful posters remind everyone to wash thoroughly, since failure to do so is akin to civic deviance in Denmark. A few favorites from my local pool:

One person who has not washed is equivalent to twenty who have washed thoroughly!

The less catchy but certainly comprehensive:

Soap + thorough washing WITHOUT SWIMWEAR
= less chlorine + cleaner bathing water
= less irritation in the eyes and mucous membranes!

Or the short and sweet:

SHOWER AGAIN after TOILET!

"Why wouldn't you wash?" says Veteran Viking when I quiz her on this.

Having spent sunny days at Tooting Lido, the largest outdoor pool in the UK, watching water cloud with sweat and sunscreen, I admit she may be onto something. A society that values cleanliness isn't the worst thing in the world, and it's no surprise that chlorine levels in UK and US swimming pools are higher than those in the Nordic countries. In Iceland, there's even a song to remind tourists which body parts to scrub, led by a fictional "director of spa etiquette" and sung to the tune of "Head, Shoulders, Knees, and Toes" ("Head, armpits, crotch and toes, crotch and toes!").[1]

Nordics don't ablute staring resolutely at their shampoo either—terrified of catching the eye of a fellow bather in a state of undress and blushing puce. Instead, they hold *actual* conversations while tackling pits and slits. *Like it's no big deal! #chalant.*

"Internationals are often surprised by how relaxed we are," says my Swedish friend Maria, "but there's nothing sexual about it. They're just bodies. And not having wet bathing costumes sticking to your skin makes everything more comfortable."

Being naked is just normal. Especially in Finnish saunas, I learn. Traditionally found in private homes and holiday cottages, these high-heat, wood-lined rooms are designed to make you sweat, flush out toxins (allegedly), improve circulation, and aid muscle recovery. The traditional hot-cold sauna cycle ends with an icy dunk or a roll in the snow if there's any around. Finns love saunas so much that there are 3.3 million saunas in a country of just 5.5 million people.[2] Emilia, the Finnish scout leader who lives near me, explain how Finns regularly sauna (it can be a verb too) with extended family—from aunts to uncles, cousins, grandparents, and in-laws.

"The first time I met Emilia's dad," her husband Andreas tells me, "we sat next to each other, naked, in a sauna. It was quite the first impression."

I'll bet.

"Many of the older generation were born in saunas," says Emilia, "since it's clean and keeps the mother and new baby warm. The sauna was often the first room anyone built in a new house." Babies take their first gentle sauna when they're a few months old, and from then on, they never stop. Andreas and Emilia now have their own sauna at their home in Denmark to continue the tradition. And the popularity of saunas is spreading across the Nordic countries, with a sharp uptick in public saunas in Norway's capital to meet demand.

Mixed-sex saunas aren't always swimsuit-free zones. "If you're not sure, look at what everyone else is doing and do that," says my friend who looks like Peter Schmeichel (a big sauna fan). "But a warning—even if everyone is naked, bring a towel to sit on. No one wants to see your sweaty butt print."

Understood.

The Nordic attitude to nudity has been profound for this former Catholic school girl raised in the UK. I was in my thirties when I moved to Denmark, which means I'd been knocking around for three whole decades before I saw the full spectrum of women's bodies in their natural form. Not film stars in carefully choreographed sex scenes or an unvarying parade of smoking-hot Nordic goddesses. I mean real bodies, naked. Tummies that pucker, C-section scars, breasts that swing, bottoms that dimple, and pubic hair that grows wherever it pleases, gloriously uncoiffed. As a result of this exposure to a whole range of real bodies, I began to accept my own a little more. Lego Man assures me that "the cock and hairy balls show" in the men's changing rooms has a similar effect. And there's a certain honesty to baring all: everyone is exposed, and everyone is equal. There's nothing funny or shaming about being naked. Now, I often feel there should be a sign outside all Danish changing rooms that reads, "Welcome to the pool. Please leave your shame here."

A survey conducted at the University of Zürich showed that

Danes are the most shameless people in the world. A mere 1.62 percent of Danes suffer from gelotophobia—fear of ridicule—the lowest proportion of the population in any country surveyed.[3] In the UK, we have the *highest* number of people with the phobia.

My own mini Vikings have grown up with nudity: in changing rooms, at the beach, in the lakes in Sweden, or even just walking past the full-frontal porny pony fountain in our town. Danes are just...*okay* about their bodies. From birth.

Children are allowed in either male or female changing rooms until they turn six, when pools ask that they change in the locker room of the sex with which they identify. So children get to see all sorts of bodies. And should they need more, there's always extra "help" on hand.

Public service broadcaster DR TV's show *Ultra Smider Tøjet* (Ultra Strips Down) prompted a scandal in 2020 for presenting children aged eleven to thirteen with a panel of nude adults. A scandal, that is, outside the Nordic countries. Danes were fine about it. As clinical psychologist Erla Heinesen Højsted said at the time, "What kind of culture are we creating for our children if it's ok for them to see 'perfect' bodies on Instagram—enhanced, digitally or cosmetically—but not 'real bodies'?"[4] So Danes focus on "real bodies" that are strong and healthy, rather than stick-thin.

"There's definitely less of a fixation on being thin in Sweden too," agrees my friend Niki in Malmö. "It's about being healthy instead. So shop mannequins vary in size for a more inclusive feel. And even advertising billboards show normal-looking women. I'm really happy about this as a parent."

Nordics "train" rather than exercise, with sport for all, regardless of age, ability, or innate skill. Simply because it feels good. I swim every Thursday, and there is a septuagenarian who spends the entire thirty-minute session climbing up metal steps, then zooming down the water slide, solo. Every. Single. Week.

The emphasis on physical activity, for *fun*, is paramount, and girls grow up playing soccer as well as boys (with great success—the US Olympic gold medal–winning women's team was coached by a Swede). Soccer is the most popular sport in Denmark, with the national team earning surprising success internationally. Then there's Denmark's national sport: handball. From what I can make out by watching Veteran Viking's daughter play, this is a cross between netball, basketball, and soccer, with players required to dribble a ball into goals instead of baskets. Denmark is officially the most successful nation at handball in the world, with a total of 104 medals.

"Is that because no one else plays?" Lego Man asks.

"No." I tell him what Veteran Viking told me: "Germans like it too, actually! The sport was even played in ancient Greece. So there!"

It gets cold in winter, so ice hockey is popular in Denmark and Sweden. Norwegians love to ski—cross-country and downhill—while Swedes and Finns are fans of floorball—a type of indoor hockey invented in the late 1960s where players whack around a ball with holes in it for twenty minutes at a time (convenient for parents on cheerleading duty).

"Being active is just for everyone. It's just what you do," says Katja from Finland, "and there isn't so much of a car culture, which helps. In North America, friends spend two, three, maybe four hours a day driving. But in the Nordic countries, it is easier to cycle or walk. We don't drive a car to a gym to sit on a stationary bike. What is that?! Many Finns just lead a good, active life, using basic common sense." According to the 2022 Active Healthy Kids Global Alliance report, Denmark and Finland top the polls when it comes to keeping children active. There are famously more bikes than cars in Copenhagen, and 82 percent of Danish children "actively transport themselves" to school twice a week—with 60 percent doing so daily.[5] "It doesn't matter who you are or what you look like," says Peter Schmeichel. "Your body is there to be used."

"And enjoyed," adds Veteran Viking, stroking her cat. "Don't forget that."

How could I forget…

Sex education has been mandatory in Denmark since 1970, and children from the age of six are taught about their rights over their own bodies during a national curriculum "Sex Week" every February (week six in the calendar, or *seks* in Danish, pleasingly). Each year, there's a theme—from consent to identity and the perfectly imperfect body.

Eleven-year-olds take a module called "adolescence" where they can submit questions anonymously for teachers to address. Student suggestions this year include the following:

"Why do some people think it's bad being gay?"

"Why does sex make a noise?"

"What is masterbathing [sic]? Is it comfy to masterbathe with your own gender?"

And my favorite: "Do you swear more after you've been through puberty?" (Answer: yes.)

"But you still have to be on top of it as parents," says my

American Mom friend, "to check kids know when and *where* to use their newfound knowledge." She reminds me of the time her eldest's class studied safer sex and teenagers were encouraged to "wrap that rascal" ("which, obviously, they found hilarious and kept chanting. All. The. Time"). "Or the year kids were given a handout of all the words for genitalia that they might encounter." American Mom flinches at the recollection. "Top of the list?"

Umm... I go blank.

"C*nt."

Oh!

"Exactly! I made them promise, 'Don't tell Grandma!'"

Unless she's anything like C-bomb Ruby, the pensioner who thrashed me at Scrabble.

By the age of thirteen, Danes have covered everything from the ins and outs of masturbation to transgender rights in frank and open discussions, an eye-opener for those of us who learned about sex from Judy Blume's *Forever*.

Public service broadcaster DR TV supports sex education in schools with *Under the Covers with Anna Lin*, where the twenty-six-year-old host discusses young people's concerns about sex. "I had a lot of questions [when I was growing up], and I can tell from the children who turn to me now that they do too," Anna Lin told DR. "You can have doubts about everything from your body's development to the very essential 'Who am I?'"[6] The show is made with consultation from BørneTelefonen, a children's help line, and Sex & Samfund, a nongovernmental family planning organization, to ensure the right tone and focus for children's needs and life stages. Sex & Samfund consultant Pernille Ane Egebæk told DR how sex education is "partly a school-based task but also a broader social task that institutions must contribute to."[7] This is an approach echoed in Sweden, the first country in the world to introduce obligatory sexual education in schools in 1955.

"We're surprised when people—often from the UK or the US— make a fuss about the way we do things in Sweden," says Kajsa Peters, mother of two and producer of youth content at Sweden's public service broadcaster SVT. "We start talking about the body and sex really early in Sweden, because isn't it better to tell kids the truth in an age-appropriate way?" When Kajsa first started at SVT, she commissioned a short video to give children between the ages of three and six an idea about the differences between male and female bodies. It was made on a shoestring, with just Kajsa, an animator, and a composer, Johan Holmström.* "We followed all the guidelines and ran it by the ministry for education," says Kajsa, "and it was intended as a playful extra for kids' TV show *Bacillakuten*, which airs on a Sunday. But it *exploded*."[8]

Snoppen & Snippan was uploaded to YouTube, classified as "adult content," and viewed 1.5 million times by Tuesday.

"Newspapers all over the world started writing about it. I had all these crazy messages, even threats, from the UK and the US."

So why the controversy?

The minute-long video opens with a catchy melody and rudimentary animation of a dancing penis, or *snoppen* in colloquial Swedish.

"Here comes a willy like a kangaroo," a cheery voice sings

---

* Who also composed the music to the game Candy Crush, downloaded by 1.7 billion worldwide. Fun fact.

as a dismembered phallus with big Disney eyes hops into the foreground.

O-kay...

"All the girls think it's excellent."

A heart-shaped *snippan* (slang for female genitalia in Swedish) with enormous eyes and thick lashes whizzes by before another snippan with a gray wig and a walking cane appears.

"Even graceful ladies think it's *elegant!*"

Other lyrics such as "the vagina is cool, you better believe it!" and "here comes the penis at full gallop" caused outrage.

Although, I think, *it can feel like a penis is coming at full gallop. Perhaps forewarned is forearmed?*

"Okay, so we ended up teaching a lot of kids in Sweden the word *snippan*," admits Kajsa, "but it's such a cute word! And it was just a fun, educational video for kids."

Eventually, YouTube agreed to remove their "adult" classification, since the video was neither targeting adults nor explicit. And everyone carried on as normal. At least in Sweden.

The Swedish National Agency for Education has a policy of "seizing every opportunity" for sex education.[9] As well as dedicated lessons, sex ed is integrated into every subject from biology to history, art, religion, physical education, even music, "looking at how gender, sexuality, and relationships are depicted in lyrics or music videos," I learn from the ministry. Then there's "the sex ed test," containing one hundred questions intended to inform pupils about relationships, love, "sexual terms they are likely to encounter," and pornography.

Pornography is included in the curriculum in several Danish

schools too, and Denmark was the first country in the world to lift the ban on pornography in 1967. Some experts want to go further still. Sexology professor Christian Graugaard of Aalborg University has suggested that pornography should be shown in schools as a way of teaching teenagers that it's nothing like real sex. "We know from research that a vast majority of teenagers have seen porn at an early age—so it's not a question of introducing youngsters to porn," he told me for a UK newspaper.[10] A Common Sense Media report from 2022 found that 73 per cent of children have watched pornography by the time they're seventeen—and more than half by the time they're thirteen.[11] Christian wants to make sure teens "possess the necessary skills" to view porn constructively and distinguish between the media's depictions of sex and everyday life.[12]

The Norwegian publicly funded broadcaster NRK has taken this into their own hands, publishing a sex guide of sixty different positions. (That's right: sixty. What have I been *doing* with my time?) This is accessible to all and modeled by real people in heterosexual and same-sex partnerships. Positions include Clamping Koala (sitting, facing one another, legs crossed at the ankle), the Speed Dump (captioned "drive carefully!"), and Can I Keep My Socks On? (okay, I made that one up).[13] At last count, the guide had six million page views—in a country of 5.4 million. NRK's editorial director explained, "I think a lot of people share the concern about how porn affects young people's sexuality, and appreciate the Sex Guide as an attempt to give a factual, nuanced, and realistic picture of what sex can be."[14]

Realistic sex? And honest depictions of what bodies look like? Whatever next?

"We just take a more practical approach," Veteran Viking tells me. "Sex is part of life so you may as well learn about it early on. Right?" I wonder whether now would be the time to remind her that I'm British and attended an all-girls school.

The age of consent is sixteen in Norway and Finland, the same as the UK and much of North America. In Denmark, Sweden, and Iceland, it's just fifteen. And for Icelanders, there's an added element to sex education for all ages. With a population of around 360,000 where almost everyone is distantly related, introductory questions at a bar to a prospective new beau can go something like, "What's your name? Do you come here often? Are you my cousin?"

Fortunately, Icelanders are now able to look each other up on an app to avoid accidental incest, technology only possible thanks to Iceland's online database holding genealogical details of almost the entire population, since most are descended from a group of ninth-century Viking settlers. The app lets users bump phones, setting off an "incest prevention alarm" if they are too closely linked. Islendinga-App—or "App of Icelanders"—is promoted with the catchy slogan, "Bump the app before you bump in bed!"

"Well, really!" is how my mother responds when I share this nugget. "It's all very no-nonsense, isn't it?" Her tone implies that she'd prefer a modicum of nonsense. But she won't find it here. Vikings don't muck about.

Later that week, I'm offered another decidedly sans-nonsense invitation. No koalas, apps, or cousins are involved, and I'm fully clothed. Although not everyone involved is.

To mark the fortieth anniversary of the definitive 1980s classic

Flashdance (anyone else feel old?), a local school is putting on a production, and would I like to come?

Would I! To see *Flashdance: The Musical*? Dialogue in Danish, songs in English? The story of Alex, welder by day, burlesque dancer by night? Yes please. Yes, I would.

After paying 25 DKK for entry and a program, sponsored by Lego Man's favorite DIY store (the one that sent him a loyalty dagger), I take my seat. As the production gets underway, it becomes clear that there are only two children with what my mother calls "the show-off gene" in a cast of fifty. They all seem pleased to be there but unwilling to take the spotlight or do anything solo. Some can sing. Some can dance. A few can act. But all three?

"It's hard to be a theater triple threat this early in life," murmurs my American Mom friend in the seat next to me. This may be true, but there is a certain irony to singing "dancing for my life" while standing stock-still. And then there are the scenes in the strip club.

"Is this appropriate? For a school production?" I whisper to American Mom. She's here to support her son, who's in the band. His younger brothers are also in attendance. I can only imagine the scenes at school tomorrow.

"You went to a play where high school kids stripped onstage? Yeah, sure you did."

Spoiler: this is not the raciest part. That comes as another actress disrobes to reveal dollar bills sticking out of her pants. And the younger brothers' jaws hit the floor.

"Don't tell Grandma!" I hear American Mom whisper.

It all ends happily as the stripper is "saved" by our heroine, who swaps welding for ballet, and they all pop on leg warmers and have a sing-along (naturally). And what would have been the stuff of *Daily Mail* fury in the UK—a comments section aflame with indignation, a school shut down even—is completely...normal.

We may not all be ready for Nordic-style liberalism just yet, but we can take steps in the right direction. To strip down, soap up, and embrace our real bodies—in all their bizarre and beautiful glory.

WHAT I'VE LEARNED ABOUT HOW TO RAISE BODY-NEUTRAL VIKINGS

- Using bodies for what they're meant for helps us feel better about them. We are all a collection of bits and should chill the heck out. If we can move our bodies, we should.

- Children shouldn't learn about bodies and sex from porn. Learning about real bodies, what they do, and our rights over them seems eminently more sensible. Sex is normal. Masturbation is normal. Everyone should have control over their own body.

- Think strong, not thin. How much disordered eating might have been avoided had we all grown up with this mantra? I wish I could go back to re-parent myself as a child and hammer this one home. Wouldn't it be lovely if the rest of the world caught on so that more young people can grow up happy, healthy, safe, and strong?

- If the opportunity arises to see an '80s musical, take it.

TEEN VIKING

THE OPENING SYNTHESIZER RIFF SOUNDS familiar. It's followed by a brassy sound as someone, somewhere, pounds a Yamaha. This isn't ideal as I'm trying to wrestle five-year-olds into the bath, persuading them it's bedtime despite bright sunshine outside. Although there's near perpetual darkness October to April, come June, it's light for twenty-one hours a day. Which means no one sleeps.

"What is that noise?" the eight-year-old demands over a galloping drum beat that sets hairs on the back of my neck on end. The music gets louder in the key of F-sharp minor as the iconic chords of Swedish rock band Europe's "The Final Countdown" power out and a truck rolls into view. It's an open-air affair with no seats, much less safety belts, probably used for livestock ordinarily. But today, the truck is equipped with massive loudspeakers and decorated with ribbons and handmade banners. Spray-painted down the side of one of these are the words *Hvem fuck er Macbeth?!*

I do a quick translation: "Who the f**k is Macbeth?" *What is going on?*

There's whooping and cheering as the truck pulls to a stop,

brakes emitting a hissing sound. A metal ladder clanks against the pavement, and teenagers in shorts and sailor caps spill out, navigating their way with sea legs (or "beer legs" as I discover). Like a clown car, they disembark in numbers that scarcely seem plausible. *Fifteen? Twenty? More?*

They arrange themselves into two lines facing each other, then join hands to form a tunnel. A boy I vaguely recognize descends from the steps to rapturous cheers.

Is that...? Could that be? The chatty neighbor's son? The boy who was playing with toy diggers in the garden only two minutes ago?

In a burst of brazen glory, he runs under the hands of his friends, arms outstretched. At the end of the human tunnel, the boy takes to one knee as a tube of plastic is lowered into his mouth...and a pint of beer is poured in the other end.

Good grief. He's not playing diggers any more, Toto.

"What is *happening*?" the redhead shouts over the regular deafening beat.

"It's the final countdown!" Lego Man is transfixed.

"Or rather graduation," I add, "Danish style." Because for two weeks in June, the streets are full of animal transporters, tractors, old army trucks, or even horse-drawn carriages carrying high school students. Nineteen-year-olds who have finished secondary education are driven around their hometown by a designated driver, visiting every classmate's house to celebrate. I've seen it from afar during our years of living Danishly, but this is the first time I've had a ringside view.

Graduating in Denmark is far more fun than cider and a scotch egg in the park circa 1998... I reflect on my own salad days and feel an overwhelming sense of goodwill for these young people and all that lies ahead of them. By the looks of it, the rest of the neighborhood is experiencing a similar swell of nostalgia. Most are now out in support, raising a glass to the neighborhood teen. I'd quite like to join this bacchanalian scene, but I have two butt-naked bath refuseniks. So instead, I watch from our balcony, like a low-rent Evita.

The smalls try every postponing ploy in their repertoire, but we finally get them to bath and bed with a mixture of Jesper Juul straight talking and basic bribery. ("Mommy and Daddy need to relax now. You can stay up late on the weekend. Yes, I'll play you 'The Final Countdown' at breakfast.") Once the coast is clear, we sneak downstairs to see if we can swing an invitation to what is clearly the hottest party in town.

Strangely, no invitation is forthcoming.

"I wonder why a load of nineteen-year-olds don't want to hang out with two really tired parents in their forties?" Lego Man asks.

"Weird," I agree.

Digger Boy's parents, however, are happy to chat—over the hedge and the dulcet tones of "Don't Leave Me This Way" by the Communards.

These people were born in the 2000s. How do they know the Communards?

"What's with the hats?" Lego Man asks. "Sailor theme?"

Our chatty neighbor explains that when the final exam of secondary school is completed, they get a *studenterhue*—the Danish word for the cap that all students wear when they graduate. This is usually white with a black peak and a ribbon to indicate what kind of education a student has. Red signifies the standard high school education, like our neighbor's son and his pals. If you've studied at a specialist trade or technical school, you go blue, farmers get green, and hairdressers get pink (please...).

I notice that many of the hats have an emblem resembling the Maltese cross.

"This symbolizes the cross on our Dannebrog—the Danish flag," says Chatty Neighbor, explaining that in more inclusive and enlightened recent years, students can also opt for the Star of David or the Islamic crescent instead. She tells me it's customary for students in the year below to decorate the truck.

"And...Macbeth?" I point at the banner.

"They studied it. Some of the kids had a hard time getting with Shakespeare."

Lego Man nods knowingly.

"But that's all over now," says Chatty Neighbor.

"Now, we party," her more taciturn husband adds, with a nod to his glass.

The partying starts early at 8:00 a.m.. Trucks pick up students to drive about, honking horns, singing, dancing, drinking, and stopping at each classmate's house for a mini party with family and family friends. The last house on the route hosts the after-party, then the bus drops everyone home ordinarily. This ritual ride is thought of so fondly that it has even been described as an expression of Danish civil religion.[1]

Because it's Denmark, there are rules attached, obviously (#rooligans). These vary from school to school, but my neighbors—and various teens who lurch up to say "hej"—fill me in on key protocols.

"If you have the biggest hat, you have to give everyone in your class a beer. If you have the smallest hat, you have to give everyone in your class a beer. If you have the highest grades, you have to give everyone in your class a beer. And if you have the lowest grades—"

"Let me guess. You give everyone in your class a beer?"

"How did you know?"

"Just a hunch. So basically, in most scenarios, you have to give everyone in your class a beer."

She grins. Tousled youths stumble over one another like drunk puppies, finishing each other's sentences in increasingly slurred Danglish. Most Danes speak excellent English, having learned it at folkeskole, but no one expects fluency after funneling beer since 8:00 a.m.

"If the party lasts until sunrise—" a blond in pigtails tells me.

"—you cut a triangle in the sweatband!" a girl in a bikini top butts in.

"And if you have *sex*—"

"—you cut a lightning bolt in it!" a reed-thin boy yells to be heard over the din. "But if you score with a teacher, you tear the white cover off your cap!"

There is a hiatus in the music. (Wham! Thanks for asking.) We all look at him.

"Has that *ever* happened?" Lego Man is suspicious.

"My brother knew a guy whose *cousin* once did."

Taciturn Neighbor shakes his head and calls it: "Bullshit." We nod in agreement, and Andrew Ridgeley starts up again.

"Oh, and there's one more," Chatty Neighbor adds, pointing at the brook running past the end of our garden. "If you jump in the water with only the student cap on, you cut a wave in the sweatband of the cap."

"Like that guy?" Lego Man asks.

"Halløj, sir!" A naked youth addresses him from the river, beaming.

Within moments, there's another. And another. And another. I haven't seen this many nineteen-year-old boys' bottoms since... well, we've all had our fun summers. I spot the neighbor's son and try to keep my eyes above waist level.

The fat-cheeked boy who used to play with toy diggers in the front garden now has a six-pack?

It's true what American Mom always says about parenting: the days are long, but the years are short.

When did this happen? And how long before it happens to my kids? The redhead is already eight. How long until I'm dealing with teenagers?

"Couple of years. Three, tops." Taciturn Neighbor shrugs. My alarm must be evident as Chatty Neighbor sends her husband away in search of "the good scissors" ("to cut the waves"). But the question of when a mini Viking tips into a teen preoccupies me. In bed that night, I stare at the ceiling, pondering, eventually dropping off before the birds begin their morning chorus at 3:00 a.m. Like sadists.

When does teenaging start? My worry machine begins again.

"When they're confirmed," says my Veteran Viking mother in arms at school drop-off. Despite being a largely secular country, Denmark has a state Lutheran church to which 74 percent of the population belong.[2] In seventh grade—age thirteen or fourteen— teens are invited to *gå til præst,* or go to the priest, to learn about the Bible and chat about life's big questions. But there's no pressure to *actually* believe since the Danish ceremony is about God saying yes to you and not the other way around. Once teens have read up on the good book, there's a church ceremony with boys in suits and girls in fancy dresses. After this, there's a lunch for family and friends where the newly confirmed give heartfelt speeches, a crippling prospect for most thirteen-year-olds but one that Danish teens take in their stride. And then? The main event: swag. Because guests gift *generously.*

The average teen will receive confirmation gifts worth between 16,000 and 20,000 DKK ($2,300–$2,900), according to a survey by Danish bank Nordea.[3] Popular wish list items include iPads, laptops, cameras, or phones, but teens also accept cold hard cash.

"The amount you give as a guest should be the amount spent on entertaining you," says Veteran Viking, adding that the closer you are to the family, the more you're expected to give. The gifting part of confirmation culture in Denmark is so entrenched that teens get the day off school after their confirmation ceremony to go on a shopping spree. I comment that this all sounds mercenary, but another parent who runs a clothes shop shut me down. She tells me *konfirmander*—the newly confirmed—are a big driver of the local economy. She's already ordered in extra stock in anticipation of "Blue Monday" as it's known.

"Okay, so they've shopped. They've had their first young adult initiation. What next?"

Veteran Viking looks at me as though I am an idiot (again). With a deep sigh that suggests this is the most obvious thing in the world, she replies, "*Efterskole* of course."

Of course!

This is the uniquely Danish boarding school her middle child has been attending for the past few months that sounds like a cross between a hippie commune and Hogwarts. So I start investigating.

"*Efterskoler* have been around for about 150 years, and they're something Denmark does really well for its teenagers," says Jakob Clausager Jensen. Jakob works for Denmark's efterskole association, but he also attended one in his youth, taught at one for eight years, and is currently sending his daughter to one (so he's a fan). Jakob tells me that a quarter of all Danish teenagers attend efterskole between the ages of fourteen and sixteen between their friskole or folkeskole (normal school) and gymnasium (the one with the sailor hats) as a sort of optional year or two out.[4] Although they offer general education, the primary task of efterskole is to prepare you for life. "You're there twenty-four seven so you have to be yourself," says Jakob. "You figure out who you really are."[5]

Working out who you really are at sixteen? Just think of the decades of therapy saved if we all took this path.

"It's not like an English boarding school either," says Jakob. I only need to walk around the light and airy yet simultaneously intimate efterskole near me to pick up this vibe. "At efterskole, everyone is equal." Each member of staff has ten students for whom they are the contact teacher, together from the time they awake to the time they go to bed. "So saying good night can take a long time as students like to talk and often have questions right before sleep," says Jakob, "but this means teachers have to be their authentic selves too. And they get to teach their hobbies or specializations. Both sides benefit."

Independence is celebrated and students are encouraged to be self-reliant, working things out with their peers or their contact teacher rather than parents. "We're trying to prepare them for life," explains teacher Michelle Brogaard from Fjordvang Efterskole in West Jutland. "So we'll say, 'Is this something you can work through with your contact teacher? Or with one of your friends?' If it's not, then they're welcome to call home, but often they feel proud that they handled something by themselves. They feel a sense of mastery and confidence—and they know for next time."[6] (#mastery.)

"Often for the first week or even the first two months, there's a no-phone policy," says Jakob. "Kids may find this annoying for the first day, but after two months, they say it's amazing. They've never felt so free." After my depressing deep dive into Denmark's digital blind spot, I believe him.

"You can go home on weekends if you want," says one of Michelle's contact students, "but actually, you make friends quickly and have this great environment, so often we don't. You know your contact teacher is there for you if you need them. And you learn to do a lot for yourself."

Students take turns cleaning the school and feeding around 150 pupils daily. It was at efterskole that Trine Hahnemann cemented her love of cooking. "We would do it on rotation normally," she tells me, "but I found I really liked it and I was good at it. And efterskoler are very democratic...so everyone took a vote, and it was decided that I should cook every day. That was quite something, age sixteen, cooking for one hundred fifty kids daily!"[7]

I ask if it's too early to sign up an eight-year-old ("or five-year-old twins...?").

How much you pay for efterskole depends on how much you earn, with the remainder paid for by the government. On the average Danish salary of 540,000 DKK (around $77,000), parents pay around 60,000 DKK ($8,500). "But that's for the whole year, including boarding, lessons, food, school trips—everything," says Jakob. This is still a significant outlay but nothing like the amount you might pay elsewhere (oh hi, England's Eton at $57,500 per year). And it's clearly accessible to many Danes. A quarter of them, in fact.

Studies show that efterskole students are more likely to complete upper secondary education (with 16 percent less risk of dropping out), and there's a "schoolmate effect," where stronger students lift weaker students up.[8] "Which is probably why the Danish government keeps funding it," says Jakob.

There's now interest in setting up efterskoler overseas. "From Japan and Korea especially," says Jakob. "I get about twenty-five groups of Korean educators each year coming to Denmark, and Korea is building five hundred efterskole-inspired schools. These are in opposition to the results-focused, high-pressured, disciplined academic schools Korea is so famous for." Parents from overseas can also enroll children in Danish efterskoler, two of which are completely in English. "There's no pupil subsidy for international students, but the price isn't more expensive than private schools around the world," says Jakob.

My teacher friend Anne from choir tells me she can always spot efterskole alumni in her gymnasium class at the start of each year. "They're much more grounded and mature. You just become centered at efterskole. Not self-centered but centered. Efterskole is like adult life with training wheels. You have someone to show you how to do your laundry, and then you *know* how to do your own laundry, age sixteen."

I once knew a thirty-year-old who didn't know how to do his laundry, so this sounds brilliant.

The next step in state-funded education for teens with more practical aptitudes or interests may be a trade school to train in skills like metalwork, electrical engineering, or mechanics. Then there are business schools where you specialize in anything from software to accounting, all completely funded by taxes. More academic students opt for gymnasium, where students continue their general education with obligatory subjects but also choose fields of study to prepare them for university. These range from math and sciences to languages, social studies, music, and arts. The student day starts at 8:00 a.m. and goes until 3:00 or 3:30 p.m., but homework ramps up to one and a half to two hours a day and ten hours a week for written assignments.

Danish gymnasiums are often a culture shock after a cozy folkeskole. They're big, for starters, with vast atriums, extensive technical facilities, and common rooms with more microwave doors pinging than can possibly be necessary for an army of ravenous teenagers. Students starting gymnasium after years of laid-back Scandinavian schooling can find the academic escalation demanding.

"These kids may have been the best in their folkeskole, with the highest grades, but now they're at gymnasium with other kids who were best in *their* school, and that's tough for many," says Anne. "We try not to dramatize the impact of grades. In the first year, you don't get a grade at all until the end of the year. But statistically, they can't all get good grades. So there's a learning curve." As local teacher Louise explained, graduating teens are given a grade between -3 ("not so good") and 12 ("the best"). It's hard work, even for those getting a double zero—or "the glasses grade." So afterward, they go *bananas*.

As another truck of beer-swigging students passes by the end of the street, I ask Anne: Has being a teenager in Denmark always been so boozy?

She laughs. "Danes do tend to drink...with enthusiasm, shall we say. And we start early."

Danes are legally allowed to buy alcohol up to 6 percent proof from the age of sixteen. For anything else, it's eighteen. Swedes and Norwegians can go to bars from eighteen, but the only way to buy anything stronger than a light beer for home consumption is by going to a state-run shop—a *systembolaget* in Sweden or a *vinmonopolet* in Norway. These have limited opening hours and are closed on Sundays, so although Swedes and Norwegians love a drink, buying alcohol isn't easy. Finns have to wait until they turn twenty to drink legally. In the US, it's twenty-one, and parents can be charged if they give their children alcohol under age.

So why are Danes so accepting of teenage drinking?

Efforts to raise the legal age in Denmark to eighteen for all types of alcohol have met with resistance, predominantly because older adults recall their own youthful intoxications with such fondness. "Being a young person in Denmark is and will be inextricably linked to alcohol and drinking. It's part of who we are," wrote anthropologist Maja Gildin Zuckerman. "We toast with them when they are 15 and pick them up at the emergency room after their stomachs are pumped when they are 16."[9] She's not joking: a WHO report found that Danish fifteen-year-olds consumed alcohol at double the European average.[10]

"We learn from our parents!" slurs a beery-smelling boy in a sailor's hat when he hears me talking teen liquor with my American Mom friend.

We're at a coffee shop in the porny pony town, and the boy has long curly hair escaping either side of his cap. His eyes look familiar. Then I notice a love bite on his neck.

Love Bite? The pool-noodle-dangling "coach" from the twins' "splash and play" swim class? He speaks!

He seems to have a vague awareness of who I am at the same moment.

"Oh, hi!"

"Hi! Sorry, I didn't recognize you with your clothes on."

American Mom's eyebrows raise, and coffee sloshes over the side of her cup.

"Swimming," I manage to mumble. "Teacher."

She flashes him a Whitestrips-bright smile. He gives a wink and lurches off.

American Mom fans herself and asks if they need any more "helpers" at swimming.

I tell her no unless she's into green bags. But his observation gets me thinking. Danes have the highest rates of heavy, episodic drinking of any country in the EU as well as the highest proportion of those who would categorize themselves as "drinkers" (97.1 percent of men and 95.3 percent of women).[11] Danish director Thomas Vinterberg explored Denmark's drinking culture in his 2020 film, *Another Round,* or *Druk* as it's called in Danish. *Druk* translates as "binge drinking." And yes: the fact that Danes have such a short, catchy word for a complete bender speaks volumes.

In the film, four teachers at a gymnasium in Copenhagen are inspired by Norwegian psychiatrist Finn Skårderud's theory that people have a natural alcohol deficiency. Skårderud speculated that a blood alcohol content of 0.05 percent could rectify this, making us more creative and relaxed. The four friends decide to try it, staying moderately drunk at all times and citing Hemingway and Churchill as inspirations (although Hemingway let a cat babysit his son, so the red flag was there).

Everyone in the film is having a lovely time ("I haven't felt this good in ages!" says Mads Mikkelsen's Martin).[12] But things don't stay that way. Because sadly, microdosing alcohol to improve performance doesn't work. Studies now show that analytical problem-solving skills suffer across *all* levels of alcohol consumption, and microdosing soon turns to macrodosing as we drink more to maintain blood-alcohol concentration.[13] But the film sparked debate, both globally and in my living room.

"Good or bad?" Lego Man stared at the screen, then his wineglass, then me. "Drinking: good or bad?"

"I don't think it's as simple as that," I began, but he was already searching for answers on his phone.

"American reviewers say bad."

I peered over his shoulder at review upon review from North America discussing the film in terms of an antialcohol polemic. But to me, it seemed largely...joyous.

I know what you're thinking: "Is this because she's a wild party animal? A debauched hedonist? A hell-raiser?" To which the answer is no. I am a tired parent of small children, someone who *used* to drink but now delivers green bags for ballet club. If anything, I am a hell-*lowerer* these days. I'm the person at a wedding who says, "Why don't we all get in a water round!" But at the start of the *Druk* film, all four men are stuck. They embark on the experiment, have a great time, until one of them—who was unhappy before—stops having fun. It's a trajectory I don't think I'd mind. This could be my fatalistic Catholic upbringing, but still.

"Or maybe you're becoming more Danish," Lego Man speculated.

I wonder...

Thomas Vinterberg spoke to the *New York Times* about Danish drinking, saying, "We have this very constant, very chaste debate about alcohol. But we also drink like Vikings. Whether it comes to sex or fighting," he added, "it helps us lose control."[14] Most Danes, when sober, are pretty controlled. So I can see where he's coming from.

The UK has its own issues with alcohol. Brits abroad have quite the reputation, and teenage drinking has been a rite of passage for generations. I drank on a weekly basis from the age of fourteen, which horrifies me now but wasn't unusual at the time. Whereas my American Mom friend grew up in the US with breathalyzers before every dance in high school. "Also, it wasn't cleaned in between students. And we wondered why we all got sick after... *But in Denmark? Everyone drinks!*"

As well as Denmark's established drinking traditions, there's a new craze most of us didn't grow up with. "The beer bong trend scares me," says Line, mother of three. These are the long tubes of plastic that I saw our neighbor's son subjected to. *Ølbonger*—or beer bongs—are available in supermarkets come graduation, and a popular online shop called Party Vikings has Europe's largest selection, describing *ølbonger* as "must-haves for festive occasions."[15]

"It wasn't like that when we were kids," reflects Veteran Viking, "but there was a lot of drinking. We feel like hypocrites if we're strict on this." So she isn't. Neither are many Danish parents. "Instead, we talk to our kids about how much to drink," says Line, "what drinks to be more careful of, to look after their friends, call us if they get in trouble." And, presumably, hope for the best.

I think about some of the messes I got myself into as a teenager. *And in my twenties. And my thirties...* Experimenting is part of growing up. We all do daft things and learn from them, hopefully. But I'd rather my kids didn't do the daft things after five beer bongs.

Binges aside, drinking culture is changing in Denmark. A study from Aarhus University found in 2021 that alcohol-related liver disease has actually been declining in Denmark for the past twenty-five years.[16] Generations born after the 1960s are more aware of the risk factors of episodic drinking and more health conscious. And global data on deaths from alcohol-associated liver diseases (cheery reading) now puts Denmark on a par with the US and the UK—far lower than Germany, Russia, and parts of Asia.[17]

Guidelines on alcohol consumption vary, and the UK government advises no more than fourteen units a week. In the US, it's fourteen for men and seven for women. The Danish health authority changed its guidelines in 2022 to recommend that adults consume no more than ten drinks a week—whatever their gender. Young people under the age of eighteen are advised not to drink *at all* under the new guidelines. And since 2023, those under eighteen have been banned from buying alcohol in nightlife areas after 10 p.m.

Line's middle child recently graduated, and she hosted the

after-party for all his friends. "Those young people were just awe-some—so kind and polite, even later in the evening. They complimented our garden, the food we served, my dress. They apologized for spilling stuff and came running to tidy up. They asked if we needed help and turned the music down when we asked them to. They looked after each other and laughed and sang the night away. I know this is not always the behavior of all Danish youth. I just think these young people give me hope for the future."

Parents enjoying the company of well-behaved teenagers? What mischief is this? Perhaps Danish teenagers are just...nicer. Does all this freedom actually pay off?

"Danish parents can seem super loosey-goosey when it comes to teenagers," says Marie Helweg-Larsen, the psychologist. "They allow alcohol at ninth grade parties, let their dating teens co-sleep, and have very little after-school supervision. At the same time, they expect teens to hold a conversation with adults around the dinner table, be polite when visiting their friends' houses, and take responsibility for their school projects. Permissiveness paired with responsibility might be the way to go. Maybe it makes for really good people in the end."[18]

Line thinks so: "My children are now sixteen, nineteen, and twenty-two, and it has never been more wholly joyful to be their parent." Every parent back home who I later recount this too will roll their eyes in disbelief or look as though they're about to vomit, cynics that we are. But for Danes, it's the truth. "In the last seven or eight years, I have just found it even more intensely gratifying to spend time with them and talk to them," says Line. "I didn't expect this at all. It's a surprise and joy after always hearing how horrible teenagers are."

"It's the same in Sweden," says Lisolette in Uppsala. "Teenagers get a bad reputation. Everyone is always asking me, 'How were the teenage years as a parent for you?!' They're expecting the answer to be 'a nightmare' but no, they were lovely. Easy, even."

Just one criticism is leveled, again and again, at teens who haven't been to efterskole.

"They can't mop for shit," Peter Schmeichel tells me.

"Sorry?"

"Have you asked an eighteen-year-old intern to mop something recently?"

I shake my head.

"I have. They can't!"

I mention this to prison guard turned pedagogue Kitta at børne-have pickup. "That sounds right," she says. "I see a big difference in the young helpers who come to work with us now to, say, ten years ago. Back then, a young person could see what needed to be done and just do it. They could take the initiative. But an eighteen- or nineteen- or even twenty-year-old these days? No! They are babied for too long!"

Chef Jacob Holmström tells me about the student helpers he works with at his restaurants in Sweden. "These kids are eighteen or nineteen, and they have no idea how to iron a shirt or vacuum or mop! At the restaurant, you iron your own chef's uniform, and they don't know how to do it! I will say to them, 'Is this the first time you're doing this?' They'll nod. I'll say things like, 'Okay, today I will show you how an iron works. Tomorrow, we'll move on to mops.' My parents would never have allowed that!"[19]

I vow here and now not to let my mini Vikings get away with it either.

Back on the street where I live, the neighbors and a few

surprisingly spritely teens are clearing up after last night's festivities. Garden furniture gets stacked, gazebos dismantled, and bottles collected until all is neat and ordered once more. The day is overcast, but my neighbors are wearing sunglasses, moving slowly, and lowering chairs with care to avoid a clang.

Ouch, that must hurt. A hangover when you're fifty is very different from a hangover when you're nineteen.

I see Digger Boy—now, thankfully, clothed—and announce to my family, "I'm buying a mop." Four faces turn to me. "For the neighbor's son! He didn't go to efterskole, so he needs to learn how to use one before university!"

My family looks at me in horror.

"That's a terrible idea," the redhead announces.

Lego Man nods in agreement.

"What? I'll put a bow on it. He'll be leaving home soon. His flatmates will thank me. As well as any future partner."

There is debate. We settle on a mop *and* an Apple music gift card. Everyone's happy. I pop to the shop after dinner, then the redhead and I troop around to deliver our bounty.

Chatty Neighbor answers the door slowly, still wearing sunglasses. "Hiii," she croaks. "Coffee?"

It's 6:30 p.m.! Who does she think I am? Ozzy Osbourne?

"No, thank you. We just wanted to pass on this."

I nudge the redhead to proffer the present and a polite if baffled teen is summoned.

"Err, thanks?" He looks at the mop and then the printout of the gift card. "Wow, thanks!"

On the way back, my son takes a final lingering look at the truck.

It belongs to a family friend, so there's less of a hurry to get it back than usual. Several stragglers are now taking selfies with it while the redhead watches with interest.

Presently, he points to the banner hanging on the truck.

"Mom?"

"Yes?"

"Who the fuck *is* Macbeth?"

Oh, so now the kid can read? Great. Just great.

WHAT I'VE LEARNED ABOUT
HOW TO RAISE A TEEN VIKING

◆ Let them do what they want, and try not to panic. They'll probably turn out quite nice. This feels radical, both in terms of permissiveness and the idea that teenagers aren't total nightmares. But perhaps they don't have to be. Perhaps, if we expect them to be polite, engaged, thoughtful human beings, they'll step up (that, or take up joyriding).

◆ Adolescents are allowed to hate us and push all the boundaries, but they also have to feel that they can talk to a trusted adult when they want to. When the fecal matter hits the rotary impeller—and it will—we need to be there. I have no desire to be one of those "cool parents" (why break the habit of a lifetime?), but I can *listen* when they need me and/or deign to speak to me. Not just for my kids but for my friends' kids and my kids' friends. I could have used this as a teenager, so I'm all in for the next generation.

◆ Teach teens how to mop, iron, clean, and do laundry. Future employers, partners, flatmates, and the general cosmos will thank us for it.

Epilogue

~~~

THE LIGHTS ARE OFF AND there's fidgeting in anticipation. I'm glancing sideways at silhouettes in the twilight when a clear note breaks the silence: the plink-plonk opening of Chris Rea's "Driving Home for Christmas." The redhead has turned on the radio and lo! By a festive fluke! It's Chris. Again. It's December, when Danes can't get enough of "Driving Home for Christmas," despite the fact that the country is so small, even the most ambitious journey tops out at around four hours. "Or sixty plays of 'Driving Home for Christmas,'" says Lego Man. He recently discovered that Chris Rea also hails from his hometown of Middlesborough and has taken him to heart like a long-lost uncle.

"Okay, here goes," I announce, plugging in fairy lights and *ta-da!* Nothing happens. The fuse has blown. Again. We live in an old house, so this is par for the course. I make my way to the under-stairs cupboard to flick on the power but notice how beautiful it is in the darkness. A sprinkling of powdery snow is falling out-side, and our neighbors' houses are lit by candles. Wafts of *gløgg*—Danish mulled wine—fill the street whenever a front door opens.

And this happens regularly, since there seems to be a near-constant stream of comers and goers. Because this is peak visiting season.

"Christmas in Denmark is all about the family," says Danish cultural sociologist Emilia van Hauen. "We celebrate on the twenty-fourth but really the whole of December is considered a special family time."[1]

In the UK, Christmas is cited as a source of major stress, up there with divorce and moving house supposedly. But Danes deck the halls with family all month long. Seeing more of them in the run-up to Christmas counterintuitively *reduces* stress on the big day. "It's less of a shock to the system," explains Veteran Viking. Familiarity can breed *content*. "So if you have a difference of opinion with a family member, you're likely to have dealt with it at some point during the year *before* Christmas."

My mother comes to stay ("You look tired, darling!" "Thank you!"), and everyone pitches in to lay the table and peel potatoes. Danes eat duck or pork with a dash of cabbage and potatoes two ways: boiled and caramelized (hence the team effort on peeling). Once we've eaten, it's time for *pakkeleg*. This a high-octane form of pass the parcel where everyone brings a wrapped gift, throws a die for the chance to win one, then throws *again* to steal other people's, stockpiling as many as possible for themselves. An early lesson for the children in life's harsh realities from the nation that brought us Nordic noir.

"Then you light real candles on the tree, and everyone holds hands and dances around it. *Carefully*," Veteran Viking emphasizes. I have experience here: early adoption of this tradition in our first year of living Danishly necessitated a fire extinguisher. Clever

Danes leave their trees outside until Christmas Eve. I, however, get overexcited and crack the first time I hear "Driving Home for Christmas" on the radio. Our tree is fully lit come December 1 and dry as an IKEA flat-pack furniture manual come the twenty-fourth. So we dance carefully and stick with tradition by singing a few songs from the ubiquitous *High School Songbook*. All manner of hygge ensues, before *presents*.

Christmas gifting can be another source of stress for those of us who aren't naturally talented shoppers. (Me. I mean me. Sorry.) There's also the angst of ingratitude and fake enthusiasm for giftees. ("What am I supposed to do with this cat bowl? I haven't got a cat." "Why have I been given a Lush bath bomb? It isn't 1995.") I read a study telling me that people in the UK spent £2.6 billion on unwanted gifts, but Danes do things differently.[2] "There's no sentimentality. If we don't like something, it's perfectly normal to take it back," says Veteran Viking. "Don't you have a saying in English, 'it's the thought that counts'?"

"We do. We just don't tend to *mean* it."

But Danes are more honest (or brutal), reducing stress all around. Most items bought from November onward come with a gift return sticker over the price to show where it came from but avoid any awkwardness over receipts. This way, everyone gets something and can exchange it for what they really want after Christmas. A gift shift that makes my festive season about 50 percent more enjoyable.

In Denmark, the big guy in the red-and-white suit comes bearing gifts for children on Christmas Eve. But there are no middle-of-the-night magic chimney antics. Whichever family member fits the Julemand (Christmas Man) outfit just dresses up and chucks some presents around. By this stage, Danes have already hosted enchanted mythical creatures for almost a month in the form of a *nisse*—the original "elf on the shelf." Mercurial and mischievous, Danish *nisser* wreak havoc on homes from the first of December. At least they do if you install a nisse door, a miniature ladder, and furniture (available at all good supermarkets). According to tradition, if nisser are treated well, they protect the family from misfortune and help with housework. In my experience, you can treat nisser like kings, and they'll still trash the place daily. Pranks vary according to who gets to nisse duty first of an evening at my house. Last year's gems included removing all furniture (Lego Man's work), covering the house in toilet paper (ditto), dyeing the milk blue with food coloring (guess who?), and leaving the kitchen table strewn with underpants (honestly, it's exhausting). They also made snow angels (adorable), lovingly crafted an advent calendar (ditto), and left heartfelt notes to each child (me, obviously).

Yuletide traditions differ across the region with Swedes gathering at 3:00 p.m. on Christmas Eve every year to watch *Donald Duck and His Friends Wish You a Merry Christmas*. The habit took hold in 1958 and is now observed by 50 percent of Swedes.[3] "And no, no one knows why," says my friend Niki in Malmö. As the credits roll, there's a knock on the door to reveal...Tomten—Santa in Swedish. Sadly, a male member of the family will usually be missing at this point, having made an untimely trip to the bathroom.

For those without any Santa-esque relatives, Stockholm's biggest taxi company offers extra services come Christmas. Jouni Talso is one of twenty-five kindly old gentlemen preapproved for the prestigious role of mobile Tomten. For the past twenty years, he's dressed up in red and white on December 24 to make house calls and spread good cheer. "Their faces light up when they see Santa, actually on their doorstep!" says Jouni. Word to the wise for anyone tempted to Tomten it: this tradition does mean that Swedish children stop believing in Santa earlier, at "around six or seven years old," Jouni tells me. "Children from the US and the UK tend to believe for longer as they never see him. He comes at night, and they think he lives far away, so they've always had to just believe. But Nordic children see Santa every year in the flesh, and they know that Santa comes from near where they live. There's less mystique so it's over quicker!"[4]

I don't want it to be over quicker. As American Mom keeps reminding me, "The days are long, but the years are short!"

Couldn't the days be slightly shorter? The years a tad longer? Would that be too much to ask?

Yesterday, my daughter had her first sleepover. I ate two rounds of jam and cheese on rye bread and rewatched *The Killing* to stave off tears. My son still calls his front teeth his "smilies," and I never want him to stop. His brother starts each day by playing C+C Music Factory's "Gonna Make You Sweat (Everybody Dance Now)" and throwing some phenomenal shapes (that he definitely hasn't inherited from his parents). I would happily take this as my wake-up call for the next decade.

The neighbor's son, Digger Boy, is home from his first term at university, while our couple-about-town neighbors on the other side are expecting.

"Expecting...Santa?" the youngest says, eyes wide.

"No, darling, a baby," I explain.

He looks disappointed. But I realize that in the space of three homes on our street, the span of all childhood is here—a selection of Vikings at various stages of their lives.

"Give me a child until they're seven, and I'll show you the adult," as Aristotle should have said. (He didn't. He just banged on about boys.) I know that the foundational elements of childhood are happening. Right now. They may have happened already in the case of the eight-year-old.

So how to make the most of the childhood they have left? I wonder, folding too-small snowsuits from the clean laundry to pass on, keenly aware that Christmas marks the passing of another year. I want to imbue my children with *sisu* like the Finns, *friluftsliv* like the Norwegians, a healthy approach to bodies like the Swedes, an Icelandic love of books, and a hefty dollop of Danish *ramasjang*.

"You're doing it! You're here, aren't you?" American Mom has dropped by to deliver Christmas gifts (complete with return stickers) and join us for a festive drink. "Growing up here, it changes them. No matter where they go or what happens next."

I wish I could be so confident ("Or just American?" Lego Man suggests). I wish I could bottle a little of that Viking spirit and export it. I know that the package of ideas can't be shipped wholesale, but there are elements we can strive toward. Like better parental leave, for the impact this has not only on parents but on children and future generations. The Nordic model is based on the idea that both parents work, so affordable high-quality childcare is a prerequisite.

"But in the US and the UK, it's increasingly necessary to have two incomes," Trine Hahnemann points out, "only there isn't the childcare in place."[5]

Remember the stats? Every dollar invested in early childhood education yields a 150 percent return. Minimum. Childcare pays for itself. And planning for a good childhood is better (and cheaper) than fixing things later.

Rather than an obsession with left hemisphere schooling, Nordics take the whole person into account. I've warmed to the idea of letting children play for longer and start school later in the hope that they'll carry on learning throughout their lives, should they choose. This helps to future proof the next generation. Economists predict that by 2050, 40 percent of current jobs will be lost to automation.[6] We don't know what jobs our children will be doing yet, but we know they'll need adaptability, curiosity, and open-mindedness to do them. Learning how to think—rather than *what* to think—feels more important than ever.

Higher education in the Nordic countries is free, so young people don't typically choose a university course based on any future income it may bring—they choose it because they're interested. Danes are even paid to study with monthly state educational support known as SU (Statens Uddannelsesstøtte), from 1,024 DKK a month if you live at home ($147) to 6,589 DKK if you don't ($949). Parents aren't obliged to remortgage the house or sell a vital organ to fund university, so there's greater opportunity for social mobility in the Nordic countries than elsewhere. The UK and the US score shamefully in terms of social mobility, and the earnings of American men are more closely tied to the earnings of their fathers than men in any other country in the world.[7] But in Denmark? Not so much.

"So you know, a good reason to stick around," as American Mom always says. She's here for the long haul and thinks I should be too. And a lot of things look better on paper in Denmark.

Mini Vikings are given freedom. With this comes responsibility and a degree of self-sufficiency that I've come to cherish. "The self-governing way we treat and raise little people is something I think Denmark gets right," says Ning de Coninck-Smith. "Take the snowsuit."[8]

Not what I was expecting, but go on.

"The snowsuit is a major emblem of Danish childhood."

I think about this. Snowsuits don't come cheap in Denmark—costing upward of $120—and they usually have to be replaced each year as the child grows. But every parent in Denmark will make the investment or borrow one for their child, then pass it on once they've outgrown it, as I'm doing now. A snowsuit is seen as something to prioritize. And this is how it should be, according to Ning. "It means you can be outdoors all day. Children can get it on and off by themselves. No rain or snow or sleet can hurt them. And they've been designed with children in mind, so there will be big zips, on both sides if needed, for whichever side is easiest for that child. I know that there are lots of issues, but we do think about children for the most part in Denmark. There is respect." It's rare that you see a wealthy society where children are taken seriously. But in Denmark, they are. By everyone. Mini Vikings have a voice, and they're taught to use it.

"You have to speak out," says Peter Schmeichel. "You have to. Otherwise..."

I know what he's going to say. "1940?"

"Exactly."

Denmark's occupation still looms large in the public consciousness, and the Second World War has influenced the way my children are being raised in ways I could never have foreseen. Growing up with grandparents' tales of wartime valor, there wasn't much thought given to how the Nordic countries fared. But the legacy of war is everywhere. I live opposite an old bomb shelter. Last week, we found the shell casing from a WWII tank in the woods. Writing at a time of the war in Ukraine and hearing first-person stories—never far away when you're on mainland Europe—brings home the realities of conflict. War lives on in our collective memory, and Danes aren't afraid of talking about it. They're not afraid of talking about anything or appearing vulnerable. "Not like when I was growing up," American Mom pinged her empty glass and reached for a refill.

US soccer icon Abby Wambach related her own introduction to the Viking way when Swedish coach Pia Sundhage took over the US women's team. On their first meeting, the Swede pulled out a guitar and began singing as the team sat, dumbfounded. Abby recalls thinking, "She has absolutely no idea what she's doing. We are screwed."[9] This was the first time they'd seen "a leader making herself vulnerable." But sharing vulnerability brought the team closer and helped them to be more collaborative. This new, more generous mindset worked wonders, and the Swede led the US team to two Olympic gold medals and a silver medal at the World Cup.

I'm not expecting my children to become World Cup champions or Olympians (though I promise I'll give two hoots about soccer if you do). But I hope they grow into useful, kind members of society. With *samfundssind*. And a robust sense of the ridiculous.

"They'll need it in this family," Lego Man mutters, giving his daily impression of someone stacking a dishwasher as our sons go outside to drink "icy water" from the hose (Danish refrigerators don't have cold water dispensers—we have to get our kicks where we can). We bumble through Christmas, eating, talking, walking, celebrating Susan the lemur's birthday, and playing Beanie Babies police raids. I take my mother to the airport on Boxing Day, and just as I'm pulling into the kiss-and-fly zone, she tells me, without warning, "They're really nice, interesting children."

I stop the car.

Shouldn't this declaration come with some kind of Klaxon? At the very least a trumpet? A kazoo?!

My mother isn't one to praise unless absolutely necessary (she recently reviewed a BBC radio documentary I presented as "nasal"), so this is big.

"Thank you," I manage, heart lodged in my throat.

"You do look tired though, darling."

"Okay, thanks." I pull on the handbrake.

"Pallor like guacamole."

Just the look I was going for... I hug her goodbye. "Cheerio!"

———

Once I get home, I find that Lego Man has dressed everyone up for "a much-needed long walk" (allegedly). We head to the beach for our customary postmortem of any family gathering, and I tell him what my mother said. He's rendered momentarily speechless.

Wind presses clothes against our bodies, and the dog tows us as we're buffeted by the elements, sea on one side, trees stripped bare on the other. The small people run ahead to explore an abandoned mobility scooter.

"A second Christmas miracle!" says Lego Man.

"What was the first?"

"That we might be doing something right as parents!"

We sink back into silence as if by mutual agreement.

Me: thinking about the improbable turns of events that have led us here and how children are like weather, changeable and impossible to control.

Lego Man: probably thinking about Chris Rea again.

It was only ever meant to be a year of living Danishly. Then I got pregnant. Then Brexit. Then IVF. Then twins. And poof! Ten years have gone by in a heartbeat. So am I a Viking now?

I've potty trained twins, I'm basically bulletproof.

But I miss my mom, notwithstanding guacamole compliments. And the rest of the family elders, who won't be around forever. And cousins who, in lieu of siblings, are important to me and who I'd like to be guiding figures in my children's lives (no pressure). I miss old friends. Godchildren. People I love who are not where I am. I miss family, both genetic and gathered, in a country where everything is centered around family. So I don't think we'll be here for good.

If only we'd been born Danish, I lament often. *If only one of us had. Why was Lego Man born in Halifax instead of Hellerup?* (A particularly leafy Copenhagen suburb.) Had at least one of us been born and bred in Denmark, I would happily stay in perpetuity. But we weren't. And no amount of *snegle* can change this. Which is why it's been even more important for me to learn all I can from the Nordics about how to build a Viking from the ground up. To find out what they do differently and how the rest of us can copy it, exporting it to use elsewhere.

I know I'm lucky to have had these experiences. This period of my life will mark me. This period of their lives will mark my children too. Forever. And Danes do "kids" well. Raising children Viking style from single cell to around age ten now seems, from all I've learned, foolproof. I love the emphasis on democracy and speaking out, since children growing up in the AI world will have to know how to analyze and interrogate information rather than just repeat it. I like the way the Nordic system nurtures independent thinkers who can work together. I maintain that the approach of utter liberalism and freedom above all else when applied to digital devices seems mad and counter to all the latest science. I'd like proper guidance on this, so it's not just up to individual parents. But the rest of the Nordic approach? It just makes sense.

"It's like a nice lunch," says Lego Man.

"Sorry?"

"You don't always want the set menu. Sometimes, you want to go à la carte," is how Lego Man puts it, only in a particularly pronounced Yorkshire accent. "That's okay, isn't it? If we've gone Viking for the first ten years of their lives and 'home' is on the menu for when the kids get older?"

Choosing where to live is a privilege, and we're all subject to the winds of change, bureaucracy, and corporate restructuring. But for now, I suppose, yes. Home could be back on the menu.

Lego Man and I have never been able to agree on where home should be, historically. We could never agree on many things, which felt like a problem. The unspoken conversations became clamorous. But actually, the Danish way has taught me that you can get along even when you don't agree. I remember what Morten from DR TV told me about how kids in Denmark grow up understanding that relationships are difficult and there is conflict—and that's okay. There's still love. Two stubborn, avoidant people are somehow making it work. Like a fractionally more mature Bamse and Kylling—Bear and Chicken (and I mean fractionally).

I look over. Lego Man is saying something, but his voice is snatched away by the wind. I cup an ear. "Sorry?"

"What I said was...'Did you know that Chris Rea had six siblings?'"

"I did not know that."

He looks pleased.

In the middle distance, a trailer arrives to pick up the mobility scooter, and the driver gives us a cheery wave. "Battery flat!"

Lego Man looks disappointed. "No Christmas miracle then?"

"Just the one," I tell him, pointing at the small people up ahead.

The redhead has picked up a stick and is giving it an experimental whack as our youngest asks questions about asteroids. My daughter is making pictures in the sand, using seaweed for hair and shells for eyes. The wind blows ribbons of hair across her face, and I feel a tug—the invisible thread between us, between them. Always.

Another kind of tug jerks me out of this reverie as the dog strains at his leash. A few youths with a puppy are ambling from the other direction. One has dark curls, twisting out from under a beanie. A down jacket is zipped to the clavicle, but there's no denying the still visible—

"Love Bite!" Lego Man starts.

Just when you thought it was safe to go back in the water.

"Hej!" Lego Man gives an exaggerated wave at the pool-noodle-dangling lothario. "I nearly didn't recognize you with your clothes on!"

My face twists with the supreme exertion of willpower required to avoid laughing. Our daughter runs over, ostensibly to greet her teacher but really to get a look at the puppy. Her cheeks are pink with cold, and she takes her mittens off to blow on icy fingers.

"You want Gore-Tex gloves," Love Bite says and nods toward my daughter's hands.

I hear a sharp intake of breath from Lego Man. "That's what I always say!"

Love Bite has just gone up several notches in his estimation.

"I don't know if you've heard," Love Bite continues.

Goodness! Silent for months, and now he's a regular Chatty Cathy.

"But we have this saying in Denmark—"

Okay, here we go.

"There's no such thing as bad weather, just the wrong—"

Lego Man finishes his sentence: "—clothes!" He beams, regarding the younger man with unconcealed admiration.

"That's it!" Love Bite points to the communal firepit where another teen is stationed, giving a pyre a desultory poke. "We're just here grilling some *pølser.*"

"Sausages? In the snow?" Lego Man is now smitten.

"Can we have sausages too? *Please?*" the other mini Vikings plead as they shuffle in snowsuits to pet the puppy/stare into the hazel eyes of their swimming teacher. Starstruck by the combination of puppy *and* pool dangler ("Wearing *clothes!*"), it takes a while to peel them away. But the light is fading so we say goodbye and head home to commence the glide path of getting smalls fed, read, and put to bed.

Finally, they sleep. All is silvery still. In the night, I wake and pad blindly to the bathroom to find Lego Man already there. Brought together by the shared human need to urinate, I wait, in a queue of one. From the skylight on the landing, I see stars out in force. The moon shines like a sickle. And then, I hear it. The distinctive peal of a newborn's cry. Plaintive. Urgent.

Lego Man emerges, blue eyes bleary with sleep, reacting to the sound with some sort of Pavlovian muscle memory. "Who needs what?" he croaks. "Diaper? Milk? Both?" I hear panic rising.

"No one. It's okay. It's not ours! We've done that part!" I hold a finger to my lips and point next door. "Listen!" There it is. Again. "It's here—the neighbor's new baby!" I feel clammy, heart racing as I'm taken back to that day, years ago, when we first became parents. *Clueless,* I think. *Completely clueless.*

I wanted a family so badly. I thought parenting was all about having a baby, then loving it, through each of its life stages. And it is. But there's much more to it than that. I wasn't prepared for questions beyond my own comprehension (see "asteroids"). Or fights about shoes. Or iPad negotiations. Or playing peekaboo for the same amount of time it takes to get a pilot's license. But we did it. We're doing it. With the best possible teachers around us: Vikings.

Everyone is doing their best when it comes to raising small people. And every day when things go wrong (see "unicorn bubble machine"), we try again the next day (see "shoehorn"). And we try again the day after that. We keep on trying. Like they will be next door with a squalling newborn. Like Digger Boy's mom and dad on the other side, whose mud magnet child, grubbing about in the dirt, has somehow become an undergraduate.

The unmistakable new baby wail rends the air again. I spot our neighbor at the window. He looks up, and I see the fear in his eyes. The same panic I had all those years ago. I give a nod—an acknowledgment of understanding. He gives me a wave before realizing he hasn't yet learned how to hold a child with one hand. He resumes cradling his precious bundle with the clutch of a drowning man as I smile back in solidarity: *You've got this. We've got this.*

And it starts all over again.

Bonus Chapter

‹‹‹

HOW TO PARTY LIKE A VIKING

TILLYKKE! (CONGRATULATIONS!) YOU'VE READ THE book, you've salivated over *snegle*, you've heard how they do Christmas, but happily, there's always an excuse to celebrate in the Nordic countries. On days when you or your small people have run out of reasons to be cheerful, why not borrow a few Viking traditions? Introducing the Nordic party lineup—or "national excuse for cake" days, as they're affectionately known in our house.

JANUARY 1: Kransekage. As the clock strikes midnight to usher in the New Year, Danes slice into a tower of eighteen or more ring-shaped layers made from almonds, eggs, and sugar (start as you mean to go on). Once everyone's surfaced at a more respectable hour, there's *vinterbadning* or "winter bathing." Locals do it in the nude near me, with a veritable buffet of bare bottoms, breasts, and dangly bits on show. But I wear a swimsuit and a woolly hat (because British). Pack plenty of towels, extra socks (the redhead requires two pairs after an icy dip), and flasks of coffee/hot chocolate as a reward afterward.

JANUARY 25 (ISH): Sólardagurinn or Sun Day. Icelanders of Ísafjörður don't see the sun *at all* for two months a year thanks to high mountains surrounding their village. When the sun makes an appearance at long last and rises high enough to be seen, Icelanders celebrate with a *sólarkaffi* or "sun coffee" and pancakes to symbolize the sun.

FEBRUARY 5: J. L. Runeberg Day. Finns love all their poets and novelists, but few get their own pastry (#writergoals). So just when winter feels like it's dragging, Finns celebrate poet Johan Ludvig Runeberg (1804–1877) with Runeberg's torte, a jam-topped cylindrical cake with almonds and rum or arrack that he ate every day for breakfast, so the story goes. Johan's wife and fellow writer, Fredrika Runeberg, came up with the recipe and was also a pioneer of historical fiction and the first Finnish author to critically analyze the status of women. Oh, and she had eight children. Unsurprisingly, Fredrika Runeberg has been chronically overlooked historically. So let's start a new campaign to rename February 5 Runeberg Day—celebrating both of them.

FEBRUARY 14: Ystävänpäivä, or Friend's Day. Forget St. Valentine, Finns dedicate today to friends, family, neighbors, and even colleagues with cards, flowers, and chocolates. Tell your pals.

SEVEN WEEKS BEFORE EASTER: Fastelavn. This Danish holiday has the second-best cake ever: chocolate-topped, marzipan-filled buns called *gammeldags fastelavnsboller*.* Fastelavn originated from the Catholic tradition of a foodie blowout before Lent, but after

---

* In first place is Trine Hahnemann's *brødtorte*, a chocolate rye bread cake. Fact.

Denmark's Reformation, Lutheran leaders weren't mad about a Roman ritual, so the celebration became secular. This meant Danes could stuff their faces with no obligation to deprive themselves after. Traditionally farmers shored up good fortune for a successful harvest by banishing cats, maligned as the embodiment of bad luck. Cats were sealed in barrels that were beaten with sticks until they splintered open and the cats escaped. "Thankfully, we just use pictures of cats now," lifelong cat lover Veteran Viking assured me. Cat-themed balsa-wood barrels are thwacked by children in fancy dress until they explode, like a piñata, showering everyone with candy. The child who knocks a hole in the barrel is crowned king or queen of cats. Afterward, smalls tout for treats door to door, singing, "Buns up, buns down, buns in my tummy. If I get no buns, I will make trouble." Loudly. Until neighbors give them more sweet treats.

In Iceland, they cut to the chase, calling this pre-Lent blowout simply Bolludagur or Bun Day. Everyone stuffs their faces with cream puffs, and children make wands to smack their parents on the bum while yelling "bolla, bolla, bolla." For each spank, they get a bun. And no, I have not made this up.

FEBRUARY 24: Konudagur or Women's Day. Icelandic custom dictates that women be utterly spoiled and treated to flowers, coffee, and cake on this day. *Marks date in diary, sends invite to all contacts*

MARCH 1: Bjordagur or Beer Day. Icelanders commemorate the end of prohibition after a seventy-four-year booze ban from 1915 to 1989 by raising a glass to celebrate. ("You need a whole day for this?" I ask Icelandic friends. "Yes," they say. In unison.)

MARCH 25: Våffeldagen or Waffle Day. Swedes eat heart-shaped waffles topped with cloudberry jam and cream to celebrate the Virgin Mary (I know: bear with me...). According to the gospels, March 25 is the day when the Archangel Gabriel came down to earth and told Mary that she would give birth to Jesus. Swedes already celebrated Our Lady's Day (Vårfrudagen) and thought it sounded a little like Våffeldagen, so they combined the two. Practical and delicious.

PALM SUNDAY: Finnish children dress up as witches and go from door to door with decorated willow twigs, offering neighbors a "magic spell" promising good health in exchange for candy (sensing a theme?). This dates back to Finland's pagan days when agrarian workers believed witches determined whether crops would thrive or fail.

EASTER: Time to exchange *gækkebreve* or Easter letters. Danish children make what look like doilies from the 1980s but are in fact anonymous letters to tease recipients into giving them chocolate. Shapes are snipped out of paper to create a snowflake-esque design, then a dot is used for each letter of the sender's name. If the recipient guesses who sent it before Easter, they receive a chocolate egg. If they don't? The sender can demand a chocolate egg from the recipient.

APRIL 15 (ISH): Dancing Cow Day. Organic cows in Denmark are kept inside during the long, cold winter before being let out to pasture mid-April. They're so happy to be back on grass that they hop, frisk, buck, gallop, and look a lot like they're dancing. Farms countrywide invite visitors to watch the spectacle and serve up dairy-based snacks for *økodag* or organic day. But we all know why we're really there, and it's the cow dancing. Outstanding.

APRIL 21: The first day of summer. Old Norse calendars were based on only two seasons: summer and winter. So essentially, this celebration means "not winter anymore." Villages, towns, and cities throughout Finland celebrate with parades, outdoor games, and community BBQs, followed by a sauna.

APRIL 30: Valborgsmässoafton or Walpurgis Night. Swedes celebrate the eighth-century German abbess St. Valborg (also known as St. Walpurgis, Walborg or Walpurga or Walburga). Born in England, she opted for a holy life in Germany. So naturally, Swedes celebrate by lighting big fires, setting off fireworks, and singing traditional folk songs. April is also the month for *utepils,* or outdoor beer—the ultimate reward for Norwegians after a long dark winter. Whatever day everyone agrees that the weather is clement—if not warm, then slightly less cold—it's time for *utepils,* and nationwide festivity ensues. Newspapers fill with pictures of people enjoying their first outdoor beer of the year.

MAY 1: May Day or Labor Day. This is a celebration of spring (and labor) throughout the Nordic countries. Finns celebrate with funnel cake constructed from deep-fried lemon-flavored batter that looks like worms but tastes surprisingly good. Best served alongside *munkki*—a Finnish doughnut—and *sima,* a lemony drink.

MAY 17: Norway's Constitution Day, also known as the Norwegian Independence Day. This is one of the biggest festivals in the country.

Cue mass merrymaking on the streets of Norwegian cities. And sausages. And perhaps a *ventepølse*—or waiting sausage—while you wait for the main-event sausage to cook.

ALSO IN MAY: Norway's World Beard and Moustache Championships, where the follicularly fortunate travel from all over to show off impressive facial hair in categories including partial beard, natural moustaches, and freestyle. Hr. Skæg a.k.a. Mr. Beard would be a shoo-in.

JUNE 5: Danish Constitution Day. Many businesses and shops close, buses fly the Danish flag, and Danes celebrate democracy with *fællessang* (group singing), open-air gatherings, *pølser*, and beer.

JUNE 6: Sweden's National Day. This day commemorates Gustav Vasa's coronation as king in 1523 and the Swedish constitution, adopted in 1809. Nationwide merriment, plus hot dogs.

JUNE 17: Iceland's Independence Day. This day marks the anniversary of the country's freedom from Danish ties in 1944 and Jón Sigurðsson who campaigned for Icelandic independence in the nineteenth century. Icelanders lay wreaths at the base of his statue in Reykjavík, and there are concerts and a parade. And sausages.

JUNE 19-25: Midsommar. Swedes commemorate midsummer on a Friday between June 19 and 25, traditionally considered a time of magic when plants acquired mysterious powers and strange things could happen. You're welcome, Shakespeare. Young Swedes pick seven different kinds of flowers and put them under their pillows to dream of their future loves. Flowers are picked in silence; otherwise, the magic is broken (and your neighbor knows you're raiding his begonias). Walking barefoot in the dew as night turns to dawn and wearing a wreath of flowers in your hair ensures health, fertility, and wet feet. Swedes play games like croquet or *kubb*, where you knock down wooden blocks by throwing sticks. Then they feast. Herring, shrimp, salmon, and shots are all on the menu, and for each toast, a new song is sung. (Swedes have more than twelve thousand toasting songs, available in a database at the Museum of Spirits in Stockholm.)

JUNE 23: Sankt Hans Eve or the eve of St. John the Baptist. This holiday is combined with the summer solstice in Denmark. It's marked by sing-alongs around a community bonfire, where an effigy of a witch is burned, historically to banish evil spirits and send them to the mountains in Germany (sorry, Germany). In our neighborhood, there are also speeches, shots, sausages, and *flødeboller* for the children—a cookie base topped with marshmallow and coated in chocolate.

JULY: Jordbærkage season. Danish strawberries are full of flavor come July, so summer is celebrated with *jordbærkage*—vanilla crème in a chocolate-coated pastry case, topped with fresh strawberries. Like eating summer and to be enjoyed at every opportunity in the name of seasonal eating.

JULY 29: St. Olaf's Day. Norwegians celebrate their patron saint (originally their king) with festivals of singing and dancing. And with sausages.

AUGUST: Kräftpremiär, a.k.a. Swedish crayfish party season! For most of the twentieth century, there were strict rules about when crayfish could be fished in Swedish waters to help the population recover to healthy levels. When the restrictions are lifted toward the end of summer each year, Swedes let loose and begin celebrating with outdoor feasts. Diners put on party hats and huddle around a long table decorated with streamers to tuck in. Noisy slurping is considered a sign of appreciation, and bibs are essential (it gets messy).

SEPTEMBER: A quieter month when Vikings catch up on garden maintenance (rock 'n' roll). Peter Schmeichel assures me that this is the time to "cut back dead perennials" and—big news—the DIY shop have at last sent him a pair of loyalty pruning shears. He is over the moon ("Next level: the dagger!"). For everyone else, it's chill time. Unless it's your birthday, your anniversary, or a Wednesday (see below). Or you're in Iceland.

Icelanders countrywide take part in September's major social event: shepherding. Locals ride horses to round up eight hundred thousand sheep from the countryside. Some tour companies even allow tourists to participate. (Let's sign up! Who's with me?)

OCTOBER: Week 42 of the year is Kartoffelferie, or potato holiday—Denmark's far-cooler rebrand of a school break with extra appreciation for spuds.

NOVEMBER 1: Jólabókaflóðið or the Christmas book flood. Icelanders exchange books on Christmas Eve, and the annual book flood begins on this date, when the list of newly published books is announced. Every home gets a free catalogue of all the new publications called the *bókatíðindi*. My friend Siggi remembers spending hours circling the ones he wanted.

THE FIRST FRIDAY OF NOVEMBER: J-Day, when the special Christmas beer, or *julebryg*, goes on sale in Denmark at precisely 8:59 p.m. Over time, J-Day has become a Christmas tradition celebrated in bars and pubs around the country (one for the grown-ups). But why not start your own tradition? Starbucks holiday cups day? Hershey's Christmas kisses day? The list is endless.

NOVEMBER 10: Mortens Aften or St. Morten's Day. This day is marked in Denmark by everyone eating duck or goose in honor of St. Martin of Tours (Morten Bisp in Danish). The story goes that Martin was so good at healing the sick that locals wanted him as their bishop, but Martin wasn't keen. So he hid, not somewhere sensible and quiet, but in a flock of geese. Unsurprisingly, their honking gave him away, and Martin was so incensed that he made everyone slaughter and eat goose as a punishment for their treachery. First documented in Denmark in 1616, Danes have stuck to this strange tradition, only allowing duck as an acceptable alternative in recent years for anyone finding a goose hard to come by (or fit in the oven).

DECEMBER 1: *Juleboller* go on sale in Denmark. A soft, sweet, and spicy delight similar to a hot cross bun without the cross. Best eaten with a good layer of *tandsmør*, or tooth butter—the Danish term for a layer of butter so thick, you see teeth marks in it after biting. Hard recommend for maximum Christmas cheer.

There are plentiful opportunities for pre-Christmas bonding, but the most popular in Denmark is baking. Early in Advent, families get together for a baking day to stock up on Christmas standards including *pebernødder* (spiced cookies) and *æbleskiver* (spherical pancake/doughnut hybrids of pure deliciousness). The only thing Vikings don't bake at this time of year is a fruited Christmas cake. Danes put their raisins in *wine* instead, along with sliced almonds. Nordic *gløgg* is like mulled wine only with added jeopardy of "bits" in every gulp so that you think you're about to choke. *Ding-dong merrily on high!*

CHRISTMAS CRAFT DAY: Julpyssla in Swedish. Vikings whittle and forage and cover their house with a medley of lichen and sprigs. Children are charged with making a *juledekoration* candle centerpiece at school or kindergarten, wedging pine cones, spruce branches, moss, and general garden detritus into a lump of clay with an Advent candle in the middle. Or *julehjerter*, the white and red woven hearts that Kitta taught all my children to make but that I still can't master (total respect to all who can).

DECEMBER 12: The first of Iceland's Yule Lads arrive. These half-troll Santa substitutes come down from the mountains to play pranks on children until Christmas, with names like Spoon Licker, Door Slammer, Doorway Sniffer, Window Peeper, and Sausage Swiper (did I mention Vikings love a sausage?). If you think this sounds creepy, there's also the Christmas Cat, who eats children who don't get new clothes. ("It seems harsh now, but I think it was to encourage parents to knit a new sock," says my friend Birna. #NordicNoir.)

DECEMBER 13: Santa Lucia Day. Commemorating the third century Sicilian who wanted to devote her life to God at a time when Christians were persecuted. According to legend, the Roman emperor commanded that Lucia be taken to a brothel, but by divine intervention, no one could move her. The emperor tried to burn her at the stake next, but she survived. So she was stabbed *and* beheaded. Just to be sure. To honor Santa Lucia today, Swedes, Danes, Norwegians, and Finns bake saffron buns and have a procession where a girl in a white dress wears a crown of candles on her head (Lucia liked to be hands-free). She's followed by candle-bearing girls and boys, also in white dresses (or, at my børnehave, sheets). They sing a translation of the Neapolitan song "Santa Lucia," and by the end of the procession, there isn't a dry eye in the house.

DECEMBER 25: Since Vikings celebrate Christmas on the twenty-fourth, on the twenty-fifth, you can just kick back, eat chocolates, and watch TV... Oh no, wait. That's in my old life. These days, we have to go on another "lovely long walk," as Lego Man puts it *sighs*. Fortunately, he makes sure we're all kitted out for it. ("You know what they say? No such thing as bad weather—" "Yes! We *know*!") And on Lasse, the *friluftsliv* fanatic's advice, I pack *all* the leftover Christmas chocolate.

DECEMBER 31: New Year's Eve. Young and old enjoy home firework displays throughout the Nordic countries (safety goggles advised).

Icelanders also sing songs and dance by the light of a neighborhood bonfire. Finns melt miniature horseshoes on a spoon over a flame (less *Trainspotting* than it sounds), then throw the contents over snow or ice to see what shape it takes. This will tell their fortunes for the year ahead. A heart means love; a coin, success; and a ship, travel.

Swedes enjoy a recitation of Alfred Tennyson's old poem "Ring Out, Wild Bells" ("Nyårsklockan"), a tradition no one seems able to explain but one that has been in place since the 1890s.

Then, everyone watches *Dinner for One*, a British two-hander comedy sketch from 1962 that has inexplicably become essential viewing in Denmark, Sweden, Norway, and Finland (as well as Germany, Austria, Switzerland, and Estonia). In the sketch, an upper-class Englishwoman has a dinner party for her ninetieth birthday—only all her friends are dead. So her butler pretends to be each of them in turn and drinks for them all. Despite being largely unknown in the UK, it's aired every year in Denmark since 1980 and in Sweden since 1969 save for a hiatus from 1963 to 1969 when it was banned due to the depiction of heavy alcohol consumption.

After that, there's more food and more drink, possibly coffee (at night! I know!), then Danes jump off the sofa as the clock strikes twelve to symbolize jumping into the new year. And then? Then, you tuck into the *kransekage* and start the cake calendar again.

But there are also Viking party perennials. Like Wednesdays.

WEDNESDAYS: Liven up hump day by observing the Danish custom of eating cinnamon buns called *onsdagssnegle* (Wednesday snails). Some bakeries sell these at reduced prices to celebrate... um...Wednesday.

BIRTHDAYS: According to Danish tradition, you're responsible for the weather on your birthday. If it's sunny, it means you've been good all year, and everyone thanks you for the lovely weather. If it's raining? You've done something dire and now everyone knows it. It's a meteorological *Picture of Dorian Gray*, only with the chance of a do-over each year.

The flag is flown on birthdays but if you don't have a flagpole (embarrassing for you), a flag outside your door will do. Most important is the mini flagpole to decorate the birthday table at mealtimes and make you feel special, regardless of your nationality, since the flag symbolizes celebration. I recently learned that Swedes get breakfast in bed on their birthday too, so if any of my family are reading: I want this.

Birthday cakes for children in Denmark tend to be *kagemand* or *kagekone*—three-foot-long mega pastries in the shape of a person, decorated with marzipan, *slik* (candy), and licorice strands for hair. The birthday girl or boy cuts the cake by slicing through the jugular, whereupon everyone screams. Because nothing says "kids party" like decapitation.

If you're over the age of ten and feel too grown-up for a *kagemand*, Danes opt for a layered sponge with cream between and berries on top. And you bring your own birthday cake, which mean everyone's spared any "oh shit, we forgot!" embarrassment. It's impossible to forget somebody's birthday when they're standing in front of you holding a three-foot cake person. Other than cake, celebrations tend to be low-key, except for milestone birthdays, when things ramp up.

"When you turn twenty-five, you get cinnamoned," my day care dad friend Peter Schmeichel told me. "I got it thrown at me from the moment I woke up. I tried to wash it off, but every time I got out of the shower, they'd attack again. I went outside, but they tied me to a lamppost and gave me swimming goggles to wear and threw more at me." *Why?* "Good question! Well, a very long time ago—sixteenth century maybe—spice salesmen were so busy travelling that they had no time for dating and became known as *pebersvends,* or pepper journeymen" Since then, unmarried Danes turning twenty-five have been showered with spices. Few Danes are married by twenty-five, so this has nothing to do with derision of the unwed and everything to do with tradition.

When you hit thirty, if you're still not married, you're upgraded to a pepper dousing and may also receive a sculpture of a pepper mill made from stacked oilcans. At least a pepper mill was the original custom. Today they're often made to look like horses or genitalia. Many happy returns!

Round birthdays, when your age can be divided by ten, are also special, celebrated with a bigger party for family and friends. And big *halvrunde* (half-round) birthdays like seventy-fifth birthdays also warrant celebration and singing. Traditionally Danes give speeches and write special song lyrics for a big birthday bash.

WEDDINGS: Viking nuptials include a lot of speeches and kissing on demand. When guests stamp their feet, newlyweds have to get under their table and kiss. When guests clang cutlery, newlyweds must stand on their chairs and kiss. When either of the newlyweds is out of the room, guests dash to kiss the lone newlywed throughout Denmark, Sweden, and Norway (sounds problematic, but apparently Vikings are okay with it).

In Sweden, bride and groom walk down the aisle together, and men get engagement rings too. And photos are taken before the ceremony so guests don't have to hang around forever afterward. Let's all agree to do Swedish-style wedding photos from now on.

In Norway, brides get a crown (vow renewal in Oslo anyone?). The *brudekrone,* or bride crown is often a family heirloom passed down through generations. ("Mom? Yes, I know I look tired, but quick question: any *crowns* knocking around?") After the wedding, the couple plant fir trees on either side of their front door to signify the children they plan to have and/or their growing relationship.

ANNIVERSARIES: In Denmark, neighbors, family, and friends make a floral arch around your front door to celebrate twelve and a half, twenty-five, and fifty years of married life. For a twelve-and-a-half-year copper anniversary, the arch is half height, so there's some ducking required. Then between 6:00 and 7:00 a.m., family, friends, and neighbors gather outside the arch and start singing for the anniversary couple to materialize before breakfasting together. There'll be bread rolls, *snegle* (of course), coffee, and possibly something stronger to toast the still-married couple having survived thus far.

———

So there you have it. Raise a glass (of anything you fancy) and *skål,* or cheers! Congratulations, you're a Viking now.

Notes

〜〜〜

INTRODUCTION: THE ACCIDENTAL DANE

1 **Danes trust most people:** K. M. Sonderskov and P. T. Dinesen, "Danish Exceptionalism: Explaining the Unique Increase in Social Trust over the Past 30 Years," *European Sociological Review* 30, no. 6 (December 2014): 782–95, https://doi.org/10.1093/esr/jcu073.

2 **Levels of trust have fallen:** Marc J. Hetherington, "The Political Relevance of Political Trust," *American Political Science Review* 92, no. 4 (December 1998): 791–808, https://doi.org/10.2307/2586304; Jack Citrin and Laura Stoker, "Political Trust in a Cynical Age," *Annual Review of Political Science* 21 (May 2018): 49–70, https://doi.org/10.1146/annurev-polisci-050316-092550; "Trust in Government, UK: 2022," Office for National Statistics, July 13, 2022, https://www.ons.gov.uk/peoplepopulationandcommunity/wellbeing/bulletins/trustingovernmentuk/2022; "Trust in Government," Organisation for Economic Cooperation and Development, 2022, https://doi.org/10.1787/1de9675e-en; "Public Trust in Government: 1958–2022," Pew Research Center, June 6, 2022, https://www.pewresearch.org/politics/2022/06/06/public-trust-in-government-1958–2022/.

3 **Nordic countries regularly top:** Charlotte Edmond, "These Are the Countries Where Children Are Most Satisfied with Their Lives," World Economic Forum, September 4, 2020, https://www.weforum.org/agenda/2020/09/child-well-being-health-happiness-unicef-report/.

4 **youngsters in the US and the UK:** "The State of the World's Children 2021," UNICEF, October 2021, https://www.unicef.org/reports/state-worlds-children-2021.

5 **UK children who are unhappy:** "State of the World's Children."

6 **a third of all teenagers:** "Any Anxiety Disorder," National Institute of Mental Health, accessed August 26, 2023, https://www.nimh.nih.gov/health/statistics/any-anxiety-disorder.

7 **around 40 percent of marriages:** "Divorces," Statistics Denmark, accessed August 26, 2023, https://www.dst.dk/en/Statistik/emner/borgere/husstande-familier-og-boern/skilsmisser.

8 **Denmark is the fifth country:** "Marriage Rates in the European Union in 2020," Statista, May 2022, https://www.statista.com/statistics/612150/marriage-rates-in-european-countries/.

9 **thirty-seven different types of family units:** Mathilde Weirsøe, "Long Live the Family," Danish School of Education, Aarhus University, May 5, 2021, https://dpu.au.dk/en/about-the-school/nyheder/single/artikel/long-live-the-family-1.

10 **"You can have happy children":** Rasmus Kjeldahl, in discussion with the author, August 29, 2022.

11 **69 percent of Icelandic babies:** "Out of Wedlock Births by Country 2023," World Population Review, accessed September 8, 2023, https://worldpopulationreview.com/country-rankings/out-of-wedlock-births-by-country.

12 **"the gentle Viking invasion":** "Trends in Egg, Sperm and Embryo Donation 2020," Human Fertilisation and Embryology Authority, November 2022, https://www.hfea.gov.uk/about-us/publications/research-and-data/trends-in-egg-sperm-and-embryo-donation-2020/.

CHAPTER 1: CONGRATULATIONS! IT'S A VIKING!

1 **"No, about frozen sperm":** Ole Schou, in discussion with the author, March 12, 2015.

2 **biologically Danish fathers:** Cryos clinic staff, in discussion with the author, August 22, 2022.

3 **one in ten children is conceived in a fertility clinic:** Søren Ziebe, head of Fertility Department, Rigshospitalet, Copenhagen, in discussion with the author, September 13, 2022; Lucy Proctor, "Why Is IVF So Popular in Denmark?," BBC News, September 21, 2018, https://www.bbc.com/news/world-europe-45512312.

4 **"a strong positive effect":** Daniel Rosenkjær et al., "Effects of Virtual Reality Erotica on Ejaculate Quality of Sperm Donors: A Balanced and Randomized Controlled Cross-Over Within-Subjects Trial," *Reproductive Biology and Endocrinology* 20 (2022): 149, https://doi.org/10.1186/s12958-022-01021-1.

5   **42 percent of Danes do volunteer work:** "Volunteering in Denmark," Frivilligjobdk, accessed July 7, 2023, https://frivilligjob.dk/Volunteering-in -Denmark-People-culture-and-history.html.

6   **46 percent of the Danish sperm donors:** Bjørn Bay et al., "Danish Sperm Donors across Three Decades: Motivations and Attitudes," *Fertility and Sterility* 101, no. 1 (January 2014): 252–57, https://doi.org/10.1016/j.fertnstert.2013.09.013.

7   **"Generally, people want a better-looking":** Helle Sejersen Myrthue, in discussion with the author, August 15, 2022.

8   **American guidelines recommend twenty-five children:** "Guidance Regarding Gamete and Embryo Donation," American Society for Reproductive Medicine, 2021, https://www.asrm.org/practice-guidance/practice-committee-documents /guidance-regarding-gamete-and-embryo-donation-2021/.

9   **donors are subject to a twelve-family limit:** "How Many Families Can Use the Same Sperm Donor?," Cryos International, accessed October 13, 2023, https:// www.cryosinternational.com/en-gb/dk-shop/private/faq/donor-children/how -many-families-can-use-the-same-donor/.

10   **there's a ten-family limit:** "Donating Your Sperm," Human Fertilisation and Embryology Authority, accessed October 13, 2023, https://www.hfea.gov.uk /donation/donors/donating-your-sperm/.

11   **the sperm shopping demographic:** Myrthue, discussion.

12   **"It's actually easier to be a *solomor*":** Karin Erb, in discussion with the author, September 9, 2015.

13   **137,000 households headed up by single women:** "Households and Families," Statistics Denmark, accessed October 13, 2023, https://www.dst.dk/en/Statistik /emner/borgere/husstande-familier-og-boern/husstande-og-familier.

14   **"Two-thirds had a partner":** Lone Schmidt, in discussion with the author, September 9, 2015, and March 20, 2023.

15   **those over the age of forty-two:** "Adoption," Familieretshuset, accessed July 7, 2023, https://familieretshuset.dk/en/your-life-situation/your-life-situation/adoption.

16   **A straw of sperm from an anonymous donor:** "Cryos Sperm Bank Prices and Payment Options," Cryos International, accessed October 13, 2023, https://www .cryosinternational.com/en-gb/dk-shop/private/how-to/how-to-order-donor -sperm/prices-and-payment/.

17   **even IUI procedures cost:** "Intrauterine Insemination (IUI)," National Health Service, updated March 10, 2020, https://www.nhs.uk/conditions/artificial -insemination/.

18 **There's a traditional idea that children:** Susan Golombok, in discussion with the author, September 9, 2015.

19 **Children conceived through medically assisted reproduction:** Anna Barbuscia, Mikko Myrskylä, and Alice Goisis, "The Psychosocial Health of Children Born after Medically Assisted Reproduction: Evidence from the UK Millennium Cohort Study," *SSM—Population Health* 7 (April 2019): 100355, https://doi.org/10.1016/j.ssmph.2019.100355.

20 **collaboration between University College London:** Hanna Remes et al., "The Well-Being of Adolescents Conceived through Medically Assisted Reproduction: A Population-Level and Within-Family Analysis," *European Journal of Population* 38 (2022): 915–49, https://doi.org/10.1007/s10680-022-09623-6; Elena Cristiana Ilioi and Susan Golombok, "Psychological Adjustment in Adolescents Conceived by Assisted Reproduction Techniques: A Systematic Review," *Human Reproduction Update* 21, no. 1 (January/February 2015): 84–96, https://doi.org/10.1093/humupd/dmu051.

CHAPTER 2: A VIKING IS BORN

1 **"There's also a hooded suit":** Katja Pantzar, in discussion with the author, September 9, 2022.

2 **Finland now has one of the lowest infant mortality rates:** "Finland (FIN): Demographics, Health & Infant Mortality," UNICEF Data, accessed October 13, 2023, https://data.unicef.org/country/fin/; "Under-Five Mortality," UNICEF Data, January 2023, https://data.unicef.org/topic/child-survival/under-five-mortality/.

3 **"and coverage has been 99 to 100 percent":** Mika Gissler, in discussion with the author, October 5, 2022.

4 **the UN secretary general:** "Guterres Calls for 'Coalition of the World' to Overcome Divisions, Provide Hope in Place of Turmoil," United Nations, accessed August 22, 2023, https://www.un.org/en/desa/guterres-calls-coalition-world-overcome-divisions-provide-hope-place-turmoil.

5 **illegal to dangle anything white out of your car:** Louise Fisher, "Kvinde fødte barn på motorvejen—mens far kørte med civil udrykning" [Woman gave birth on the motorway—while father was driving with civil emergency services], TV2 Østjylland, January 31, 2020, https://www.tv2ostjylland.dk/aarhus/kvinde-foedte-barn-paa-motorvejen-mens-far-koerte-med-civil-udrykning.

6 **"I loved my new baby":** Nanna Schultz, in discussion with the author, November 1, 2022.

7   **Icelandic hospitals even import supplies of breast milk:** Helen Russell, "Iceland to Import Breast Milk from Denmark," *Guardian*, October 22, 2014, https://www.theguardian.com/world/2014/oct/22/iceland-to-import-breast -milk-denmark.

8   **The average Dane pays 35.4 percent:** OECD, *Taxing Wages 2023: Indexation of Labour Taxation and Benefits in OECD Countries* (Paris: OECD Publishing, 2023), https://doi.org/10.1787/8c99fa4d-en.

9   **the average monthly salary:** "The Average Dane," Statistics Denmark, accessed August 26, 2023, https://www.dst.dk/en/Statistik/laer-om-statistik /gennemsnitsdanskeren.

10   **Danes are taking home:** "Income Tax Calculator Denmark," Talent.com, accessed July 7, 2023, https://dk.talent.com/en/tax-calculator.

11   **In the US, it's $5,048:** "National Average Wage Index," Social Security Administration, accessed June 16, 2023, https://www.ssa.gov/oact/cola/AWI.html.

12   **According to the Forbes tax calculator:** "Florida Income Tax Calculator 2022–2023," Forbes Advisor, accessed July 7, 2023, https://www.forbes.com /advisor/income-tax-calculator/florida/?deductions=0&filing=single& income=56000&ira=0&k401=0.

13   **the cost of living in Denmark:** "Cost of Living in Denmark," Numbeo, updated June 2023, https://www.numbeo.com/cost-of-living/country_result.jsp?country =Denmark.

14   **thirty-three hours a week:** "Average Usual Weekly Hours Worked on the Main Job," OECD, 2018, https://stats.oecd.org/Index.aspx?DataSetCode= AVE_HRS.

15   **Shigehiro Oishi from the University of Virginia:** Shigehiro Oishi, Selin Kesebir, and Ed Diener, "Income Inequality and Happiness," *Psychological Science* 22, no. 9 (2011): 1095–1100, https://doi.org/10.1177/0956797611417262.

16   **leading to a rise in addiction:** Richard Wilkinson and Kate Pickett, *The Inner Level: How More Equal Societies Reduce Stress, Restore Sanity and Improve Everyone's Well-Being* (New York: Penguin, 2019); Richard Wilkinson and Kate E. Pickett, "The Enemy between Us: The Psychological and Social Costs of Inequality," *European Journal of Social Psychology* 47, no. 1 (February 2017): 11–24, https:// doi.org/10.1002/ejsp.2275; Dawn Foster, "Kate Pickett and Richard Wilkinson: 'Inequality Strikes at Our Health and Happiness,'" *Guardian*, September 18, 2018, https://www.theguardian.com/inequality/2018/sep/18/kate-pickett-richard -wilkinson-mental-wellbeing-inequality-the-spirit-level.

CHAPTER 3: BABY DANE

1 **"in enunciating the words":** Julia Samuel, in discussion with the author, September 17, 2019.

2 **Finnish researchers found that babies sleep longer:** Marjo Tourula, Arja Isola, and Juhani Hassi, "Children Sleeping Outdoors in Winter: Parents' Experiences of a Culturally Bound Childcare Practice," *International Journal of Circumpolar Health* 67, no. 2–3 (June 2008): 269–78, https://doi.org/10.3402/ijch.v67i2–3.18284.

3 **the last reported case was in 1966:** "Kidnapped Danish Baby Is Found after Four Weeks," *New York Times*, January 12, 1966, https://www.nytimes.com/1966/01/12 /archives/kidnapped-danish-baby-is-found-after-four-weeks.html.

4 **"Today, 90 percent of all Swedish fathers":** Niklas Löfgren, in discussion with the author, August 18, 2022.

5 **the Norwegian government recently valued:** Christa Clapp, "The Smart Economics of Norway's Parental Leave, and Why the U.S. Should Consider It," *Washington Post*, January 11, 2016, https://www.washingtonpost.com/news /parenting/wp/2016/01/11/the-smart-economics-of-norways-parental-leave/.

6 **Women make up almost half of the workforce:** "Employment: Share of Female Managers," OECD, accessed October 13, 2023, https://stats.oecd.org/Index.aspx ?QueryId=96330.

7 **In the UK, it's 32 percent:** "Number of Women in Senior Management Positions Reaches New High," Consultancy.uk, March 8, 2022, https://www.consultancy .uk/news/30635/number-of-women-in-senior-management-positions-reaches -new-high.

8 **Swedish women making up 43 percent of managers:** "Employment: Share of Female Managers."

9 **"This is largely down to Sweden's use-it-or-lose-it policy":** Lise Johansen, in discussion with the author, January 9, 2023.

10 **a woman's earnings rose 7 percent:** Gwynn Guilford, "The Economic Case for Paternity Leave," Quartz, September 24, 2014, https://qz.com/266841/economic -case-for-paternity-leave.

11 **paternity leave also improves maternal health:** May Wong, "It's Good for New Moms When Dads Can Stay Home," Stanford Institute for Economic Policy Research, June 3, 2019, https://siepr.stanford.edu/news/its-good-new-moms -when-dads-can-stay-home.

12 **depression and anxiety in new mothers:** Qual, J, Healthcare Eco, and Hunter Rm. 2021. "Committed to Create Value for Researchers the Role of Maternity Services

in Reducing the Prevalence and Cost of Perinatal Depression and Anxiety during COVID-19 in England the Role of Maternity Services in Reducing the Prevalence and Cost of Perinatal Depression and Anxiety during COVID-19 in England Commentary Volume 4 Issue 4." https://doi.org/10.23880/jqhe-16000234.

13 **Only 1 percent of employees:** "Work-Life Balance," OECD Better Life Index, accessed August 26, 2023, https://www.oecdbetterlifeindex.org/topics/work-life-balance/.

14 **Danes are the second most productive workers in Europe:** "Work-Life Balance," Denmark.dk, accessed October 13, 2023, https://denmark.dk/society-and-business/work-life-balance.

15 **This "sickness gap" carries on:** Nikolay Angelov, Per Johansson, and Erica Lindahl, "Gender Differences in Sickness Absence and the Gender Division of Family Responsibilities," Institute of Labor Economics, Discussion Paper 7379 (2013), https://ideas.repec.org/p/iza/izadps/dp7379.html.

16 **Something now proven to take:** Michael Price, "Study of Marathon Runners Reveals a 'Hard Limit' on Human Endurance," *Science*, June 5, 2019, https://www.science.org/content/article/study-marathon-runners-reveals-hard-limit-human-endurance.

17 **"so much so that it's like":** Johannes Romppanen, in discussion with the author, September 5, 2022.

18 **Neuroscientists from Tel Aviv University:** Daphna Joel et al., "Sex beyond the Genitalia: The Human Brain Mosaic," *Proceedings of the National Academy of Sciences* 112, no. 50 (November 30, 2015), 15468–73, https://doi.org/10.1073/pnas.1509654112.

19 **A study from Bar-Ilan University:** Eyal Abraham et al., "Father's Brain Is Sensitive to Childcare Experiences," *Proceedings of the National Academy of Sciences* 111, no. 27 (May 27, 2014): 9792–97, https://doi.org/10.1073/pnas.1402569111.

20 **Men who take parental leave:** Linda Haas and C. Philip Hwang, "The Impact of Taking Parental Leave on Fathers' Participation in Childcare and Relationships with Children: Lessons from Sweden," *Community, Work & Family* 11, no. 1 (2008): 85–104, https://doi.org/10.1080/13668800701785346.

CHAPTER 4: BRINGING UP *BØRN*

1 **Anthropologist Abigail Page:** Abigail E. Page et al., "Testing Adaptive Hypotheses of Alloparenting in Agta Foragers," *Nature Human Behaviour* 3 (November 2019): 1154–63, https://doi.org/10.1038/s41562-019-0679-2.

2   **Psychologist Sheina Lew-Levy:** Sheina Lew-Levy et al., "Who Teaches Children to Forage? Exploring the Primacy of Child-to-Child Teaching among Hadza and BaYaka Hunter-Gatherers of Tanzania and Congo," *Evolution and Human Behavior* 41, no. 1 (January 2020): 12–22, https://doi.org/10.1016/j.evolhumbehav.2019.07 .003.

3   **Studies show that while motor development:** Klaus Libertus and Dominic A. Violi, "Sit to Talk: Relation between Motor Skills and Language Development in Infancy," *Frontiers in Psychology* 7 (2016): 475, https://doi.org/10.3389/fpsyg .2016.00475; Hayley C. Leonard and Elisabeth L. Hill, "Review: The Impact of Motor Development on Typical and Atypical Social Cognition and Language: A Systematic Review," *Child and Adolescent Mental Health* 19, no. 3 (September 2014):163–70, https://doi.org/10.1111/camh.12055; Esther Thelen, "Development as a Dynamic System," *Current Directions in Psychological Science* 1, no. 6 (December 1992): 189–93, https://doi.org/10.1111/1467-8721.ep10770402; Jana M. Iverson, "Developing Language in a Developing Body: The Relationship between Motor Development and Language Development," *Journal of Child Language* 37, no. 2 (March 2010): 229–61, https://doi.org/10.1017%2FS0305000909990432.

4   **In his book Den danske sang:** Phillip Faber, Den danske sang (Politikens Forlag, 2020).

5   **London School of Economics researchers:** "Big Change Starts Small," Royal Foundation Centre for Early Childhood, June 2021, https:// centreforearlychildhood.org/report/.

6   **"You notice from the very beginning":** Pantzar, discussion.

7   **"Kindergarten in Finland doesn't focus":** Pasi Sahlberg, *Finnish Lessons 3.0: What Can the World Learn from Educational Change in Finland?* (New York: Teachers College Press, 2021), 52.

8   **the state pays 75 percent:** "Income-Based Allowance, Sibling Allowance, and Other Allowances," Life in Denmark, last updated April 11, 2023, https:// lifeindenmark.borger.dk/family-and-children/day-care/income-based-allowance —sibling-allowance—and-other-allowances.

9   **Britain has the second highest:** "Coram Family and Childcare Survey 2022," Coram Group, 2022, https://www.coram.org.uk/resource/resource-coram -family-and-childcare-survey-2022/; "Earnings and Hours Worked, All Employees," Office for National Statistics, June 27, 2022, https://www.ons.gov.uk /employmentandlabourmarket/peopleinwork/earningsandworkinghours/datasets /earningsandhoursworkedallemployeesashetable8; "Cost of Childcare Has Risen by

over £2,000 a Year since 2010," Trades Union Congress, June 13, 2022, https://www
.tuc.org.uk/news/cost-childcare-has-risen-over-ps2000-year-2010.

10 **for every dollar invested:** "$10 a Day Child Care for Canadian Families," Prime
Minister of Canada, April 21, 2021, https://www.pm.gc.ca/en/news/news-releases
/2021/04/21/10-day-child-care-canadian-families.

11 **high proportion of working mothers:** Laura Oliver, "This Is Where Mothers
Work the Longest Hours," World Economic Forum, May 12, 2017, https://
www.weforum.org/agenda/2017/05/this-is-where-mothers-work-the-longest
-hours/.

12 **in many hunter-gatherer societies:** Michaeleen Doucleff, *Hunt, Gather, Parent:
What Ancient Cultures Can Teach Us about the Lost Art of Raising Happy, Helpful
Little Humans* (New York: Avid Reader Press, 2022), 138.

13 **the World Health Organization commissioned a report:** John Bowlby, "Mental
Health and Maternal Care," *Public Health* 65 (October 1951-September 1952): 128,
https://doi.org/10.1016/s0033–3506(51)80146-x.

14 **US anthropologist Margaret Mead:** Marga Vicedo, "Putting Attachment in Its
Place: Disciplinary and Cultural Contexts," *European Journal of Developmental
Psychology* 14, no. 6 (2017): 684–99, https://doi.org/10.1080/17405629.2017
.1289838; Michael Rutter, "Maternal Deprivation, 1972–1978: New Findings, New
Concepts, New Approaches," *Child Development* 50, no. 2 (June 1979): 283–305,
https://doi.org/10.1111/j.1467–8624.1979.tb04110.x; "Michael Rutter," Royal Society,
accessed October 13, 2023, https://royalsociety.org/people/michael-rutter-12215/.

15 **"There's a lot of attention to attachment":** Henriette Cranil, in discussion with
the author, August 31, 2022.

16 **daughters of working moms:** Dina Gerdeman, "Kids of Working Moms Grow
into Happy Adults," Working Knowledge, Harvard Business School, July 16, 2018,
https://hbswk.hbs.edu/item/kids-of-working-moms-grow-into-happy-adults.

17 **study from the University of North Carolina:** Cheryl Buehler and Marion
O'Brien, "Mothers' Part-Time Employment: Associations with Mother and Family
Well-Being," *Journal of Family Psychology* 25, no. 6 (December 2011): 895–906,
https://doi.org/10.1037%2Fa0025993.

18 **"the weight of the evidence":** Emily Oster, "We Need to Stop Shaming Women
for Wanting (or Not Wanting) to Return to Work," *Fast Company*, April 23, 2019,
https://www.fastcompany.com/90338409/we-need-to-stop-shaming-women-for
-wanting-or-not-wanting-to-return-to-work.

19 **Kindergarten staff in central Denmark:** "Danish Nursery Offers Parents Time for Making Babies," *BBC News*, September 13, 2012, https://www.bbc.com/news/world-europe-19585136.

20 **Hvem passer vores børn?** Hvem Passer Vores Børn? 2019. DR2.

CHAPTER 5: NO SUCH THING AS BAD WEATHER

1 **"Plus, the more you know about nature":** Per Nilsson, in discussion with the author, June 1, 2015.

2 **spending time outdoors can improve:** "Stressed? Take a 20-Minute 'Nature Pill,'" ScienceDaily, April 4, 2019, https://www.sciencedaily.com/releases/2019/04/190404074915.htm; Richard Mitchell, "Is Physical Activity in Natural Environments Better for Mental Health than Physical Activity in Other Environments?," *Social Science & Medicine* 91 (August 2013): 130–34, https://doi.org/10.1016/j.socscimed.2012.04.012.

3 **Researchers in Norway:** Eivind Aadland et al., "Active Learning Norwegian Preschool(er)s (ACTNOW)—Design of a Cluster Randomized Controlled Trial of Staff Professional Development to Promote Physical Activity, Motor Skills, and Cognition in Preschoolers," *Frontiers in Psychology* 11 (2020): 1382, https://doi.org/10.3389/fpsyg.2020.01382.

4 **"Because kids don't have to fight":** Karen Marie Eid Kaarby, in discussion with the author, August 30, 2022.

5 **The Swiss psychologist Jean Piaget:** Les Smith, "About Piaget | Jean Piaget Society," accessed 2021, https://piaget.org/about-piaget/. Saul Mcleod, "Sensorimotor Stage of Cognitive Development | Simply Psychology," accessed April 9, 2019, https://www.simplypsychology.org/sensorimotor.html.

6 **children showed signs of heightened microbial diversity:** Marja I. Roslund et al., "Biodiversity Intervention Enhances Immune Regulation and Health-Associated Commensal Microbiota among Daycare Children," *Science Advances* 6, no. 42 (October 14, 2020), https://doi.org/10.1126/sciadv.aba2578.

7 **"as water and air molecules collide":** Carina Grafetstätter et al., "Does Waterfall Aerosol Influence Mucosal Immunity and Chronic Stress? A Randomized Controlled Clinical Trial," *Journal of Physiological Anthropology* 36 (2017): 10, https://doi.org/10.1186/s40101-016-0117-3.

8 **researchers from Stony Brook University:** Sean A. P. Clouston, Olga Morozova, and Jaymie R. Meliker, "A Wind Speed Threshold for Increased Outdoor

Transmission of Coronavirus: An Ecological Study," *BMC Infectious Diseases* 21 (2021): 1194, https://doi.org/10.1186/s12879-021-06796-z.

9 **"You can't wait for a sunny day in life":** Lasse Heimdal, in discussion with the author, August 19, 2022.

10 **"positive wintertime mindset":** Kari Leibowitz, in discussion with the author, November 10, 2020.

11 **"Parents not born into this culture":** Bente Lier, in discussion with the author, September 2, 2022.

12 **Exposure to green space:** Caoimhe Twohig-Bennett and Andy Jones, "The Health Benefits of the Great Outdoors: A Systematic Review and Meta-Analysis of Greenspace Exposure and Health Outcomes," *Environmental Research* 166 (October 2018): 628–37, https://doi.org/10.1016/j.envres.2018.06.030.

13 **three-quarters of UK children:** Damian Carrington, "Three-Quarters of UK Children Spend Less Time Outdoors than Prison Inmates—Survey," *Guardian*, March 25, 2016, https://www.theguardian.com/environment/2016/mar/25/three-quarters-of-uk-children-spend-less-time-outdoors-than-prison-inmates-survey.

CHAPTER 6: FORAGING AND FAMILY MEALS

1 **Denmark has the highest per capita consumption:** "Organic Food Market: Leading Countries Based on Consumption per Capita, 2021," Statista, March 13, 2023, https://www.statista.com/statistics/263077/per-capita-revenue-of-organic-foods-worldwide-since-2007/.

2 **Sweden and Norway also make:** Louise Kaad-Hansen, "Facts & Figures about Danish Organics," Organic Denmark, February 2022, https://www.organicdenmark.com/facts-figures-about-danish-organics.

3 **"But there's a technique to it":** Trine Hahnemann, in discussion with the author, November 1, 2022.

4 **Children from poorer households:** Petter Lundborg, Dan-Olof Rooth, and Jesper Alex-Petersen, "Long-Term Effects of Childhood Nutrition: Evidence from a School Lunch Reform," *Review of Economic Studies* 89, no. 2 (March 2022): 876–908, https://doi.org/10.1093/restud/rdab028.

5 **"We've got it good in Sweden":** Jacob Holmström, in discussion with the author, August 24, 2022.

6 **"The Swedish approach is about seasonal":** Liselotte Forslin, in discussion with the author, August 29, 2022.

7   **14 percent of British five-year-olds:** Carl Baker, "Obesity Statistics," UK Parliament, January 12, 2023, https://commonslibrary.parliament.uk/research-briefings/sn03336/.

8   **In the US, it's one in five:** "Childhood Overweight and Obesity," Centers for Disease Control and Prevention, last updated April 1, 2022, https://www.cdc.gov/obesity/childhood/index.html.

9   **In Denmark? It's 5 percent:** "WHO European Childhood Obesity Surveillance Initiative (COSI)," World Health Organization, accessed August 26, 2023, https://www.who.int/europe/initiatives/who-european-childhood-obesity-surveillance-initiative-(cosi).

10 **adult obesity has doubled:** Jannie Nielsen et al., "Body Mass Index Trajectories from Childhood to Adulthood and Age at Onset of Overweight and Obesity: The Influence of Parents' Weight Status," *American Journal of Epidemiology* 191, no. 11 (November 2022): 1877–85, https://doi.org/10.1093/aje/kwac124; "Adult Obesity Facts," Centers for Disease Control and Prevention, last updated May 17, 2022, https://www.cdc.gov/obesity/data/adult.html.

11 **a diet high in ultra-processed foods:** Reynalda Cordova et al., "Consumption of Ultra-Processed Foods Associated with Weight Gain and Obesity in Adults: A Multi-National Cohort Study," *Clinical Nutrition* 40, no. 9 (September 2021): 5079–88, https://doi.org/10.1016/j.clnu.2021.08.009.

12 **13 percent of Danish children were now overweight:** Christine Frithioff-Bøjsøe et al., "Early Detection of Childhood Overweight and Related Complications in a Danish Population-Based Cohort Aged 2–8 Years," *Obesity Research & Clinical Practice* 16, no. 3 (May-June 2022): 228–34, https://doi.org/10.1016/j.orcp.2022.04.001.

13 **World Health Organization data:** "Country Profiles on Nutrition, Physical Activity and Obesity in the 53 WHO European Region Member States: Methodology and Summary," World Health Organization, September 10, 2021, https://www.who.int/europe/publications/i/item/9789289050036.

14 **"Safety belts are used in case of a collision":** Peter Opsvik, in correspondence with the author, August 2, 2022.

15 **consumption of meat has doubled in forty years:** "Finns 3rd in Global Meat-Eating Table," Yle, December 20, 2013, https://yle.fi/a/3-6994566; Kjersti Kildahl, "Nine Facts about Norwegian Agriculture," Nibio, March 5, 2020, https://www.nibio.no/en/news/nine-facts-about-norwegian-agriculture.

CHAPTER 7: SINGING, *SAMFUNDSSIND*, AND THE SOCIAL BRAIN

1 **"Today it's quite common to sing together":** Kristian Kongshøj, in discussion with the author, February 17, 2023.

2 **Joining together in song has been proven:** Nick Alan Joseph Stewart and Adam Jonathan Lonsdale, "It's Better Together: The Psychological Benefits of Singing in a Choir," *Psychology of Music* 44, no. 6 (November 2016): 1240–54, https://doi.org /10.1177/0305735615624976; Jason R. Keeler et al., "The Neurochemistry and Social Flow of Singing: Bonding and Oxytocin," *Frontiers in Human Neuroscience* 9 (2015): 518, https://doi.org/10.3389/fnhum.2015.00518.

3 **a study from Aarhus University:** "Antologi: Fællessang og fællesskab" [Anthology: Community song and community], Videncenter for Sang, accessed September 14, 2023, https://videncenterforsang.dk/tema/faellessang-og-faellesskab/; "Ny lancering: Sang bygger bro mellem mennesker og knytter os sammen" [New launch: Song builds bridges between people and connects us], Sangens Hus, September 10, 2019, https://sangenshus.dk/sang-bygger-bro-og-knytter-os-sammen/.

4 **In his book *Den danske sang*:** Phillip Faber, *Den danske sang* (Politikens Forlag, 2020).

5 **"The genders are more equal in Denmark":** Marie Helweg-Larsen, in discussion with the author, February 17, 2023.

6 **Sweden is ranked as the most feminine society:** "Country Comparison Tool," Hofstede Insights, accessed October 13, 2023, https://www.hofstede-insights.com /country-comparison-tool?countries=sweden, https://www.hofstede-insights .com/country-comparison-tool?countries=norway.

7 **the famous wallet study:** Alain Cohn et al., "Civic Honesty around the Globe," *Science* 365, no. 6448 (June 20, 2019): 70–73, https://doi.org/10.1126/science .aau8712.

8 **more caring countries are also happier:** "Why Are Danish People So Happy?," Denmark.dk, accessed October 13, 2023, https://denmark.dk/people-and-culture /happiness; "World Happiness, Trust and Social Connections in Times of Crisis," World Happiness Report, March 20, 2023, https://worldhappiness.report /ed/2023/world-happiness-trust-and-social-connections-in-times-of-crisis/.

9 **research from Arizona State University:** "Parents Should Avoid Pressuring Young Children over Grades, ASU Study Says," Arizona State University, November 28, 2016, https://news.asu.edu/20161128-discoveries-parents-should -avoid-pressuring-young-children-over-grades-asu-study-says.

10 **Family therapist and mother of three:** Sofie Münster, in discussion with the author, February 28, 2023.

11 **we are wired for empathy:** Soyoung Q. Park et al., "A Neural Link between Generosity and Happiness," *Nature Communications* 8 (2017): 15964, https://doi .org/10.1038/ncomms15964.

12 **90 percent of Icelandic women:** Kirstie Brewer, "The Day Iceland's Women Went on Strike," *BBC News*, October 23, 2015, https://www.bbc.com/news /magazine-34602822.

13 **"A letter to the future":** "Iceland Holds Funeral for First Glacier Lost to Climate Change," *Guardian*, August 19, 2019, https://www.theguardian.com/world/2019 /aug/19/iceland-holds-funeral-for-first-glacier-lost-to-climate-change.

14 **"And becoming an activist":** Tom Daley, "Greta Thunberg," March 12, 2023, in *Made with Love*, produced by Spiritland Productions, podcast, 38:59, https://podcasts.apple.com/gb/podcast/greta-thunberg/id1671846653?i= 1000603841617.

15 **"The decision on life choices":** Kjeldahl, discussion.

16 **A Boston Consultancy Group report:** Nanna Gelebo et al., "Cost of Living Crisis: Nordic Consumer Sentiment 2022," BCG Global, November 28, 2022, https://www.bcg.com/publications/2022/nordic-cost-of-living-crisis-consumer -sentiment-report.

17 **One in four households in Norway:** Jo Arne Marvik, Halldor Asvall, and Line Tomter, "Ny rapport: Ein av tre hushaldningar har fått ein dårlegare økonomi sidan januar" [New report: One in three households have had worse finances since January], NRK, July 29, 2022, https://www.nrk.no/norge/ny-rapport_-ein-av-tre -hushaldningar-har-fatt-ein-darlegare-okonomi-sidan-januar-1.16052465; Jon Henley, "'Sweden Has a Poverty Problem': The Social Stores Offering Food at Rock-Bottom Prices," *Guardian*, December 5, 2022, https://www.theguardian.com/world /2022/dec/05/sweden-has-a-poverty-problem-the-social-stores-offering-food -at-rock-bottom-prices; Simon Johnson, "Analysis: Sweden's Cost of Living Crisis Spooks Voters ahead of Election," Reuters, September 5, 2022, https://www.reuters .com/world/swedens-cost-living-crisis-spooks-voters-ahead-election-2022-09-02/.

CHAPTER 8: SHOW, DON'T TELL: DISCIPLINE DANISH STYLE

1 **"Everyone is just so calm here":** Niki Brantmark, in discussion with the author, October 28, 2022.

2 **"The Danish way isn't to focus":** Münster, discussion.

3 **Brain scans show that getting told off:** Daniel J. Siegel and Tina Payne Bryson, *The Whole-Brain Child: 12 Revolutionary Strategies to Nurture Your Child's Developing Mind* (New York: Bantam Books, 2012), 42

4 **Danish family therapist Jesper Juul:** Jesper Juul, *Your Competent Child: Toward a New Paradigm in Parenting and Education* (Bloomington, IN: Balboa Press, 2011), 38.

5 **"Not thinner? Not cleverer?":** *Bridget Jones's Diary*, directed by Sharon Maguire (Universal Pictures, 2001).

6 **"children learn that they cannot always get":** Juul, *Your Competent Child*, 125.

7 **the tenets of Jante's law:** Aksel Sandemose, *A Fugitive Crosses His Tracks*, trans. Eugene Gay-Tifft (New York: A. A. Knopf, 1936), 78.

8 **"children older than five":** Juul, *Your Competent Child*, 154.

9 **"Now listen, when you were young":** Juul, *Your Competent Child*, 155.

10 **"When children are hungry":** Hahnemann, discussion.

11 **we ruin the child's sensible sense:** Juul, *Your Competent Child*, 72.

12 **Rats deprived of the opportunity:** Michael Potegal and Dorothy Einon, "Aggressive Behaviors in Adult Rats Deprived of Playfighting Experience as Juveniles," *Developmental Psychobiology* 22, no. 2 (March 1989): 159–72, https://doi.org/10.1002/dev.420220206.

13 **"it's about self-governance":** Ning de Coninck-Smith, in discussion with the author, November 14, 2022.

CHAPTER 9: PLAY (WELL)

1 **"He leaves a loving wife":** Mark John Stafford (@LEGO_Nabii), "On Wed19th Feb former Chief Designer at LEGO, and creator of the LEGO Minifig Jens Nygaard Knudsen passed," X (formerly Twitter), February 21, 2020, 9:20 a.m., https://twitter.com/LEGO_Nabii/status/1230859764365692928.

2 **"Play is a sign of well-being":** Marc Malmdorf Andersen, in discussion with the author, September 19, 2022.

3 **"probably the most important factor":** Stuart L. Brown and Christopher C. Vaughan, *Play: How It Shapes the Brain, Opens the Imagination, and Invigorates the Soul* (New York: Avery, 2009), 6.

4 **play makes us happier and healthier:** Amy Jo Dowd and Bo Stjerne Thomsen, "Learning through Play: Increasing Impact, Reducing Inequality," Philanthropy Europe Assocation, January 1, 2021, https://philea.issuelab.org/resource/learning-through-play-increasing-impact-reducing-inequality.html.

5 **Many US children:** Kenneth R. Ginsburg et al., "The Importance of Play in Promoting Healthy Child Development and Maintaining Strong Parent-Child Bonds," *Pediatrics* 119, no. 1 (January 2007): 182–91, https://doi.org/10.1542/peds .2006–2697.

6 **Playtime for UK and US children:** Sandra L. Hofferth and John F. Sandberg, "Changes in American Children's Time, 1981–1997," *Advances in Life Course Research* 6 (January 2001): 193–229, https://doi.org/10.1016/s1040–2608(01)80011–3.

7 **"Children are increasingly under pressure":** Paul Ramchandani, in discussion with the author, February 9, 2022.

8 **"People are reaching the physical limits":** Alex Soojung-Kim Pang, in discussion with the author, June 28, 2021.

9 **Microsoft Japan found that staff productivity:** Kazuaki Nagata, "Four-Day Workweek Boosted Productivity by 40%, Microsoft Japan Experiment Shows," *Japan Times*, November 5, 2019, https://www.japantimes.co.jp/news/2019/11/05 /business/microsoft-japan-says-four-day-workweek-boosted-productivity-40/.

10 **New Zealand finance company Perpetual Guardian:** Eleanor Ainge Roy, "Work Less, Get More: New Zealand Firm's Four-Day Week an 'Unmitigated Success,'" *Guardian*, July 18, 2018, https://www.theguardian.com/world/2018/jul/19/work -less-get-more-new-zealand-firms-four-day-week-an-unmitigated-success.

11 **Delaying kindergarten for a year:** Valerie Strauss, "Delaying Kindergarten until Age 7 Offers Key Benefits to Kids—Study," *Washington Post*, October 7, 2015, https://www.washingtonpost.com/news/answer-sheet/wp/2015/10/07/delaying -kindergarten-until-age-7-offers-key-benefits-to-kids-study/; Thomas S. Dee and Hans Henrik Sievertsen, "The Gift of Time? School Starting Age and Mental Health," National Bureau of Economic Research, Working Paper 21610, October 2015, https://doi.org/10.3386/w21610.

12 **Researchers from Michigan State University:** "Nearly One Million Children in U.S. Potentially Misdiagnosed with ADHD, Study Finds," ScienceDaily, August 17, 2010, https://www.sciencedaily.com/releases/2010/08/100817103342.htm.

13 **a Harvard study of 407,000 children:** Timothy J. Layton et al., "Attention Deficit-Hyperactivity Disorder and Month of School Enrollment," *New England Journal of Medicine* 379, no. 22 (November 29, 2018): 2122–30, https://doi.org/10.1056 /nejmoa1806828.

14 **"In Finland, we have ADHD too":** Pasi Sahlberg and William Doyle, *Let the Children Play: Why More Play Will Save Our Schools and Help Children Thrive* (New York: Oxford University Press, 2019), 159.

15 **Denmark is home to a global play experiment:** "What Is PZ?," Project Zero, Harvard Graduate School of Education, accessed October 13, 2023, https://pz .harvard.edu/who-we-are/about.

16 **"less than four hours a week":** "Ingka Centres Open Pop-Up PlayLabs," Ingka Group, November 2, 2022, https://www.ingka.com/news/ingka-centres-open -pop-up-playlabs-bringing-parents-and-children-together-in-the-spirit-of-play/.

17 **53 percent of parents struggle to find time:** Floriane Laroche, "Parents Spend a Total of 1,300 Hours Playing with Their Kids during Their First Five Years," SWNS Digital, September 29, 2022, https://swnsdigital.com/uk/2022/09/parents-spend -a-total-of-1300-hours-playing-with-their-kids-during-their-first-five-years/.

18 **Researchers from Harvard University:** "Serve and Return," Center on the Developing Child, Harvard University, accessed August 26, 2023, https:// developingchild.harvard.edu/science/key-concepts/serve-and-return/.

19 **"The ideas around attachment theory":** Sabilah Eboo Alwani, in discussion with the author, September 20, 2022.

20 **According to a Lego "Play Well" study:** "What Do Children (and Grown-Ups) Have to Say about Play?," Learning Through Play, accessed August 26, 2023, https://learningthroughplay.com/explore-the-research/what-do-children-have -to-say-about-play.

21 **four different types of play:** "Engaging Young Children in Play," Learning Through Play, accessed July 6, 2023, https://learningthroughplay.com/explore -the-research/engaging-young-children-in-play.

CHAPTER 10: RISK (A.K.A. VIKING HEALTH AND SAFETY)

1 **"children have the right to freeze":** Gunnar Breivik, *Sug i magen og livskvalitet* [Thrills and quality of life] (2001). Gunnar Breivik, "The quest for excitement and the safe society," Philosophy, Risk and Adventure Sports, ed. Mike McNamee. Bente Routledge, January 2007, 10–24. https://www.researchgate.net/publication /262600436_The_quest_for_excitement_and_the_safe_society.

2 **"be hungry once in a while":** Gunnar Breivik, "The Quest for Excitement and the Safe Society," in *Philosophy, Risk and Adventure Sports*, ed. Mike McNamee (New York: Routledge, 2007), 10–24, https://www.researchgate.net/publication /262600436_The_quest_for_excitement_and_the_safe_society.

3 **"The way children approach risky play":** Ellen Beate Hansen Sandseter, in discussion with the author, October 3, 2022.

4 **In Germany, insurers recently demanded:** Philip Oltermann, "Learning the

Ropes: Why Germany Is Building Risk into Its Playgrounds," *Guardian*, October 24, 2021, https://www.theguardian.com/world/2021/oct/24/why-germany-is-building-risk-into-its-playgrounds.

5 **take part in *isvaksovning*:** "Swedish Kids Take the Plunge in Icy Lake Survival Lessons," France 24, February 9, 2023, https://www.france24.com/en/live-news/20230209-swedish-kids-take-the-plunge-in-icy-lake-survival-lessons.

6 **"risk and benefit" assessment:** "Resources," Play Safety Forum, March 4, 2015, https://playsafetyforum.wordpress.com/resources/.

7 **parents suing local authorities in the US:** Sue Dremann, "Palo Alto School District Sued for Negligence over Kindergartener's Broken Leg," Palo Alto Online, August 3, 2023, https://www.paloaltoonline.com/news/2023/08/03/palo-alto-school-district-sued-for-negligence-over-kindergarteners-broken-leg.

8 **"We grew up believing children should learn":** Lier, discussion.

9 **"It's quite useful as a parent":** Hrund Þrándardóttir, in discussion with the author, October 5, 2022.

10 **Iceland is ranked the safest country in the world:** "Global Peace Index," Vision of Humanity, 2023, https://www.visionofhumanity.org/maps/#/.

11 **"It was a tough life":** Jacob Hindhede, in discussion with the author, September 28, 2022.

CHAPTER 11: DIGITAL BLIND SPOT

1 **"It is for boys":** Søren Hebsgaard, in discussion with the author, August 18, 2022.

2 **Half of all Danish children:** "Online Games Gamble with Children's Data," Danish Society of Engineers' Working Group on Ethics and Technology and DataEthics.eu, March 2021, https://dataethics.eu/wp-content/uploads/GameTechEnglishVersion.pdf.

3 **A Common Sense Media study:** "The Common Sense Census: Media Use by Kids Age Zero to Eight, 2020," Common Sense Media, November 17, 2020, https://www.commonsensemedia.org/research/the-common-sense-census-media-use-by-kids-age-zero-to-eight-2020.

4 **majority of children in the US now own a smartphone:** "The Common Sense Census: Media Use by Tweens and Teens, 2019," Common Sense Media, October 28, 2019, https://www.commonsensemedia.org/research/the-common-sense-census-media-use-by-tweens-and-teens-2019.

5 **"It's not just that spending time":** Hindhede, discussion.

6 **Researchers from the University of Copenhagen:** Anne Cathrin Joergensen

et al., "Spinal Pain in Pre-Adolescence and the Relation with Screen Time and Physical Activity Behavior," *BMC Musculoskeletal Disorders* 22, no. 1 (2021): 393, https://doi.org/10.1186/s12891-021-04263-z.

7   **a US study found that:** Jeremy J. Walsh et al., "Associations between 24 Hour Movement Behaviours and Global Cognition in US Children: A Cross-Sectional Observational Study," *Lancet Child & Adolescent Health* 2, no. 11 (November 2018): 783–91, https://doi.org/10.1016/s2352–4642(18)30278–5.

8   **there's growing concern for the eyesight:** Joshua Foreman et al., "Association between Digital Smart Device Use and Myopia: A Systematic Review and Meta-Analysis," *Lancet Digital Health* 3, no. 12 (December 2021): E806–18, https://doi.org/10.1016/s2589–7500(21)00135–7.

9   **Danish children spend:** Learning Through Play, "What Do Children."

10   **"Parents allowed children to be at home":** Lier, discussion.

11   **number of Norwegian children who played outside:** Linn Elise Jakhelln, "Barn leker mindre ute i nærområdet" [Children play less outside in the immediate area], *Norsk Friluftsliv*, May 5, 2022, https://norskfriluftsliv.no/barn-leker-mindre-ute-i-naeromradet/.

12   **a dramatic increase in myopia rates:** Jessica Mudditt, "Why Short-Sightedness Is on the Rise," BBC, October 4, 2022, https://www.bbc.com/future/article/20220927-can-you-prevent-short-sightedness-in-kids.

13   **"the real digital divide":** Naomi Schaefer Riley, "America's Real Digital Divide," *New York Times*, February 11, 2018, https://www.nytimes.com/2018/02/11/opinion/america-digital-divide.html.

14   **screen time recommendations for under-fives:** "To Grow Up Healthy, Children Need to Sit Less and Play More," World Health Organization, April 24, 2019, https://www.who.int/news/item/24-04-2019-to-grow-up-healthy-children-need-to-sit-less-and-play-more.

15   **China went further:** "China Cuts Children's Online Gaming to One Hour," *BBC News*, August 30, 2021, https://www.bbc.com/news/technology-58384457.

16   **The UK keeps things vague:** "The Health Impacts of Screen Time: A Guide for Clinicians and Parents," Royal College of Paediatrics and Child Health, January 2019, https://www.rcpch.ac.uk/resources/health-impacts-screen-time-guide-clinicians-parents.

17   **a digital task force:** "Demokratisk kontrol med tech-giganternes forretnings-modeller: Delafrapportering fra regeringens ekspertgruppe om tech-giganter" [Democratic control of the tech giants' business models: Partial report from

the government's expert group on tech giants], Regeringens ekspertgruppe om tech-giganter, June 2023, https://em.dk/aktuelt/udgivelser-og-aftaler/2023/jun /demokratisk-kontrol-med-tech-giganternes-forretningsmodeller; "Regeringens ekspertgruppe om tech-giganter udgiver første rapport med konkrete anbefalinger" [The government's expert group on tech giants publishes its first report with concrete recommendations], Medierådet for Børn og Unge [Media Council for Children and Young People], June 13, 2023, https://www.medieraadet.dk/medieradet/regeringens -ekspertgruppe-om-tech-giganter-udgiver-foerste-rapport-med-konkrete.

18   **the government has agreed:** "Tech-giganterne skal begrænses: Regeringen vil beskytte børn bedre" [The tech giants must be limited: The government will protect children better], Erhvervsministeriet [Ministry of Business], June 12, 2023, https://em.dk/aktuelt/nyheder/2023/jun/tech-giganterne-skal-begraenses -regeringen-vil-beskytte-boern-bedre

19   **"to protect children from potential negative consequences":** Silas Bay Nielsen, "Minister vil have iPads væk fra børnehave og vuggestuer" [Minister wants iPads out of kindergartens and nurseries], DR, June 5, 2023, https://www.dr.dk/nyheder /politik/minister-vil-have-ipads-vaek-fra-boernehave-og-vuggestuer.

20   **"I'm determined to wait for hard evidence":** Stine Liv Johansen, in discussion with the author, August 15, 2022.

21   **"It's like saying that all children":** "Forældre sætter regler for børns skærmfor-brug: Fristelsen er for stor" [Parents set rules for children's screen use: The temp-tation is too great], TV2, May 10, 2022, https://nyheder.tv2.dk/samfund/2022 -05-10-foraeldre-saetter-regler-for-boerns-skaermforbrug-fristelsen-er-for-stor.

22   **"The WHO data is just so black and white":** Johansen, discussion.

23   **"take an interest":** Anbefalinger om børn, unges og forældres brug af skærm" [Recommendations about children, young people and parents' use of screens], Sundhedsstyrelsen [National Board of Health], last updated January 5, 2023, https://www.sst.dk/da/fagperson/forebyggelse-og-tvaergaaende-indsatser /mental-og-digital-sundhed/digital-sundhed/skaermbrug

24   **"I make one video a week for my channel":** Naja Münster, email correspondence with the author, August 22, 2022.

25   **"Screens aren't in opposition to an outdoorsy life":** Johansen, discussion.

26   **"meet an animal and want to find out more":** "Pædagoger ser ikke skærmprob-lem i dagtilbud" [Educators do not see a screen problem in day care], DR, June 5, 2023, https://www.dr.dk/nyheder/politik/paedagoger-ser-ikke-skaermproblem -i-dagtilbud.

27 **"A lot of people say everything is worse":** de Coninck-Smith, discussion.

28 **"So kids need their phones for everything":** Brantmark, discussion.

29 **"The challenge must be to be able":** Hanne Münster, email correspondence with the author, August 22, 2022.

30 **Research from the University of Michigan:** Diane Swanbrow, "Empathy: College Students Don't Have as Much as They Used To," University of Michigan News, May 27, 2010, https://news.umich.edu/empathy-college-students-don-t -have-as-much-as-they-used-to/.

31 **"being on the iPad, computer, or PlayStation":** Jeppe Kyhne Knudsen, "To timer foran skærmen dagligt kan skade dit barns indlæring" [Two hours in front of the screen daily can harm your child's learning], DR, October 1, 2018, https://www.dr .dk/nyheder/viden/kroppen/timer-foran-skaermen-dagligt-kan-skade-dit-barns -indlaering.

32 **"Now when kids are seven or eight":** Kjeldahl, discussion.

33 **a post from psychologist Adam Grant:** Adam Grant (@AdamMGrant), "The earlier kids get smartphones, the worse their mental health as adults," X (formerly Twitter), May 15, 2023, 10:46 a.m., https://twitter.com/AdamMGrant/status /1658121692416204801.

34 **a Sapien Labs study:** "Study out from Sapien Labs Links Age of First Smartphone to Mental Wellbeing," Sapien Labs, May 14, 2023, https://sapienlabs.org/whats _new/study-out-from-sapien-labs-links-age-of-first-smartphone-to-mental -wellbeing/.

35 **Smartphones should wait:** Jon Haidt and Zach Rausch, "Kids Who Get Smartphones Earlier Become Adults with Worse Mental Health," After Babel, May 15, 2023, https://jonathanhaidt.substack.com/p/sapien-smartphone -report.

36 **A UCLA study of eleven- to thirteen-year-olds:** Yalda Uhls et al., "Five Days at Outdoor Education Camp without Screens Improves Preteen Skills with Nonverbal Emotion Cues," *Computers in Human Behavior* 39 (October 2014): 387–92, https://doi.org/10.1016/j.chb.2014.05.036.

CHAPTER 12: THE NEW NORSE SAGAS

1 **"It's always in the top five":** Kajsa Peters, in discussion with the author, August 25, 2022.

2 **"Pippi has a huge influence":** Morten Skov, in discussion with the author, October 11, 2022.

3 **"People have got both eyes and ears"**: Astrid Lindgren, *Pippi in the South Seas*, trans. Susan Beard, illus. Ingrid Vang-Nyman (New York: Puffin Books, 2022), 18.

4 **"If you are very strong"**: Astrid Lindgren, *Meet Pippi Longstocking*, trans. Elisabeth Kallik Dyssegaard, illus. Ingrid Vang-Nyman (Oxford: Oxford University Press, 2022), 53.

5 **"she had this understanding"**: "Astrid Lindgren, Creator of Pippi Longstocking," *Great Lives*, BBC, accessed July 6, 2023, https://www.bbc.co.uk/programmes/m001c6gv.

6 **"he had more playing to do"**: Astrid Lindgren, *Nothing but Fun in Noisy Village*, trans. Susan Beard, illus. Mini Grey (Oxford: Oxford University Press, 2021), 21.

7 **"Pippi taught us never to underestimate children"**: Kim Fupz Aakeson, in discussion with the author, September 13, 2022.

8 **Researchers from Oxford Brookes University:** John Stansfield and Louise Bunce, "The Relationship between Empathy and Reading Fiction: Separate Roles for Cognitive and Affective Components," *Journal of European Psychology Students* 5, no. 3 (2014): 9–18, https://doi.org/10.5334/jeps.ca.

9 **"the sea's just a weak character"**: Tove Jansson, *Moominpappa at Sea*, trans. Kingsley Hart (London: Puffin Books, 2019), 198, 23, 22.

10 **"people find themselves in what she writes"**: Sophia Jansson, in discussion with the author, September 14, 2022.

11 **"doesn't notice quite how lonely"**: Tove Jansson, *Who Will Comfort Toffle?: A Tale of Moomin Valley*, trans. Sophie Hannah (Montreal, QC: Enfant, 2010), 26.

12 **"always wore a dress he inherited"**: Tove Jansson, *Finn Family Moomintroll*, trans. Elizabeth Portch (Harmonsworth, UK: Penguin Books, 1961), footnotes.

13 **A Florida State University sociologist:** Janice McCabe et al., "Gender in Twentieth-Century Children's Books," *Gender & Society* 25, no. 2 (April 2011): 197–226, https://doi.org/10.1177/0891243211398358.

14 **"a dreadful little boy"**: Astrid Lindgren, *Emil and the Sneaky Rat*, trans. Susan Beard, illus. Mini Grey (Oxford: Oxford University Press, 2020), 3.

15 **"We love him just as he is"**: Lindgren, *Emil and the Sneaky Rat*, 4.

16 **"We ought to think"**: Lindgren, *Emil and the Sneaky Rat*, 5.

17 **"I like this approach"**: Hahnemann, discussion.

18 **"It comes naturally to Bamse"**: Brian Patterson, the actor who plays Kylling, sharing original 1960s character breakdown from cast documents, in discussion with the author, October 19, 2022.

19 **Danish anthropologist Christian Groes:** Katherine J. Wu, "'To Me, This

Penis Is Out of Control,'" *Atlantic*, February 26, 2021, https://www.theatlantic
.com/health/archive/2021/02/john-dillermand-danish-kids-show-giant-penis
/618153/.

CHAPTER 13: SCHOOLTIME (BARELY)

1 **"a typical thing to do":** Peter Sandøe, in discussion with the author, June 19, 2014.

2 **"It's very different from the situation in the UK":** de Coninck-Smith, discussion.

3 **"the early onset of lots of homework":** Alwani, discussion.

4 **confidence, motivation, resilience, and communication:** Carl Cullinane and
Rebecca Montacute, "Life Lessons," Sutton Trust, October 11, 2017, https://www
.suttontrust.com/our-research/life-lessons-workplace-skills/.

5 **pressuring children to read too early:** Nancy Carlsson-Paige, Geralyn Bywater
McLaughlin, and John Almon, "Reading Instruction in Kindergarten: Little to
Gain and Much to Lose," Defending the Early Years, January 2015, https://eric.ed
.gov/?id=ED609172.

6 **A study from the University of Regensburg:** Sebastian P. Suggate, Elizabeth
A. Schaughency, and Elaine Reese, "Children Learning to Read Later Catch up
to Children Reading Earlier," *Early Childhood Research Quarterly* 28, no. 1 (2013):
33–48, https://doi.org/10.1016/j.ecresq.2012.04.004.

7 **"no discernible benefits":** Sebastian P. Suggate, "School Entry Age and Reading
Achievement in the 2006 Programme for International Student Assessment
(PISA)," *International Journal of Educational Research* 48, no. 3 (2009): 151–61,
https://doi.org/10.1016/j.ijer.2009.05.001.

8 **Program for International Student Assessment data:** "PISA 2018 Results,"
OECD, 2018, https://www.oecd.org/pisa/publications/pisa-2018-results.htm.

9 **By age fifteen, Danish students:** "PISA 2018 Database," OECD, 2018, https://
www.oecd.org/pisa/data/2018database/.

10 **UNICEF's latest global league table:** Edmond, "These Are the Countries."

11 **"there is no evidence":** D. Hofkins and S. Northen, *Introducing the Cambridge
Primary Review* (Cambridge: University of Cambridge, 2009), https://eprints
.whiterose.ac.uk/76337/1/R_Alexander_CPR_revised_booklet.pdf.

12 **they're happier too:** Frank Martela et al., "The Nordic Exceptionalism: What
Explains Why the Nordic Countries Are Constantly among the Happiest in the
World," World Happiness Report, March 20, 2020, https://worldhappiness
.report/ed/2020/the-nordic-exceptionalism-what-explains-why-the-nordic
-countries-are-constantly-among-the-happiest-in-the-world/.

13 **"We get a child to where we want them"**: Tobias Heiberg, in discussion with the author, September 2, 2022.

14 **"deeply shaken by the reports"**: Emma Bubola and Jasmina Nielsen, "Bullying and Sex Abuse Scandal Engulfs Elite Danish School," *New York Times*, August 28, 2022, https://www.nytimes.com/2022/08/28/world/europe/denmark-bullying -private-school.html.

15 **2 percent of schools are private**: "Frequently Asked Questions," Ministry of Education and Culture, Finland, accessed October 14, 2023, https://okm.fi/en /frequently-asked-questions.

16 **average time spent at school each year**: "State Education Practices (SEP)," National Center for Education Statistics, 2020, https://nces.ed.gov/programs /statereform/tab1_1–2020.asp; "How Many Days and Hours of School Time Each US State Requires by Grade," PlaygroundEquipment.com, accessed October 14, 2023, https://www.playgroundequipment.com/how-many-days-and-hours-of -school-time-per-us-state/.

17 **teacher autonomy is linked with happier classrooms**: Omar T. Al-Bataineh, Ahmad M. Mahasneh, and Zohair Al-Zoubi, "The Correlation between Level of School Happiness and Teacher Autonomy in Jordan," *International Journal of Instruction* 14, no. 2 (April 2021): 1021–36, https://doi.org/10.29333/iji.2021 .14258a; Ahmet Şakir Yazici, "The Relationship between the Teacher Autonomy and Learner Autonomy Support Behaviors," *Journal of Educational Sciences Research* 6, no. 2 (October 2016): 1–23, https://www.eduscires.com/articles/the -relationship-between-the-teacher-autonomy-and-learnerautonomy-support -behaviors.pdf.

18 **"We pay high taxes in Denmark"**: Hahnemann, discussion.

CHAPTER 14: *GOD FERIE!* HOLIDAYING LIKE A VIKING

1 **"collective restoration"**: Terry Hartig et al., "Vacation, Collective Restoration, and Mental Health in a Population," *Society and Mental Health* 3, no. 3 (November 2013): 221–36, https://doi.org/10.1177/2156869313497718; Oliver Burkeman, "This Column Will Change Your Life: A Holiday Shared Is a Break for Us All," *Guardian*, August 16, 2014, https://www.theguardian.com/lifeandstyle/2014/aug /16/change-life-holidays-collective-restoration-oliver-burkeman.

2 **51 percent of Swedes have access**: "Norwegian Ownership of Swedish Holiday Homes Largest," Statistics Sweden, March 24, 2022, https://www.scb.se/en /finding-statistics/statistics-by-subject-area/housing-construction-and-building

/housing-construction-and-conversion/dwelling-stock/pong/statistical-news
/foreign-ownership-and-expatriate-swedes-ownership-of-holiday-homes-in
-sweden-2021/.

3   **"We looked out for him in return":** Lars Kruthof, in discussion with the author, March 13, 2018.

4   **"There's a strong history of fear":** Casper Steinfath, in discussion with the author, May 1, 2019.

5   **"Salt crystals found in the air":** Niels Poplens, email correspondence with the author, January 29, 2020.

6   **"We take it for granted":** Rikke Johansen, in discussion with the author, January 30, 2020.

7   **Being around a large expanse of water:** M. P. White et al., "The 'Blue Gym': What Can Blue Space Do for You and What Can You Do for Blue Space?," *Journal of the Marine Biological Association of the United Kingdom* 96, no. 1 (2016): 5–12, https://doi.org/10.1017/S0025315415002209.

8   **Experiencing nature on holiday:** Salvatore Bimonte and Valeria Faralla, "Happiness and Nature-Based Vacations," *Annals of Tourism Research* 46 (May 2014): 176–78, https://doi.org/10.1016/j.annals.2014.02.002.

9   **Researchers from Northwestern University:** Nelly A. Papalambros et al., "Acoustic Enhancement of Sleep Slow Oscillations and Concomitant Memory Improvement in Older Adults," *Frontiers in Human Neuroscience* 11 (March 2017): 109, https://doi.org/10.3389/fnhum.2017.00109.

10 **a National Trust study:** Steven Morris, "A Stroll by the Sea Will Help You Sleep Longer, Study Finds," *Guardian*, September 17, 2015, https://www.theguardian.com/uk-news/2015/sep/17/a-stroll-by-the-sea-will-help-you-sleep-longer-study-finds.

CHAPTER 15: LET'S GET PHYSICAL

1   **In Iceland, there's even a song:** Guy Martin, "How to Get Naked in Iceland: New 'Spa Etiquette' Tourist Video Is Viral Comedy Gold," *Forbes*, March 1, 2016, https://www.forbes.com/sites/guymartin/2016/03/01/how-to-get-naked-in-iceland-spa-etiquette-tourist-video-gudmundur/?sh=750f0d233635.

2   **3.3 million saunas in a country of just 5.5 million people:** Steven Beschloss, "Finland's Sauna Obsession." *National Geographic*, November 3, 2015.

3   **A mere 1.62 percent of Danes:** Pippa Stephens, "Gelotophobia: Living a Life in Fear of Laughter," *BBC News*, June 27, 2014, http://www.bbc.co.uk/news/health-27323470.

4 **"What kind of culture are we creating"**: Nina Siena, "New Danish Children's TV Show Features Man with Giant Penis," *Latin Times*, January 8, 2021, https://www.latintimes.com/new-danish-childrens-tv-show-features-man-giant-penis-464759; Erla Heinesen Højsted, in discussion with the author, August 8, 2022.

5 **82 percent of Danish children:** "Denmark," Active Healthy Kids Global Alliance, accessed July 3, 2023, https://www.activehealthykids.org/denmark/.

6 **"I had a lot of questions"**: Andreas Relster, "Ny serie imødekommer unges usikkerhed om pubertet og sex" [New series addresses young people's uncertainty about puberty and sex], DR, February 8, 2021, https://www.dr.dk/om-dr/nyheder/ny-serie-imoedekommer-unges-usikkerhed-om-pubertet-og-sex.

7 **"partly a school-based task"**: Relster, "Ny serie."

8 **"We're surprised when people"**: Peters, discussion.

9 **"seizing every opportunity"**: "Sex Education: Gender Equality, Sexuality and Human Relationships in the Swedish Curricula," Swedish National Agency for Education, 2014, https://www.skolverket.se/download/18.6bfaca41169863e6a65bd27/1553966490106/pdf3580.pdf.

10 **"We know from research"**: Helen Russell, "Porn Belongs in the Classroom, Says Danish Professor," *Guardian*, March 16, 2015, https://www.theguardian.com/culture/2015/mar/16/pornography-belongs-classroom-professor-denmark.

11 **A Common Sense Media report:** Michael Robb and Supreet Mann, "Teens and Pornography," Common Sense Media, 2022, https://www.commonsensemedia.org/sites/default/files/research/report/2022-teens-and-pornography-final-web.pdf.

12 **"possess the necessary skills"**: Russell, "Porn Belongs in the Classroom."

13 **a sex guide of sixty different positions:** "Sexguiden," NRK, accessed September 13, 2023, https://www.nrk.no/spesial/sexguide.

14 **"I think a lot of people"**: Jonathan Gaathaug Nielsen, "NRKs sexguide skaper overskrifter over hele verden" [NRK's sex guide makes headlines all over the world], NRK, June 22, 2021, https://www.nrk.no/kultur/nrk-sin-sexguide-tar-av-i-utlandet-1.15547837.

CHAPTER 16: TEEN VIKING

1 **This ritual ride:** Margit Warburg, "Graduation in Denmark: Secular Ritual and Civil Religion," *Journal of Ritual Studies* 23, no. 2 (2009): 31–42, http://www.jstor.org/stable/44368808.

2 **Denmark has a state Lutheran church:** "Types of Tax: Direct Tax—Church Tax,"

Danish Customs and Tax Administration, accessed October 14, 2023, https://skat
.dk/data.aspx?oid=2244282.

3   **average teen will receive confirmation gifts:** Ann Lehmann Erichsen,
"Konfirmationsfest på afbud" [Confirmation party canceled], Nordea, April 19,
2021, https://nytfranordea.nordea.dk/da/artikler/konfirmationsfest-paa-afbud.

4   **"*Efterskoler* have been around for about 150 years":** Jakob Clausager Jensen,
in discussion with the author, February 28, 2023.

5   **a quarter of all Danish teenagers attend efterskole:** Magnus Nørtoft,
"Rekordstor andel tager efterskole i 10. klasse: Især andelen af unge med forældre
med relativt høje indkomster er stigende" [A record-breaking proportion take
post-secondary education in the 10th grade: The proportion of young people
with parents with relatively high incomes in particular is increasing], Statistics
Denmark, September 4, 2020, https://www.dst.dk/da/Statistik/nyheder-analyser
-publ/bagtal/2020/2020-09-04-rekordstor-andel-paa-efterskole.

6   **"We're trying to prepare them":** Michelle Brogaard, in discussion with the
author, August 26, 2022.

7   **"We would do it on rotation normally":** Hahnemann, discussion.

8   **efterskole students are more likely to complete:** "The Danish Efterskole,"
Efterskolen ved Nyborg, accessed September 13, 2023, https://evn.dk/skolen/the
-danish-efterskole.

9   **"Being a young person in Denmark":** Lisa Abend, "A Cinematic Love Letter to
Denmark's Drinking Culture," *New York Times*, December 4, 2020, https://www
.nytimes.com/2020/12/04/movies/another-round-vinterberg-denmark.html.

10 **a WHO report:** Jo Inchley et al., eds., *Spotlight on Adolescent Health and Well-Being:
Findings from the 2017/2018 Health Behaviour in School-Aged Children (HBSC)
Survey in Europe and Canada*, vol. 2, *Key Data* (Copenhagen: WHO Regional Office
for Europe, 2020), https://apps.who.int/iris/handle/10665/332104.

11 **highest rates of heavy, episodic drinking:** Camille Bello, "Europe Is Home
to the World's Heaviest Drinkers. Which Country Drinks the Most Alcohol?,"
Euronews, June 30, 2023, https://www.euronews.com/next/2023/06/30/so-long
-dry-january-which-country-drinks-the-most-alcohol-in-europe; "Denmark:
Consumption Patterns," Nordic Alcohol and Drug Report, accessed October 14,
2023, https://www.nordicalcohol.org/denmark-consumption-patterns.

12 **"I haven't felt this good in ages!":** *Another Round*, directed by Thomas Vinterberg
(Zentropa Entertainments, 2020).

13 **analytical problem-solving skills suffer:** W. Dean Chiles and Alan E. Jennings,

"Effects of Alcohol on a Problem Solving Task," Civil Aeromedical Institute, March 1, 1972, https://rosap.ntl.bts.gov/view/dot/20990; Harry Sumnall, "Another Round? What Really Happens When You Microdose Alcohol," *Conversation*, October 11, 2021, https://theconversation.com/another-round-what-really -happens-when-you-microdose-alcohol-166433.

14 **"We have this very constant":** Abend, "Cinematic Love Letter."

15 **"must-haves for festive occasions":** "Beer Bongs," Party Vikings, accessed September 13, 2023, https://partyvikings.co.uk/products/party-gadgets/beer-bong.

16 **A study from Aarhus University:** Frederik Kraglund et al., "Decreasing Incidence of Alcohol-Related Liver Disease in Denmark: A 25-Year Nationwide Study," *Clinical Epidemiology* 13 (January 2021): 1–11, https://doi.org/10.2147/clep .s287870.

17 **global data on deaths:** Harshad Devarbhavi et al., "Global Burden of Liver Disease: 2023 Update," *Journal of Hepatology* 79, no. 2 (August 2023): P516–37, https://doi.org/10.1016/j.jhep.2023.03.017.

18 **"Danish parents can seem super loosey-goosey":** Helweg-Larsen, discussion.

19 **"These kids are eighteen or nineteen":** Holmström, discussion.

EPILOGUE

1 **"Christmas in Denmark is all about the family":** Emilia van Hauen, in discussion with the author, November 25, 2015.

2 **people in the UK spent £2.6 billion:** Paloma Kubiak, "Brits Spend £2bn on Unwanted Christmas Presents," Your Money, December 9, 2019, https://www .yourmoney.com/household-bills/brits-spend-2bn-on-unwanted-christmas -presents/.

3 **Yuletide traditions differ across the region:** Jeremy Stahl, "Sweden's Bizarre Tradition of Watching Donald Duck Cartoons on Christmas Eve," *Slate*, December 22, 2009, https://slate.com/culture/2009/12/sweden-s-bizarre-tradition-of -watching-donald-duck-kalle-anka-cartoons-on-christmas-eve.html.

4 **"Their faces light up when they see Santa":** Jouni Talso, in discussion with the author, August 23, 2022.

5 **"But in the US and the UK":** Hahnemann, discussion.

6 **Economists predict that by 2050:** Carl Benedikt Frey and Michael A. Osborne, "The Future of Employment: How Susceptible Are Jobs to Computerisation?," *Technological Forecasting and Social Change* 114 (January 2017): 254–80, https:// doi.org/10.1016/j.techfore.2016.08.019.

7   **the earnings of American men:** Ron Haskins, Julia B. Isaacs, and Isabel V. Sawhill, "Getting Ahead or Losing Ground: Economic Mobility in America," Brookings Institution, February 20, 2008, https://www.brookings.edu/articles/getting-ahead-or-losing-ground-economic-mobility-in-america/.

8   **"The self-governing way we treat":** de Coninck-Smith, discussion.

9   **"she has absolutely no idea":** Abby Wambach, *Wolfpack: How to Come Together, Unleash Our Power, and Change the Game* (New York: Celadon Books, 2019), 74.

Index

〰

A

Aakeson, Kim Fupz, 201
activism, 116
adaptability, 293
addiction, 28
ADHD, 151–152
adolescents. See teenagers
adoption, 11
adventurous play, 168. See also risk
aesthetics, 94
age of consent, 264
agriculture, 95, 156, 174, 214
alarm clocks, 134–135, 138
alcohol, 129, 278–282, 314
Allemansrätten, 78
alloparents, 51
Alwani, Sabilah Eboo, 156–159, 160,
　　219, 223
Andersen, Hans Christian, 203
Andersen, Marc Malmdorf, 147, 148,
　　149, 150, 167–168, 169–170, 173
anniversaries, 317
annual leave, 56. See also holiday time

Another Round (Druk), 279–281
anxiety, xii, 37. See also mental health
attachment theory, 58, 156
authority, external, 137
autonomy, 93, 116, 127–128
　　modeling, 139

B

baby box, 19–20
baby gear, 19, 29, 34
baking, 97, 312. See also cake
Ball, David, 171
barnevogne (child wagons), 34
beaches, 241–242, 244
bedtime, 134–135, 139
beer. See alcohol; celebrations
beer bong, 281
behavior. See also discipline
　　autonomy and, 127–128
　　changing, 226
　　empathy and, 128–129
　　feelings behind, 128
　　reasons for, 123, 124

Bergman, Ingmar, 237
birth, 22–27, 29
    recovery from, 32
birthdays, 65–66, 315–316
births, outside marriage, xvii
boarding schools, 227
    efterskole, 273–276, 284
bodies, 292. See also health, physical;
    movement
    age of consent and, 264
    learning about, 266
    nudity, 253–257, 303
    pornography, 262–263, 266
    sex education, 259–264, 266
    thinness, 257, 266
books, 202–203, 292, 310–311. See also
    literature; reading
børnehave (kindergarten), 49, 51, 55,
    151. See also day care
boundaries, 63–64, 66, 107, 137
boundary age, 127
bøvl, 175–176
Bowlby, John, 57–58
brains, 44
Brantmark, Niki, 122
breastfeeding, 26–27
Breivik, Gunnar, 167, 169
Brogaard, Michelle, 275
Brown, Stuart, 148
bullying, 107, 111

C
cake, 96–98, 303, 315. See also
    celebrations
calmness, 122
camping, 78–81

Canada, 57, 186
candles, 94
candy, 136
caring, 111, 117
caring cultures, 107–108
cars, 258–259
cats, 305
celebrations, 303–317
    birthdays, 65–66, 315–316
    Christmas, 287–292, 310–311,
        312–313
chaos, 66
charity, 112
child care, 292–293. See also day care;
    parents, working
    cost of, 55–56
    men in, 59–60
    return on, 293
    subsidized, 39
    in UK, 56
    in US, 56
child development, 59, 72
child endangerment, 36
childbirth, 22–27, 29
    recovery from, 32
childhood, 117, 152, 292
children, donor-conceived, 2, 9–15
China, screen time in, 186
chips, 87–88
choices, 137
chores, 138, 284, 286
Christianity, 202
    confirmation, 272–273
Christmas, 287–292, 310–311, 312–313
cinnamon, 315–316
cleanliness, 253–254

climate change, 116

clothing, 68, 75–77, 81, 82, 124, 294, 300

cohesion, 102, 104. See also community

Common Sense Media, 182, 263

community. See also cohesion; samfundssind; togetherness
    childhood and, 117
    COVID-19 and, 106
    education and, 116
    helping, 115–116 (See also volunteering)
    rules and, 66
    singing and, 103–105

competencies, 172, 176

confirmation, 272–273

conflict, 140–142, 209, 295, 299

conformity, 126

connections, 108. See also community

control, 24

cooking, 90, 275

cooperation, 126–127

corporal punishment, 200

cost of living, 20, 28

COVID-19, 74, 105–106, 185

cows, 306–307

coziness, 94. See also hygge

Cranil, Henriette, 11–13, 37, 58

Creasy, Stella, 56

creativity, 150

Cribsheet (Oster), 59

criticism, 128

Cryos, 1–4, 6, 7–8

cultural competence, 172

curfew, 173

curiosity, 293

curling, 124, 142

D

danger, desire for, 168. See also risk

Danske sang, Den (Faber), 104

darkness, in literature, 202–203, 212

data, personal, 186. See also screens

day care, 12. See also child care; parents, working
    birthdays and, 65–66
    børnehave (kindergarten), 51, 172
    child-to-child teaching in, 51
    food at, 84, 86–87
    goals and, 53–56, 63
    hours of, 62
    in Iceland, 55
    outdoor naps and, 60–61
    paperwork, 63
    security, 60
    staff, 48, 62
    student helpers, 60
    Tripp Trapp and, 94
    vuggestue (nursery), 49, 50–52

days, names of, xiv

de Coninck-Smith, Ning, 141, 152–153, 191, 216, 223, 294

December, 288. See also Christmas

democracy, 103, 217, 298, 308

Denmark, xiii, xiv

dental treatment, 28. See also healthcare

design, 94

digital blind spot. See screens

digital divide, 185

Dinner for One, 314

discipline. See also behavior
  corporal punishment, 200
  fighting, 140–142, 143
  food and, 135–137
  modeling autonomy, 139
  praise and, 130–132
  reducing friction, 124, 142–143
  respect and, 128
  responsibility and, 137–138
  ultimatums, 123
discomfort, tolerance for, 176
dissections, 213–215
diversity, 225
divorce, xvi, xvii, 13
donor-conceived children, 2, 9–15
drinking culture, 278–282. See also
  alcohol
driving, 258–259

E

eating. See also food
  disordered, 266
economic challenges, 117
economy, parental leave and, 39–43
Eddas, 198. See also literature
education, xi–xii, 5. See also day care;
  schools; teachers
  age and, vii, 151
  boarding schools, 227, 273–276
  community and, 116
  cooking and, 90, 275
  cost of, 216
  dissections, 213–215
  efterskole, 273–276, 284
  in Finland, 54–55, 218, 220,
    228–229

folkeskole, 215, 274, 277
food and, 88–89
free, 28, 293
friendship class, 225
grades, 220, 277
graduation, 268–272, 281
gymnasium, 274, 277
homework, 219, 230
international students, 276
pace of, 218–223
parental involvement and, 223–224
paying for, 229, 275–276
pressure in, 220–222
private schools, 216, 228
public speaking and, 218, 231
screens and, 182, 185, 190, 191, 275
social skills and, 225
special needs and, 226, 229
in Sweden, 219
tests, 220, 222, 228, 230
trade school, 277
in UK, 218, 219, 229
university, 293
in US, 229
education, early childhood, 48, 293.
  See also child care; day care
efterskole, 273–276, 284
egalitarianism, 131. See also equality
Egebæk, Pernille Ane, 260
emotions, 51–52, 126, 209. See also
  discipline
empathy, 128–129, 192, 201
employment, female, xvi. See also
  women, working
environment, 20, 116. See also nature;
  outdoors

equality, xi–xii, xvi, 108, 131, 274. See also inequality
Erb, Karin, 9
European Union, 39
Everyday Sisu (Pantzar), 55, 172
eyesight, 183–184, 185

F

Faber, Phillip, 104–105
failure, 129–130, 211
faith, 37, 46, 230
family time, 91–92
family units, types of, xvi–xvii, 9, 16
Faroe Islands, xv note
fathers, 38–39, 41, 42–44, 46
fear, 168–169
feelings, 51–52, 126, 209. See also discipline
feminine ideals, 108
fertility treatments, 1, 2–16
fighting, 140–142, 143. See also conflict
Finding Sisu (Pantzar), 55
Finland, xii, xiii
    academic achievement in, 222
    age of consent in, 264
    alcohol in, 278
    baby box, 19–20
    celebrations in, 303–317
    clothing in, 77
    day care in, 55
    education in, 54–55, 218, 220, 228–229
    food in, 88, 89, 96
    healthcare in, 20–21
    kindergarten in, 55
    literature in, 204–206

parental leave in, 38
risky play in, 172
saunas in, 255
screen time in, 186
sisu (grit), 55, 172, 176, 292
summer cabins in, 234
Vikings and, xiv
women in management in, 40
Finnish Lessons (Sahlberg), 55
flags, 315
Flashdance, 265–266
folkeskole, 215, 274, 277. See also education
food. See also celebrations
    cake, 96–98, 303, 315
    candy, 136
    chips, 87–88
    control around, 136
    cooking, 90, 275
    at day care, 84, 86–87
    discipline and, 135–137
    education and, 88–89
    family meals, 91–92, 99
    foraging, 89
    health and, 83, 88–89
    hunger, 135–136
    leverpostej (liver pâté), 18, 85–86
    lunch, 86–88
    meat, 95–96
    obesity and, 90–91
    organic, 84
    outdoors and, 79, 82
    pølser, 95–96, 99
    rye bread, 86, 88, 91
    snacks, 83, 85, 87–88, 91, 98
    in UK, 95

ultra-processed, 90–91
in US, 95
food waste, 115
foraging, 89
Forslin, Liselotte, 89, 92
Frederiksen, Mette, xvii, 105
free/critical thinking, 217, 230, 293
freedom, 116
parents', 138–140
responsibility and, 134
fresh air. See nature; outdoors
friction, reducing, 124, 142–143
friends, 46
friendship class, 225
friluftsliv (free air life), 71, 74, 78, 79, 292
Fugitive Crosses His Tracks, A (Sandemose), 131
fundraising, 112

G

gaming. See screens
garbage bags, 115, 120
gelotophobia, 257
gender
in literature, 206
screens and, 182
gender equality, xvi, 108
Germany. See also World War II
risky play and, 171
gifts, 273, 288, 289
Gill, Tim, 171
Gissler, Mika, 20
Gjedde, Albert, 192
Global Peace Index, 173
goals, 63

Golombok, Susan, 13
good, greater, 106, 116. See also samfundssind
grades, 220, 277
graduation, 268–272, 281
Grant, Adam, 193
Graugaard, Christian, 263
greater good, 106, 116. See also samfundssind
green bags, 115, 120
Greenland, xv note
grit (sisu), 55, 172, 176, 292
Grundtvig, N. F. S., 102, 217
gymnasium, 274, 277

H

Hahnemann, Trine, 85–86, 91, 97, 135, 208, 229–230, 275, 293
Hansen, Lise, 51–52
happiness, viii, xi–xii, xvi, 16, 28, 108, 111
health, mental. See mental health
health, physical, 53
food and, 83, 88–89
mud and, 72–73
obesity, 90–91
outdoors and, 78, 82
rain and, 73
responsibility and, 137
sickness gap, 41–42
wind and, 73–74
health and safety, xi, 171, 246. See also risk; safety
health visitors, 33
healthcare, 5, 107, 166
baby box, 19–20

childbirth, 22–27, 29, 32
in Finland, 20–21
free, 28
pregnancy, 17–21
risky play and, 171
in US, 171
Hebsgaard, Søren, 181–182, 185, 194
Heiberg, Tobias, 225, 226
Heimdal, Lasse, 74, 76, 79
helicopter parenting (curling), 124, 142
helping, 115–116, 138. See also volunteering
Helweg-Larsen, Marie, 108, 118, 283
Herlufsholm School, 227
high chair, 92–94
Hindhede, Jacob, 174, 183, 184
Hofstede, Geert, 108
Højskolesangbogen (High School Songbook), 103
Højsted, Erla Heinesen, 257
hole stones, 241–242, 244, 251
holiday time, 56, 233–234. See also celebrations
nature and, 243
screens and, 251
summerhouses, 234–251
Holmström, Jacob, 89, 90, 284
home decor, 94
homework, 219, 230
honesty, 212
MAR and, 16
hot dogs (pølser), 95–96, 99
hulsten, 241–242, 244, 251
hunger, 135–136
hygge, xvi, 94, 96, 99, 222, 224, 289

Iceland, xiii. See also sagas, Norse
age of consent in, 264
books and, 202–203, 292, 310–311
celebrations in, 303–317
day care in, 55
food in, 96
incest prevention in, 264
names in, 45
parental leave in, 38
risky play in, 172–173
safety in, 173
screen time in, 186
summer cabins in, 234
Vikings and, xv
ICI (intracervical insemination), 3, 4. See also fertility treatments
illness. See also health, physical; healthcare; mental health
sickness gap, 41–42
incest prevention, 264
inclusivity, 205–207, 212, 270
income, xvi, 27–28, 292–293
parental leave and, 41
taxes and, 39
independence, 93, 274
individualization, 116–117
inequality, 20, 21, 28, 29. See also equality
infant mortality rates, 20
infertility, 10. See also fertility treatments
innovation, 150
intracervical insemination (ICI), 3, 4. See also fertility treatments
intrauterine insemination (IUI), 3, 4. See also fertility treatments

islands, 238, 240–243, 244
 Faroe Islands, xv note
IUI (intrauterine insemination), 3, 4.
 See also fertility treatments
IVF, 3–4. See also fertility treatments

J

jail, 52–53
Jansson, Sophia, 204–205, 207
Jansson, Tove, 204, 207
Jante's law, 131, 218, 242
Japan, 151
Jensen, Jakob Clausager, 274, 275, 276
Johansen, Lise, 40, 42
Johansen, Rikke, 240
Johansen, Stine Liv, 186, 190, 191
Julemand (Christmas Man), 289–290
junk playgrounds, 152–153
Juul, Jesper, 126, 127, 130, 131, 134, 135,
 137, 139

K

Kaarby, Karen Marie Eid, 71–72
kidnapping, 35–36
kindergarten (børnehave), 49, 51, 55,
 151. See also day care
Kjeldahl, Rasmus, xvii, 116–117, 192, 194
Klitmøller, 239
Knudsen, Jens Nygaard, 146
Kompan, 153
Kongshøj, Kristian, 102, 106
Kristiansen, Godtfred, 146
Kristiansen, Ole Kirk, 146
Krogh, Diana Ringe, 109–110, 117
Kruthof, Lars, 237
kvajebajer, 129

L

labor market. See women, working;
 work
lakris (licorice), 18
land, 78
language
 choice of, 128
 swearing, 132
language development, 53
learning. See also education
 lifelong, 293
 through play, 222
leave, 56. See also holiday time; parental leave
leg, 147, 162. See also play
legepatruljen (play patrol), 111
Lego, 96, 145–147, 158, 184
Leibowitz, Kari, 75, 76
leverpostej (liver pâté), 18, 85–86
Lew-Levy, Sheina, 51
LGBTQ+ community
 children's literature and, 205–207
 pronouns, 206–207
 same-sex couples, xvii, 9, 11
 transgender rights, 260
licorice (lakris), 18
Lier, Bente, 78, 79, 172, 185
life choices, 116–117
life satisfaction, xvi
Lin, Anna, 260
Lindgren, Astrid, 198–201, 207–208
Lindhardt, Tom, 153
Lingaard, Louise, 214–215, 220
listening, 286
literature. See also books; reading
 content, 201–209

darkness in, 202–203, 212

gender in, 206

inclusivity and, 205–207

Moomins, 204–206, 207

Norse sagas, xiii, 198, 209

Pippi Longstocking, 197–201, 207–208, 210–211

litigation, risky play and, 171

liver pâté (leverpostej), 18, 85–86

lockdowns, 106, 185. See also COVID-19

Löfgren, Niklas, 38–40, 41

Lomborg, Mikkel, 210

Longstocking, Pippi, 197–201, 207–208, 210–211

M

Mägi, Marika, xiv

Marin, Sanna, xvii

masculinity, 108

mastery, 175, 176, 275

masturbation, 260, 266

Maya people, 57

Mead, Margaret, 58

meals. See food

meat, 18, 85, 95–96, 99

medically assisted reproduction (MAR), 9–15

men, 46

in day care, 59–60

parental leave and, 38–39, 41, 42–44

mental health, xii

anxiety, xii, 37

caring and, 111

child care and, 53

outdoors and, 71

screens and, 185, 193

stress, 149–150, 288, 289

stress leave, 107

work hours and, 151

midwives, 17, 25

Minecraft, 181, 182, 183. See also screens

Modern Families (Golombok), 13

Monstrum, 153

Moomins, 204–206, 207

mothers, single, xvii, 9–13

mothers, working, 41–42, 56–59, 292–293. See also women, working

mother's groups, 33–34

motor development, 53

movement, 53, 173, 257–259. See also play

mud, 72–73, 81, 82

Münster, Hanne, 191

Münster, Naja, 189–190, 191

Münster, Sofie, 112, 123, 125, 132

music. See singing

Myrthue, Helle Sejersen, 8, 9

mythology, Norse, 202. See also literature

N

names, 44–46

naps, outdoor, 35–37, 60–61

national identity, community singing and, 103–104

nationalism, xvi

nature. See also outdoors; weather

health and, 78, 82

holiday time and, 243

play and, 71–72, 153

prioritizing, 52

screens and, 190, 195

New Zealand, 151

Nielsen, Carl, 104

Nilsson, Per, 71

nisser, 290

"Nordic", use of term, xiii

Nordic countries, xii–xiii, xv, xvi. See
    also Denmark; Finland; Iceland;
    Norway; Sweden

"Norse", use of term, xiii

Norway, xiii

    academic achievement in, 222

    age of consent in, 264

    alcohol in, 278

    celebrations in, 303–317

    day care in, 55

    economic challenges of, 117

    feminine ideals and, 108

    food in, 96

    friluftsliv (free air life), 71, 74, 78,
        79, 292

    health and safety in, 167

    obesity in, 91

    parental leave in, 38

    screen time in, 185, 186

    sex education in, 263

    summer cabins in, 234

    Vikings and, xiv

    women in management in, 40

nudity, 253–257, 303

nursery (vuggestue), 49, 50–52. See
    also day care

nursing, 26–27

O

obedience, 126

obesity, 90–91

OECD (Organization for Economic
    Cooperation and Development),
    27, 28, 39, 53

Oishi, Shigehiro, 28

ølbonger, 281

only children, 16, 169

Ø-PAS, 240

open-mindedness, 293

Opsvik, Peter, 92–93

oracy, 218, 231

Organization for Economic
    Cooperation and Development
    (OECD), 27, 28, 39, 53

Oster, Emily, 59

outdoor library, 77

outdoors, 59, 66, 71. See also nature;
    weather

    camping, 78–81

    child development and, 72

    food and, 79, 82

    friluftsliv (free air life), 71, 74, 78,
        79, 292

    health and, 78, 82

    mental health and, 71

    napping in, 35–37, 60–61

    screens and, 190, 195

P

Page, Abigail, 51

pakkeleg, 288

Palmberg, Johan, 199

pandemic, 74, 105–106, 185

Pang, Alex Soojung-Kim, 150

INDEX

Pantzar, Katja, 19, 54–55, 77, 89, 172, 228
parental leave, 37–42, 292
    economy and, 39–43
    fathers and, 38–39, 41, 42–44
    in Iceland, 38
    in Sweden, 38–39, 40–43
parenting, Viking, xviii
parents
    help for, 117–119
    needs of, 138–139
    screens and, 188–189, 192
    support for, 32
parents, new, 46, 302
parents, single, xvii, 9–13
parents, working, 292–293. See also
    parental leave; women, working
parties, 65–66, 303–317
paternity leave, 41, 42–44. See also
    parental leave
peace table, 140
pedagogues, 48. See also teachers
peekaboo, 155–156
pepper, 316
Peters, Kajsa, 198, 261, 262
phones, 191, 193, 196, 275. See also
    screens
Piaget, Jean, 72
Pickett, Kate, 28
Pietilä, Tuulikki, 205
play, 59, 147, 154. See also risk
    adults and, 149–151, 154–161, 162
    importance of, 162
    learning through, 222
    Lego, 145–147
    nature and, 71–72, 153
    prioritizing, 52–53

    reading as, 223
    types of, 159–160, 162
    "wild times", 156
    words for, 147, 162
    work and, 150
play fighting, 140–142, 143
play patrol (legepatruljen), 111
playgrounds, 152–154, 171
playgroups, multiage, 51. See also day
    care
pølser, 95–96, 99
Poplens, Niels, 239
pork, 85
pornography, 262–263, 266
poverty prevention, 53
praise, 130–132, 143
pregnancy, 17–21, 29. See also child-
    birth; fertility treatments
    unplanned, 13
prenatal care, 20
prison, 52–53
privilege, 228
process, focus on, 125
productivity, 41, 151
Program for International Student
    Assessment (PISA), 222
pronouns, 206–207
public access, right of, 78
public speaking, 218, 231
punishment, 126. See also discipline
pyt, 129–130

R
rain, 73, 81, 82
ramasjang, 53, 138, 292. See also
    movement

Ramchandani, Paul, 149, 155
reading, 222, 223. See also books;
    education; literature
relationships, xvi, 299
religion, 202, 272–273
rent, 28
reproduction, 2–16. See also sex
    education
resilience. See also sisu
    risk and, 171
respect, 128, 142, 294
responsibility, 134–135, 137–138, 176,
    283, 294
restoration, collective, 234
ridicule, fear of, 257
Riley, Naomi Schaefer, 185
Rimpler, Elisa, 190
risk, 180. See also health and safety;
    safety
    benefits of, 167–168, 170–171
    cultural competence and, 172
    healthcare and, 171
    in Iceland, 172–173
    importance of, 174–175
    negative, 170
    positive, 170
    repressed, 169–170
    resilience and, 171
    scouts and, 175–177
    screens and, 188
    sisu (grit) and, 172
    Wow Park Billund, 174–175
rocks, 241–242, 244, 251
Romppanen, Johannes, 44
rules, 66
Runeberg, Fredrika, 304

Runeberg, Johan Ludvig, 304
Rutter, Michael, 58
rye bread, 86, 88, 91

S
safety. See also health and safety; risk
    high chairs and, 93
    risky play and, 173
    screens and, 188, 190
sagas, Norse, xiii, 198, 209. See also
    literature; television
Sahlberg, Pasi, 55, 151–152
sailing, 245–248
same-sex couples, xvii, 9, 11. See also
    LGBTQ+ community
samfundssind, 105–106, 120, 296
    building, 112–113
    children and, 117–119, 120
    scouts and, 106–107
    volunteering and, 109–115
Samuel, Julia, 33
Sandemose, Aksel, 131
Sandøe, Peter, 214
Sandseter, Ellen Beate Hansen, 168–
    169, 170–172, 173
Santa, 289–291
saunas, 255–256
sausage (pølser), 95–96, 99
Scandinavia, xii–xiii, xv. See also
    Denmark; Norway; Sweden
Scandinavian Baking (Hahnemann),
    97
Schmidt, Lone, 10
schools. See also education; teachers
    boarding schools, 227, 273–276,
    284

INDEX

efterskole, 273–276, 284
    free meals at, 88–89
    islands and, 243
    private schools, 216, 228
    screens and, 182, 185, 190, 191, 275
Schou, Ole, 1, 3, 5, 9
Schultz, Nanna, 24, 86, 90, 91
science, 16
scouts, 106–107, 175–177
screens, 181–196, 237
    addiction to, 184–185
    age and, 182–183, 193–194, 196
    benefits of, 191–192
    education and, 182, 185, 190, 191, 275
    effects of, 183, 185, 192
    eyesight and, 183–184, 185
    gender and, 182
    holiday time and, 251
    lockdowns and, 185
    mental health and, 185, 193
    outdoors and, 190, 195
    parents and, 188–189, 192
    phones, 191, 193, 196, 275
    recommendations for, 186, 193–194
    risk and, 188
    safety and, 188, 190
    time spent on, 181, 182, 184, 186
sea, 238–250
self-esteem, 28, 130–132
self-reliance, 274
self-sufficiency, 124, 294
sex education, 259–264, 266
shame, 256–257
shyness, 127
sickness gap, 41–42
simplicity, 236, 250

Simsick, Louise, 24–25
singing, 101–105, 120, 217, 295
single parents, xvii, 9–13
sisu (grit), 55, 172, 176, 292
Skagen, 239
Skårderud, Finn, 280
Skov, Morten, 198, 202, 203, 207, 208–209, 210, 299
Skrammellegepladsen (de Coninck-Smith), 153
sleep, 243
    babies and, 35–36
    naps, 35–37, 60–61
smartphones, 191, 193, 196, 275. See also screens
snacks, 83, 85, 87–88, 91, 98
Snoppen & Snippan, 261–262
snowsuits, 294
soccer, 258, 295
social cohesion, 102, 104. See also community
social connections, 108. See also community
social media, 186. See also screens
social mobility, 293
social privilege, 228
social skills, 51, 225
socialization, 57
solomor (single mothers), xvii, 9–13
Sørensen, Anette, 36
special needs, 229
sperm donors, xvii–xviii, 1–16
    anonymous, 6
    applications to be, 4–9
    demand for, 2, 9–13
    limits on, 9

spille, 147, 162. See also play

sports, 131, 258, 295

status, 28

Steinfath, Casper, 239

Stokke chair, 92–94

stones, 241–242, 244, 251

storytelling, Nordic, 203. See also
    literature

stress, 149–150, 288, 289

stress leave, 107

student helpers, 60

sudden infant death syndrome (SIDS),
    20

Suggate, Sebastian, 221

summer. See holiday time

summerhouses, 234–251

Sundhage, Pia, 295

swearing, 132

Sweden, xiii

    academic achievement in, 222

    age of consent in, 264

    alcohol in, 278

    bodies and, 292

    celebrations in, 303–317

    child care in, 53

    Christmas in, 290–291

    economic challenges, 117

    education in, 219

    feminine ideals and, 108

    food in, 88–89, 90, 96

    nature and, 71

    obesity in, 91

    parental leave in, 38–39, 40–43

    pronouns in, 206–207

    risky play and, 171

    screens in, 186, 191

    sex education in, 261–262

    shyness in, 127 note

    summerhouses in, 234, 236–237

    teenagers in, 283–284

    Vikings and, xiv

    women in management in, 40

swimming, 239, 253–254

T

Talso, Jouni, 290–291

taxes, 27–28, 29, 39, 56, 96, 111,
    229–230

teachers, 51–52, 217. See also educa-
    tion; schools

    autonomy of, 231

    in Finland, 228

technology. See screens

teenagers

    alcohol and, 278–279

    chores and, 284, 286

    confirmation and, 272–273

    efterskole, 273–276, 284

    expectations for, 283–284, 286

    graduation, 268–272, 281

    gymnasium, 274, 277

    listening to, 286

    in Sweden, 283–284

television

    children's programming, 139,
        209–211

    sex education and, 257, 260–262

Tesfaye, Mattias, 186

tests, 220, 222, 228, 230

thinking, free/critical, 217, 230, 293

thinness, 257, 266

Þrándardóttir, Hrund, 173

Thunberg, Greta, 116
tillid, 37, 46, 230. See also trust
time, 291–292
     giving, 125 (See also discipline;
          volunteering)
togetherness, 99, 103. See also
     community
tolerance, 225
trade schools, 277
transgender rights, 260. See also
     LGBTQ+ community
Tripp Trapp, 92–94
trodsalder, 127
trouble (bøvl), 175–176
trust, x–xi, 5, 20, 35, 37, 46, 120, 230
truth, 212
twins, 12–13

U
UK
     academic achievement in, 222
     age of consent in, 264
     alcohol in, 281, 282
     child care in, 56
     Christmas in, 288
     cost of living in, 292–293
     Denmark compared to, ix–x
     education in, 218, 219, 229
     fertility treatments in, 11
     food in, 95
     health and safety in, 171
     masculinity and, 108
     mental health in, xii
     obesity in, 90
     parental leave and, 43
     play in, 148–149

     risky play and, 171
     safety in, 173
     screen time in, 186
     sex education and, 261
     sperm donation and, 9
     swimming pools in, 254
     women in management in, 40
ultimatums, 123
Ultra Smider Tøjet (Ultra Strips
     Down), 257
Under the Covers with Anna Lin,
     260
United States, 228
     academic achievement in, 222
     age of consent in, 264
     alcohol in, 278, 281, 282
     child care in, 56
     cost of living in, 292–293
     Denmark compared to, 36
     education in, 229
     food in, 95
     happiness in, 28
     healthcare in, 171
     masculinity and, 108
     mental health in, xii
     obesity in, 90
     parental leave and, 43
     play in, 148–149
     safety in, 173
     screen time in, 186
     sex education and, 261
     sperm donation in, 9
     swimming pools in, 254
     wages in, 27, 292–293
     women in management in, 40
university, 293

V

vacation. See holiday time
validation, external, 132
van Hauen, Emilia, 288
Velling, Mette Bay, 217
video games. See screens
Vikings, xiii–xv
Vinterberg, Thomas, 279, 281
volunteering, 5, 109–115, 119
vuggestue (nursery), 49, 50–52. See also day care
vulnerability, 295

W

wages, xvi, 27–28, 292–293
Wambach, Abby, 295
war, 295. See also World War II
water, 238–250
wealth, redistribution of, 28
weather, 73, 75–77, 81, 82
weddings, 316–317
Wednesdays, 314
welfare safety net, 5, 108
well-being, xi–xii. See also happiness; health, physical; mental health
WHO (World Health Organization). See World Health Organization (WHO)
wieners (pølser), 95–96, 99
"wild times", 156. See also play
Wilkinson, Richard, 28
Willemoes, Peter, 102
wind, health and, 73–74
wind power, 116
women, working, xvi, 39, 40, 41–42, 56–59, 292–293

work. See also parental leave; women, working
    annual leave, 56 (See also holiday time)
    play and, 150
    stress leave, 107
    women in management, 40
work hours, 28, 41, 91, 107, 109, 150–151
World Economic Forum, 39
World Happiness Report, 108
World Health Organization (WHO)
    on alcohol, 278
    on day care, 57–58
    on obesity, 91
    screen time and, 186, 187
World War II, 137, 217, 239, 295
    junk playgrounds and, 152
    working women during, 57
Wow Park Billund, 174–175

Y

Year of Living Danishly, The (Russell), x
yeast, 97–98
Your Competent Child (Juul), 126

Z

Zuckerman, Maja Gildin, 278

Acknowledgments

〰〰

To all the small people who have made this book possible, thank you. From sharing stories to fetching warm paper from the printer and making two hundred paper airplanes with my penultimate draft, *tak* (thank you, in Danish).

Thank you to Anna Power for always believing in me and to Louise Haines, Anna Michels, and Liv Turner, who let me write books for a living and be a part of that magical place where ideas can wrestle it out.

To the rest of the team at Harper Collins UK—Mia Colleran, Victoria Pullen, Nicola Webb, Eve Hutchings, and Kate Quarry. A huge thank you to the team at Sourcebooks and Penguin Random House in the US and to the rest of the Johnson and Alcock crew—Michael Alcock, Anna Dawson, Helene Butler, Saliann St-Clair, and Kroum Valtchkov.

Thank you to all the experts named in the book for their generosity and to all those who helped me to get to them, including Denise Lauritsen, Bryony Lester, Lasse Ribergård Rasmussen, and Neeni Lomborg. To Pia Nielsen and Kitta Pust, the best pedagogues in town.

To all the Viking parents for their support, especially Camilla Bjerre, Rikke Bruntse Dahl, Camilla Uhre Fog, Kimie Sandborg Randorf, Johanne Lucie Ertok, Sille Aarlit Jensen, and Maria Gustavsson (as well as honorary Viking parents John Hassall and Tracii Guns). Special thanks to Sanne Moth and Annika Friis for fellow twin mom sanity checks and early reader excellence. And to my own mother, for raising me.

To fellow "outsiders" Tim, Amy, Sean, Graham, Louise, Viv, Ian, Jono, Fee, Chesney, and Nichole for sharing insights and observations. To Tara, for keeping my children in rollerblades (crucial) and Fen for invaluable early brainstorming. I am ever grateful to my UK crew, Ali, Caroline, Chrissy, Emily, Sarah, Kate, and Jill, for helping to turn off Shit FM if the volume ever gets too loud. And to you for reading. Thank you.

About the Author

© Simon Meyer

Helen Russell is a bestselling author, journalist, and speaker. Formerly editor of marieclaire.co.uk turned Scandinavia correspondent for the *Guardian*, her first book, *The Year of Living Danishly*, became an international bestseller and has been optioned for television. She's the author of five other books, translated into twenty-one languages. Helen writes for magazines and newspapers globally, including pieces in the *Times*, *National Geographic*, and the *Wall Street Journal*. She's spent the past ten years studying cultural approaches to emotions and now writes and speaks about her work internationally (when not chasing after three small people and an unruly dog).